SO-BPI-673

New Thinking in Economics

New Thinking in Economics

Edited by J R Shackleton
Principal Lecturer in Economics
Polytechnic of Central London

HB
171
.N497
1990
West

Edward Elgar

© J R Shackleton 1990

All rights reserved. No part of this publication may be reproduced, stored in a retrieval system, or transmitted in any form or by any means, electronic, mechanical, photocopying, recording, or otherwise without the prior permission of the publisher.

Published by

Edward Elgar Publishing Limited
Gower House
Croft Road
Aldershot
Hants GU11 3HR
England

Edward Elgar Publishing Company
Old Post Road
Brookfield
Vermont 05036
USA

British Library Cataloguing in Publication Data

New thinking in economics.
   1. Economics
   I. Shackleton, J. R. (John Richard)
   330

Library of Congress Cataloguing in Publication Data

New thinking in economics / edited by J.R. Shackleton.
      p.   cm.
     ISBN 1–85278–341–9
     1. Economics. I. Shackleton, J.R.
  HB171. N497 1991
  330–dc20   90–41645
                                                         CIP

ISBN 1 85278 341 9

Printed in Great Britain by
Billing & Sons Ltd, Worcester

Contents

List of Figures and Tables   vii
List of Contributors   ix

1.   Introduction   1
     J R Shackleton
2.   Has there been a Classical Liberal Revival?   10
     John Burton
3.   Financial Change and Macromonetary Control   27
     Tad Podolski
4.   Open-Economy Macroeconomics   48
     Peter Spencer
5.   Rational Expectations and the New Macroeconomics   72
     David Peel
6.   The Ups and Downs of Business Cycle Theory   88
     Brian Morgan and J R Shackleton
7.   Neo-Keynesian Theories of Unemployment   109
     G K Shaw
8.   Some Recent Developments in Econometric Modelling   124
     M J Pokorny
9.   Public Choice: The Economics of Politics   140
     Rosalind Levačić
10. Post-Keynesian Economics: Recent Developments and
     Future Prospects   160
     Philip Arestis
11. The New Industrial Economics   179
     Brian Haines and J R Shackleton

References   205
Index   231

Figures and Tables

FIGURES

3.1   Different levels of 'money' with a given monetary base   40
A4.1   The symmetric situation
       (a)   Inflation   68
       (b)   Unemployment   68
A4.2   The asymmetric situation   71
5.1   The Phillips curve   77
5.2   Expectations-augmented Phillips curve   78
5.3   Vertical Phillips curve   79
6.1   The time path of real UK GDP and trend growth   91
6.2   The cycle: percentage deviations of GDP from trend   91
7.1   Keynesian unemployment   111
8.1   Consumer expenditure and personal disposable income, 1958–75 133
8.2   Annual rate of inflation in the UK, 1958–75   138
9.1   Sources of rent-seeking: the example of import controls   150
10.1   Post-Keynesian circular flow   167
11.1   The structure-conduct-performance approach   181
11.2   The firm versus the market   188

TABLES

3.1   Injecting 100 units of currency into a banking system   31
3.2   Impact of public and private finance on growth of M3, 1982–89 43
4.1   Assumptions of the Mundell-Fleming (MF) model and its
       derivatives   52
4.2   Five models of international linkage   63
11.1   Outcome of MMC investigations, 1965–85   193

List of Contributors

Editor:
J R Shackleton
Principal Lecturer in Economics, Polytechnic of Central London

Other Contributors:
Philip Arestis
Professor and Head of Department of Applied Economics, Polytechnic of East London
John Burton
Professor and Head of Department of Economics and Public Policy, Leeds Polytechnic
Brian Haines
Senior Lecturer in Economics, Polytechnic of Central London
Rosalind Levačić
Lecturer in Economics, The Open University
Brian Morgan
Government Economic Service
David Peel
Professor of Economics, University College of Wales, Aberystwyth
Tad Podolski
Professor and Head of Faculty of Business, Economics and Management, Portsmouth Polytechnic
M J Pokorny
Head of Department, The Business School, Polytechnic of North London
G K Shaw
Rank Foundation Professor of Economics, University of Buckingham
Peter Spencer
Chief UK Economist, Shearson Lehman Hutton

1 Introduction

J R Shackleton

ABOUT THIS BOOK

Sisyphus, the founder of Corinth, was punished for various misdemeanours by having to roll a heavy stone up a hill forever. Each time he approached the top, the stone rolled back down and he had to start all over again. This sort of punishment is out of favour with the courts these days, but many of us nevertheless inflict it on ourselves. Anyone wishing to keep abreast of developments in economic thinking faces just such a Sisyphean task. Each year many thousands of academic books and papers spew forth from universities, colleges and research institutes all over the world. Time and again those of us who profess to teach economics in a halfway up-to-date manner seem to have to scrap much of our accumulated human capital and start again.

I suppose we have an incentive to do so. Our jobs, or our promotion prospects, may depend on it. In any case some of us, poorly paid and overworked though we are, actually enjoy it. However there are many other people who have some interest in economics but, understandably, rather less commitment. It is at them that this book is aimed. They include that great mass of students who are unlikely to make careers as professional economists, but have to absorb a fair amount of economics in their degrees. Many of them may be studying the subject as part of a joint honours programme or, increasingly, as an element in a business studies degree. Although such students are well catered for at an introductory level (the market for basic texts must be almost saturated), they are less well supplied at an intermediate level. Books ostensibly aimed at senior undergraduates are frequently almost ludicrously over the heads of all but a handful of the students I come into contact with. They are written in a technical language which is incomprehensible to most normal students, and usually with far more of an eye to the opinions of the authors' professional peers than to the needs of their readers.

This book's potential readers also include people whose work involves or builds on a basic knowledge of economics. They have a professional concern with being aware of new developments, but have neither the time nor the inclination to plough through the journals or attend academic conferences. Such people include economists working in government or business: their work is often highly technical, but with a narrow focus. They also include journalists and financial analysts. Then there are schoolteachers, academics in related disciplines (sociologists, political scientists, statisticians), trade union officials and professional lobbyists. Perhaps even some politicians ('madmen in authority' as Keynes so politely put it) are still sufficiently open to new ideas to want to know what economists are currently thinking, rather than relying on their recollections of 'academic scribblers of a few years back'.[1] Well, perhaps.

So much for the book's target readership. What of the content? The idea is to cover the major changes in economic thinking in the last decade or so. A flip through the references listed at the back of the book will indicate that something over two-thirds have a publication date after 1980. But no hard and fast rule was drawn up for the time span covered, and some writers have looked back further than others.

Each chapter takes an area of economics which is widely taught on undergraduate courses, or is of practical significance, or is of political concern: where possible, all three. The authors have attempted to provide straightforward surveys of recent developments, as far as possible in a non-mathematical manner which assumes only limited prior knowledge. Where appropriate the material is critically commented on, and likely future developments sketched out. Any particularly difficult material has been dealt with in appendices, and the aim has been to ensure that the reader can actually *read* each chapter with some enjoyment and profit, rather than struggle through it line by line. However the notes, appendices and extensive references enable readers to follow up in more detail any subject which interests them.

'NEW' THINKING IN ECONOMICS

Of course, the title of the book invites knowledgeable readers to turn up their noses. Some of the topics covered have been discussed for some time, and anyway 'newness' dates very rapidly. Given writing, dissemination and publication lags (and despite modern technology, bringing out a book is a much slower process than 50 years ago), no book of this sort can ever be as up-to-date as you would like. More fundamentally, however, it should be pointed out that superficially novel analysis may really be a restatement in modern dress of long-established ideas – old wine in new bottles, as one of the economics profession's favourite cliches has it.

There's some truth in this. While emphasising newness we should not lose sight of the recurrent oscillations in economic thinking. There are 'long waves' in economics between emphasis on belief in the unfettered workings of private enterprise and stress on its weaknesses. After the extended heyday of Keynesianism and statism, the last 10 or 15 years have seen the apotheosis of the market. This may not last indefinitely for reasons I shall touch on later. But there can be no doubt that the 1980s saw the biggest revival of market liberalism this century. Under conservative administrations in Britain, the United States and several other developed economies, both practical politicians and a large section of the intelligentsia swung away from state intervention in industry, welfarism and discretionary demand management. It seemed that the political success of this tendency in the West was echoed at the end of the 1980s by the collapse of the Communist regimes of Eastern Europe.

Such developments, discussed by John Burton in Chapter 2, were accompanied by a great deal of 'new' analysis which was in reality a revival of older ideas, forgotten or downplayed in the 1950s, 1960s and much of the 1970s. Thus we had the resuscitation of monetarism, a doctrine understood in outline by David Hume in the 18th century and perhaps even by John Locke in the 17th. This was tarted up into a modern, scientifically testable hypothesis by Milton Friedman and later by 'New Classicals' such as Robert Lucas – although both freely admitted their debts to writers of the past.

More bizarrely, there has been a notable revival in the ideas of the Austrian School of economists, whose most notable modern adherent has been Friedrich Hayek. Its emphasis on the role of the market as a transmitter and coordinator of knowledge, and its hostility to almost all forms of economic activity by the state, have been combined with a denial of the twentieth-century's 'modernist' faith in quantification as the touchstone of scientific analysis. The neo-Austrian approach is much discussed here.

So you could say that the 'newness' of much recent analysis is spurious. However nobody steps twice into the same stream, and revivals of older ideas are necessarily changed by new circumstances and by new modes of expression. There may be perennial tension between defenders and critics of the free market, but its form changes and areas of disagreement have been narrowed as the workings of the market have become rather better understood by both sides. So no future swing back towards interventionism (a possibility in the 1990s, whether you like it or not) will be a *simple* return to the ideas of the past.

ECONOMICS TODAY

In particular, any return will surely not involve a replay of the macroeconomics of the years of the 'Keynesian consensus'.[2] For it is in macroeconomics that the greatest changes have occurred, and the language of this subject can never be the same again.

Twenty years ago, economics was taught in two separate boxes. 'Microeconomics' was concerned with the workings of prices and markets and substitution at the margin. The concept of equilibrium between demand and supply was a basic working principle. 'Macroeconomics', at least in its popular versions, was something else entirely. It concerned economic aggregates which behaved very differently from their components. Here consumption depended on income rather than price variables, and investment was barely affected by the interest rate. Governments, often seen as benign correctives to 'market failure', were faced with the problem of maintaining the appropriate level of aggregate demand so as to avoid the Scylla of unemployment and the Charybdis of inflation. This was usually seen as a problem of fiscal policy, involving the balance between taxation and government spending, supplemented in the case of inflation with incomes policies which were supposed to restrain wage increases.[3]

Most readers know that these policies were discredited by their failure adequately to deal with the inflationary problems of the 1970s. A popular response was to swing over to the sort of economic fundamentalism favoured by Milton Friedman, with his belief that inflation was 'always and everywhere a monetary phenomenon', curable by tight control of the money supply. But this in its turn was largely discredited, at least in any simple form, by the experience of the 1980s. Rapid technological and institutional change (discussed in some detail by Tad Podolski in Chapter 3) made monetary control difficult and uncertain in its effects. Perhaps even more fundamentally, Friedman's monetarism was seen by many to suffer from the same flaw as the Keynesianism it challenged – an emphasis on macroeconomic relationships with suspect microeconomic underpinnings. What have been called 'monetarists mark II' (aka the New Classicals) have argued the need for a macroeconomics firmly founded in microeconomic reasoning. In a nutshell, they have argued for complete commitment to the principle of equilibrium modelling – the assumption that all markets clear simultaneously and thus the problem of effective demand is inconceivable. This has led to a revival in the equilibrium theory of the business cycle (discussed in Chapter 6), albeit recently in directions which the New Classicals didn't originally envisage.

The principle of market-clearing has been justified on the grounds that *uncleared* markets seem to imply irrational behaviour by firms, households or workers. And nowadays adherence to the assumption of utility-maximising individuals out to do the best they can for themselves is seen by many as the criterion demarcating the economist from the non-economist. Even the neo-Keynesian writers discussed by G K Shaw in Chapter 7 broadly accept this position. They have tried in a number of ways to explain in microeconomic terms the rigidities – such as wage stickiness – which prevent markets from generating an optimal pattern of employment. Their explanations involve a close examination of the incentive patterns facing individuals and firms as well as the nature of bargaining and production institutions, rather than *ad hoc* hypotheses about 'money illusion' and so forth favoured by earlier generations of Keynesians.

The focus on the economic analysis of institutions is also found in much of the interesting new literature on the theory of the firm (see Chapter 11) and on public choice (Chapter 9). Indeed many of the ideas of the new institutional economics, developed and extended in the last decade, have application right across the whole field of economics.

Institutional structures inhibiting complete market flexibility are often responses to the pervasiveness of uncertainty and the absence of full information. These problems have also given rise to the overwhelming importance now placed, particularly in macroeconomics, on the problem of forming expectations about the future. David Peel (Chapter 5) discusses some of the implications of the acceptance of the principle of rational expectations; further ramifications are explored in Chapters 4 and 6. One major policy conclusion from this literature has been scepticism about the ability of governments to manipulate aggregate demand in order to stabilise the economy. A fascinating analysis of the need for governments to secure 'credibility' for their policy commitments ensues. This has again fed back into analysis of institutions, with many theorists claiming that we need constitutional reform to limit governments' ability to renege on their promises. This has been associated in turn with further arguments for limiting the role of the state in the economy at the micro as well as at the macro level: for example, the arguments of Hayek and the Austrians. The related ideas of James Buchanan, with his emphasis on wasteful 'rent-seeking' by interest groups seeking market intervention on their behalf, are explored by Rosalind Levačić in Chapter 9.

Another development in macroeconomics deserves emphasis: the general recognition of the openness of national economies and the need for macromodelling to incorporate this. Until quite recently it was common for basic expositions of macroeconomics to use models of closed economies onto which a foreign trade sector was grafted, if at all, as an afterthought. This is understandable given the limited role played by foreign trade in the 1930s when modern macroeconomics was born, as well as restrictions on capital mobility coupled with the hegemony of the US dollar in the 1950s and 1960s. In this period American economists, often more insular than their European counterparts in any case, could largely ignore developments in the rest of the world.

In the 1970s and 1980s, with the rise of Japanese and West German industrial power, the collapse of the Bretton Woods system, the oil price shocks and the emergence of the US as a net debtor, it became increasingly obvious that in any consideration of the domestic economy the world economy had to be explicitly modelled. Peter Spencer devotes Chapter 4 to Open Economy macroeconomics.

Finally, in concluding this rapid sketch of recent developments in economics, a comment on the use of mathematics and econometrics. One reason for books like this is the need to 'translate' the analysis and empirical findings of experts into something comprehensible to the non-specialist. The mathematisation of economics has gathered pace for more than a century, though the econometric revolution is largely a characteristic of the postwar period. These developments have never been unanimously accepted within the discipline. Despite his own ability as a mathematician, Marshall was an early sceptic of the mathematical possibilities of economics,[4] whilst Keynes showed a distinctly lukewarm attitude to early developments in econometrics.

The extensive growth in the use of mathematical reasoning and statistical analysis in economics is nowadays almost certainly irreversible. In a technical sense, mathematics saves time and critical effort (for example, much of the endless controversy over Keynes' writings stems largely from his unwillingness to spell out precisely his assumptions and derivations).[5] And econometrics is a natural response to the inability of mathematical models alone to provide anything other than indications of the direction of economic changes (and often not even that). Their use also owes much to economic factors in a quite specific sense – the mathematically trained have a comparative advantage in an increasingly competitive profession – and also to sociological factors such as the professionalisation of the discipline and the need to enhance status and create a rationale for the exclusion of the untrained.

However there remain strong currents in economics which largely eschew mathematical and quantitative work. Some theorists, most notably the Austrians, have always insisted that economics, as a *social* science, differs fundamentally from the natural sciences from which mathematical techniques have (allegedly inappropriately) been borrowed. The recent resurgence of Austrian economics and much of the work of fellow spirits such as Buchanan (see Chapter 9) need little mathematical facility to grasp. If these writers are normally associated with the political right, substantial interest also remains, certainly in the UK and Italy, in the post-Keynesian tradition (see Chapter 10) which similarly tends to downplay quantitative analysis.

Perhaps these currents have been strengthened by the indifferent performance of econometrics over the last 15 years or so: much of the earlier postwar optimism about the use of econometrics to resolve theoretical and policy issues has evaporated, at least for the time being.[6] In macroeconomics the Lucas critique[7] has undermined much of the econometric work done in the Keynesian tradition, which assumed the stability of parameters that more recent theory suggests will be variables. More generally, critical work by writers such as David Hendry has attacked the reliance on statistical modelling of the Box-Jenkins variety and argued for a much more rigorous form of econometric model-building involving an exhaustive range of new tests (see Chapter 8).

In view of this, it is perhaps less surprising than it might have once have seemed that much of the most influential policy writing of the last decade has come neither from mathematical theorists nor tooled-up number-crunchers. I think particularly of the work flowing from the Heritage Foundation in the USA, and from the Institute of Economic Affairs and the Adam Smith Institute in the UK (discussed in Chapter 2) – all of which is perfectly comprehensible to the mathematical and statistical dud.

These developments are unlikely to reverse the whole drift of the last hundred years or more. But they serve as a salutary reminder of the continuing methodological pluralism within economics, and of the need for keeping open the lines of communication within – and beyond – the discipline.

THE FUTURE

Nobody can foretell the future, but many economists make a good living by pretending to. In finishing this Introduction I cannot resist peering into my crystal ball in an attempt to discern likely themes in the economics of the next decade or so. There are a number of related topics which suggest themselves as we approach the end of the century.

One obvious area of immense significance is the collapse of central planning in Eastern Europe and the impending transition to the market – a process fraught with danger as well as promise. In the past the study of command economies has been an underfunded backwater in the West, inhabited largely by eccentrics and ideologues of left and right. Now this area is going to be invaded by large numbers of economists who will not be content with analysing and explaining. They will be looking for a slice of the action, pressing their favourite remedies on countries which, emerging blinking into the sunlight after 45 years of seclusion, may be too ready a prey for the snake-oil salesmen.

It is very likely that Eastern Europe – possibly China too – will become much more like the capitalist countries of the West over the next decade. But there is more than one model of successful capitalist development, and it does not necessarily follow that the preferred solution to the problems of the former planned economies will be a reversion to red-blooded laissez-faire. An alternative option (given these countries' histories, possibly a more attractive one) would be a welfarist, interventionist capitalism on, say, Swedish lines.

For it may be the case that the high point of free market liberalism has passed, at least for the moment. For example in countries like Britain and the USA it seems likely that over-hasty deregulation in the 1980s will throw up problems calling for 'reregulation' in the 1990s; the financial sector and the public utility monopolies spring to mind. In the UK, too, there is concern across the political spectrum about the inadequacy of education and training: the argument is about the extent and nature of the public intervention required, not about the principle of government involvement. Economists, as always, will have much to say.

More importantly, environmental issues are likely to be high on the political
agenda in coming years throughout the world, with inevitable pressure for
increased regulation. Although the economics of environmentalism made an
impact in the early 1970s, this was largely in the form of a neo-Malthusian
concern about resource availability. Today's concern is with pollution: past
concern about the 'quality of life' has escalated into fear concerning the ultimate
threat to planetary survival. Economic analysis can be a highly effective antidote
to hysteria in this area as elsewhere, but the case against panic measures will have
to be made forcefully.

Within the European Community, the movement towards economic integration is likely to stimulate community action on environmental issues – action
which, to be successful, will need to spread to Eastern Europe too. Economic
integration at all levels is the aim of most EC governments for the 1990s, though
opinions differ about the plausibility and desirability of destroying all those
barriers (of custom, language and residual concern about national security)
which inhibit complete integration. Doubts remain, too, about the likely division
of costs and benefits from integration: these doubts may grow as pressures
develop to increase the Community's membership. Again economists have
useful things to say, and their discussions of policy will need to take on a much
wider perspective over the next few years. The number of British authors whose
empirical work and policy analysis are confined to UK problems must surely
begin to fall.

This has to be most important with respect to macroeconomic policy.
Whatever the elusiveness of the microeconomic gains from integration, it is clear
that there would be tangible benefits from greater macroeconomic coordination
in Europe (or, indeed, more widely – though the problems of coordination rise
exponentially with the numbers of countries involved). A narrowing of the
spread of inflation rates among EC countries (a likely consequence of a
strengthened ERM), for example, would surely also tend to be associated with
a greater convergence of unemployment rates and economic growth.

A further topic which I would guess will enjoy a resurgence is the economics
of long-run growth. This area of the subject, popular in the 1960s, vanished
almost entirely from the journals in the 1970s and 1980s as concern with short-
run problems of inflation and unemployment increased. It is due for a revival, for
it is concerned with dependency rates, human capital and savings ratios, topics
which will be of increasing policy concern because of the rapid ageing of the
populations of most developed countries as the 21st century gets under way.

So there is no shortage of practical and theoretical issues for economists to
attend to over the next few years. A discipline which has such a constant turnover
of problems and concerns is likely to continue to generate 'new thinking' into the
indefinite future.

ACKNOWLEDGEMENTS

I must thank Mark Blaug and Edward Elgar for asking me to put this book together. Philip Cox provided some useful advice and a footnote in Chapter 6. Jeanette Purcell helped me to get the references sorted out.

For part of the time the book was in preparation, I was working at the Department of Social Security. It should be obvious that nothing written here is in the slightest way the responsibility of that Department, though prudence dictates that I add the customary disclaimer.

NOTES

1. See Keynes (1936) p. 383.
2. In the 1950s and 1960s, theoretical elaboration of the Keynesian model undermined its claim to be a 'general' theory: its assumptions were seen rather as special cases of the classical approach. However 'Keynesianism' as a policy framework was believed to *work*, and thus had a central place in the textbooks even if the theoretical honours went elsewhere.
3. They may even have worked at times, at least in the short run – but that is another story.
4. 'The chief use of pure mathematics in economic questions seems to be in helping a person to write down quickly...some of his thoughts for his own use...But when a great many symbols have to be used, they become very laborious to anyone but the writer himself...it seems doubtful whether anyone spends his time well in reading lengthy translations of economic doctrines into mathematics, that have not been made by himself'(Marshall, 1890, p. ix).
5. See Backhouse (1985) p. 334.
6. I would expect it to return. The quantum leap in computer power and the emergence of cheap user-friendly econometric software is putting into the hands of quite ordinary undergraduates skills and facilities which were once the prerogative of a tiny minority of elite researchers.
7. See 'Econometric Policy Evaluation: A Critique' in Lucas (1981)

2. Has there been a Classical Liberal Revival?

John Burton

In this chapter Professor Burton discusses the observation made in the Introduction, that much of the 'new' thinking of recent years is actually a restatement of older ideas. In particular he examines the revived interest in classical liberalism, and its considerable impact on policy-makers in the USA, the UK and even in Eastern Europe. He analyses the parallel phenomena of Reaganomics and Thatcherism; despite the apparently stronger intellectual commitment to liberalism in the USA, changes in economic policy have been more dramatic in the UK. Although there are some contradictions in the way in which classical liberals conceptualise political economy, Professor Burton sees their approach as both illuminating and likely to become still more influential during the rest of the century.

INTRODUCTION

The contributions in this volume are generally concerned with 'new' ideas in, and 'new' schools of, economic thought and analysis. As a variant, this essay discusses whether, and to what extent, an 'old' school of economic thought and policy analysis – classical liberalism – has staged a revival in recent decades. It also examines theories of why this may have come about, and in particular the extent to which – and how – classical liberal rhetoric and policy prescription have been translated into policy *action* (concentrating on the experience of the US and the UK).

Before starting on this task, it would seem advisable to offer some summary notes on the nature and origins of classical liberalism. This school of political economy originates with the work of such philosophers and economists as David Hume (1711-76), Adam Smith (1723-90), David Ricardo (1772-1823) and John Stuart Mill (1806-73). By the nineteenth century it had become the ruling intellectual paradigm in political and economic thought in the then most advanced nations. But its dominance was to wane towards the end of that century, and by 1945 its position can only be described as that of an acutely endangered species of thought. In April 1947, a small band (39) of academics – primarily economists – gathered in a remote mountain retreat (Mont Pelerin) near Vevey, Switzerland, at the instigation of Friedrich Hayek. There they formulated a programme for the survival of the precepts of classical liberalism in a world that seemed to be hurtling away from their system of ideas towards government planning and ownership of industry, towards the precepts of Marxism (and more general brands of socialism), and towards a rejection of the idea of freedom under the Rule of Law. The Mont Pelerin Society – the international 'debating association' of classical liberalism – was thereby born.

It is more difficult to state summarily the precise content of classical liberalism. As with any massive apparatus of politico-economic thought and ideology (and, arguably, there are only two others of similar extent – Marxism and conservatism), there are many subtle variations in the positions of its expositors, even sometimes downright disagreement.[1] Very broadly, however, classical liberals adopt an anti-statist policy stance and argue for the socially beneficial consequences of economic freedom in open markets. But classical liberalism is not simply, or at all, propaganda for pro-capitalist economic policy such as issues from the presses of industrial confederations of all Western countries (and, now, many Eastern ones too!).[2]

The foundations of classical liberalism lie in far more fundamental matters: in ideas about a free society under Rule of Law, and about the need to protect the Citizen from the State by the two devices of maintaining free market exit/entry, and of constitutional disciplining of government discretion. Nor is it, importantly, a narrow nationally-oriented programme. Free trade amongst independent and constitutionally separate nation-states has always been a keystone of the classical liberal credo.

THE EVENTS OF THE 1980s

There is no doubt, in retrospect, that the 1980s can only been seen, on a global scale, as a decade of momentous upheaval and movement in the rhetoric of economic policy debate and prescription in a classical liberal direction. (We shall later examine the question of what this entailed in policy practice.) In two key (primarily) Anglo-Saxon nations, the US and the UK, political leaders came to power – in 1980 and 1979 respectively – who espoused free-market rhetoric and doctrines. Both attempted to break with the postwar social democratic consensus on policy, and both were subsequently to be re-elected with substantial majorities. But the promotion of free market ideas and policies was not to be the sole preserve of Atlanticist conservative political leaders. Across the other side of the globe, ostensibly Labour governments in both Australia and – in particular – New Zealand were to adopt free market and deregulation measures which, arguably, were even more drastic than those pursued by either Mrs Thatcher or Ronald Reagan.

Nor was the surge towards free market policies a uniquely 'Anglo-Saxon' development in the 1980s, as the above examples may seem to imply. The implementation of the Tax Reform Act of 1980 in the USA (TRA-86, hereafter) set off a wave of similar 'competitive' tax structure reforms across many countries around the globe. Again, Mrs Thatcher's development of privatisation programmes in the 1980s were to be followed by similar experiments in a large medley of other countries, numbering some 50 by 1986.[3]

To all of this must be added the momentous – even astounding – political and policy developments that occurred in Eastern Europe towards the end of 1989. At the very time of writing, privatisation, pro-enterprise, and pro-trade laws are due to be passed by the legislatures of many countries of Eastern Europe (such as Poland and Yugoslavia), or already have been (as in Hungary). Hungary and Yugoslavia have infant securities markets in existence. The new Polish economic programme announced on 1 January 1990 involves a rapid transformation of the ownership structure of their economy towards a private-sector market economy within the space of only one year. It is also relevant to note that the economic adviser to both the Polish and Yugoslavian governments, Professor Jeffrey Sachs of Harvard University, has recently written as a categorical basis for policy in the East that:

> ...Eastern countries must reject any lingering ideas about a 'third way' such as a chimerical 'market socialism', based on public ownership or worker self-management, and go straight for a western-style market economy.[4]

Another straw in this vast wind of policy change might be seen as the commitment by Treaty (The Single European Act of 1986) of the 12 nations of the European Community to the 'completion of the internal market' by the end of 1992. Quite how far this will actually go (e.g. regarding differences across member-states in relation to excise and VAT rates) remains to be seen. Yet there can be no doubt that the '1992 Project' in general constitutes a massive programme of deregulation in the world's largest economic bloc.

However, we should beware, first, of assuming that all of these events are linked together (to which we shall return below). We should beware, secondly, of assuming that all political rhetoric that is indulged in actually becomes translated into policy practice; politicians of all parties are not unknown to adopt catchphrases from academic scribblers if that serves their political purpose. We shall examine this matter with respect to the US and the UK below also.

Yet the general direction of events in the policy arena in the 1980s *could* be – and in some accounts is – read as a profound, widespread revival in free-market ideas and policies, underpinned by a growing revival in classical liberal political economy and philosophy that continues to expand its influence. It is an open fact that such free-market think-tanks as the Institute of Economic Affairs play host to a growing army of visiting economists from East Europe and Russia who gesticulate with reverence and excitement at the photographs adorning its walls of Milton Friedman, Friedrich Hayek, and other doyens of classical liberal thought. (Meanwhile, the Adam Smith Institute, also of London, now holds major conferences on privatioation techniques not in London alone, but increasingly in East European capitals such as Warsaw and Budapest, with the open welcome of government authorities.) Something of a decisive shift in attitudes and policies is clearly going on. But why?

TIDES AND TIMES

It is useful to start by turning back the clock nearly fifty years to examine Hayek's (1944) work on this topic. Hayek had previously been viewed as a somewhat austere pure economic theorist, indulging primarily in arcane debates on capital and monetary theory, but his *Road to Serfdom* (1944) was a very different offering from similar previous publications. It proved to be a bestseller and also appeared in condensed form in the *Reader's Digest*.[5]

In that book, Hayek sought to analyse why it was that the world was turning away from the classical liberal conception of freedom under the Rule of Law towards socialistic conceptions of planning of the economy by government, and what the consequences of such a development would be. It painted a sombre picture of the future. The adoption of socialistic principles, Hayek forewarned, would lead to both economic stagnation and political dictatorship: a 'road to serfdom'. The postwar experience of many East European countries, and of the Soviet Union and the Republic of China, bears out the general thrust of Hayek's prescient analysis.

Yet in general this did *not* happen in the West, although some considerable growth of government spending and regulation was witnessed across Western countries for much of the postwar period (Nutter, 1978; Burton, 1985; Swann, 1989). Moreover, as recounted above, the 1980s has seen some (variable) recoil in policy practice from the 'socialistic tide' that Hayek feared in 1944. It has been important for classical liberals to try to explain to themselves, and others, why the sombre forecast of one of their most noted luminaries has not come about, and why they now, on some accounts, seem to be on the 'winning side/tide'.

As a preface to a consideration of these contemporary debates, it is only fair to note that Hayek himself in 1944 did not propose any 'historical inevitability' thesis about the collapse of capitalism as a result of growing 'socialistic' tendencies in thought and policy at the time. Hayek's proposition was that the adoption of 'wrong' policy stances and ideas would lead to profound economic and political consequences (of which the world was generally unaware). If however, as he hoped, the world rejected those ideas and policies, then those consequences would not obtain.

It is certainly not unnatural, and perhaps rather predictable, that many intellectuals share with Hayek and John Maynard Keynes (another classical liberal, and friendly towards Hayek) the belief that the world is ruled by ideas (in Keynes' famous phrase 'and by very little else'). Also, the acceptance that there may be considerable delay in policy practice, as ideas filter only slowly from scholars and thinkers, via generations of students in higher education and the activities of the media, to the wider populace. But, as we shall see, this proposition comes into conflict with some of the strands of thinking in the classical liberal revival, notably public-choice-type analysis.[6]

How to Explain the 'Turning Tide'

Nowhere is this conflict more apparent than in the various recent works of two of the most prominent classical liberals of our times, Milton and Rose Friedman. In some of their accounts (e.g. M and R Friedman, 1980, ch. 10; 1988; 1989), general fundamental 'tides' in the affairs of men and women develop in the realm of ideas and specifically, in this context, in political economy. These waves of ideas are refined through the work of scholars; they expand and deepen, and eventually come to some sort of 'maturity' as a paradigm-cum-general philosophy. Eventually, through their commanding influence on the general climate of opinion and tenor of discussion, they infuse politics and pass into policy and legislation.

Specifically, the Friedmans diagnose three such major waves of influential political-economic ideas since the eighteenth century, which they label as the Adam Smith tide, the Fabian tide, and the Hayek tide.[7] One does rather wonder from their accounts where the Marxist and Keynesian tides come in (or rather disappeared to). But their general point is clear: ideas have consequences.

Yet in other accounts of the interaction of ideas and policy, they draw heavily upon the public-choice notion of the blockage to policy change posed in democratic societies by the existence of a multiplicity of competing interest groups in the political process; these, they argue, will stymie reform along classical liberal lines. They detect an 'iron triangle' of interests in contemporary political democracy, composed of politicians (legislators), bureaucrats and powerful interest groups. The system is underpinned by an asymmetry of costs and benefits in political market decision-making. The costs of any political decision (regulation or legislative act) may be diffused across huge numbers of taxpayers (including future taxpayers via the techniques of inflationary finance and/or bond finance of government expenditure) or via 'hidden' redistributive taxation in the form of regulation.[8] Yet the average taxpayer is, in Downs' (1957) phrase, 'rationally ignorant' of the various tax exactions made from him/her (and in the case of tax burdens thrown onto as yet unborn generations, utterly ignorant). Meanwhile, the benefits attaching to fiscal and regulatory redistribution may be concentrated upon politically important interest groups. The bureaucracy that administers the entire process also has a vested interest in its retention – and, indeed, expansion. Thus the 'iron triangle' that prevents a classical liberal break-out and process of sound reform. According to this account by the Friedmans (1984), a reform-minded government has but a small window of opportunity in terms of time after election to office before the 'tyranny of the status quo' reasserts itself.

There is something of an inconsistency, amounting almost to schizophrenia, in these two classical liberal analyses of policy determination. It cannot be that the world is 'ruled' by both ideas and interests. The clash of the two models continues to excite classical liberal controversy, with no clear resolution in sight (Barry, 1984; Gamble *et al*, 1989).

The Constitutionalist 'Escape Route'

There is one possible escape-route from this dilemma of the classical liberal analysis of policy determination and change. This is offered by the constitutionalist economics of James Buchanan (see Chapter 9 of this book) who, with the Friedmans and Hayek, is one of the leading classical liberals of our times. In this analysis, even if politics is driven by interests, it might yet be possible to convince all of the players in the political/lobbying 'game' that it is of negative-sum nature; also of the general benefit of changing the rules of the game by the *constitutional* disciplining of government (for example, to mandate a balanced budget). There have certainly been moves in this direction in the US, underpinned by its strong constitutionalist tradition. For example, in 1983 some 32 States of the Union (of the required 34) passed a resolution calling for a constitutional convention to establish a balanced Federal government budget. The fact is, however, that this did not come off, and economic reform in the US has not been affected by constitutional (Amendment) means.

The rejection of the 'constitutional solution' to the prisoner's dilemma involved in classical liberal reform programmes is even clearer in the UK. Britain has virtually no written constitution, so it would be difficult to 'rewrite' it. Mrs Thatcher's successive governments have, moreover, shown no interest in this idea whatsoever.

How then, and to what extent, has there been a revival of classical liberal policy? And why did it occur? It would be impossible adequately to assess these matters on a global scale, so we confine our attentions here to the experience of the USA and the UK during the 1980s.

REAGANOMICS AND ALL THAT

To what extent did 'Reaganomics', the economic policy pursued during Ronald Reagan's presidency (1980-88), constitute a classical liberal 'revolution' in economic policy? There is a diversity of views on this matter. Indeed, we need turn only to the memoirs of two of Reagan's top economic aides to obtain entirely different views.

The negative view has been powerfully expressed by David Stockman (1986, pp. 14-15), formerly Reagan's Director of the Office of Management and the Budget:

> By 1982, I knew the Reagan Revolution was impossible. It was a metaphor with no anchor in political and economic reality....In the final analysis, there has been no Reagan Revolution in national economic governance. All of the umbilical cords of dependency [upon the state] still exist because the public elects politicians who want to preserve them.

The Stockman analysis is thus that there was no classical liberal revival in US economic policy practice. Change was thwarted by the 'tyranny of the status quo', the log-jam imposed by vested interests on the policy process. Stockman – naturally enough, given his former Office – concentrates upon what happened to government spending, revenues and the (Federal) deficit as a test of the success or failure of Reaganomics. In his analysis, Reagan's attempt to 'roll back the state' by planned Federal expenditure cuts got blocked early on in his first term of office. Subsequently, attempts to remove the looming Federal budget deficit by (tax) revenue increases also got blocked by powerful coalitions and interest groups in the political process. Thus, in Stockman's phrase, 'politics' (quickly) 'triumphed' over ideas, and the 'Reagan Revolution' was soon aborted.

The positive, contrary view is taken by another important Reagan economist, his Chief Adviser on domestic and economic policy, Martin Anderson (1988, p.6):

> ...by any reasonable standard, what was happening in America [in the Reagan years] was a revolution, not a violent physical revolution driven by guns, but a revolution of ideas....The intellectual and political revolution [then] occurring in the United States is known throughout the world as conservative.[9]

Which view is correct? Was there a classical liberal revival in US economic policy? To test these questions we might address two matters: the sources of ideas behind Reaganomics and their implementation in policy practice.

The Intellectual Sources of Reaganomics

It is not widely appreciated that Ronald Reagan – generally seen simply as an ex-film actor, albeit 'The Great Communicator' (as the press later dubbed him) – received his intellectual training primarily through the discipline of economics. He majored in economics at Oberlin College, where he obtained a considerable grounding in the classical liberal world-view. We should not find it surprising that, in his subsequent political life, he was to draw heavily upon classical liberal ideas, those of economists in particular.

There is *no* disagreement between Stockman and Anderson as to the *source* of the ideas and ideology behind Reagan's economic policy. It was unquestionably classical liberal doctrine and, most especially, the work of classical liberal economists who, in modern guise, are sometime labelled as 'The New Right' or 'The New Right Enlightenment' (Barry, 1987; Seldon, 1985).

The nine charter members of Reagan's economic team (formed in 1975) reads like a Mont Pelerin Society roll of honour, including such figures as Milton Friedman, C Lowell Harris, Arthur Laffer, William Niskanen and Murray Weidenbaum. The Economic Policy Coordinating Committee, established in 1980 to coordinate Reagan's six economic policy task forces, was chaired by George Schultz (a former Dean of the Business School of the University of Chicago, subsequently to become Reagan's Secretary of State). Others in Reagan's team of (74) economic advisers in the 1980 Presidential campaign included Alan Greenspan, Norman Ture, Paul Craig Roberts, Arthur F Burns, James Buchanan and William Simon – all, again, New Right notables.

In short, the programme of Reaganomics was undoubtedly forged and written by a massive team of committed free marketeers and 'New Right' thinkers. At no other time in this century has the classical liberal 'movement' been given such direct access to, and control over, the policy-formation process. *Policy Memorandum No. 1*, written by Anderson in August 1979 to summarise the general (and specific) economic strategies advocated by this large group of economists of the New Right, read like a classical liberal charter of economic policy[10] – which is precisely what it was. It called for a reduction of federal tax rates; deregulation; the control of federal spending; the balancing of the Federal budget, and consistency over time in the application of economic policy in order to give an environment of predictability to business decision-making. Also, an Economic Bill of Rights that would *constitutionally* limit the amount that the Federal government could spend, would impose a balanced Federal budget, and prohibit recourse to price and wage controls. Much of this, although not all (specifically, the Economic Bill of Rights) Reagan committed himself to in the 1980 Presidential campaign; subsequently, it formed the basis of the 'economic game plan' announced by President-Elect Reagan four months before he was due to take formal office.

The classical liberal credentials and sources of 'Reaganomics' are undeniable. But what *actually* happened?

The Implementation of 'Reaganomics'

Overall, it must be recorded that not much of this programme ever got put into policy practice in the Reagan years. In particular, Federal government spending was not brought down which, combined with a policy of avoiding tax increases, led to a large and looming Federal government deficit (amounting to 6.3% of US GNP in 1983, though brought down to 3% by 1988). Perhaps the more crucial test of Reaganomics in practice lies in the area of microeconomics, rather than macroeconomic policy.[11] Here, we might have especial regard to two classically-liberal oriented programmes of action: privatisation and the deregulation of markets.

'Privatisation' has two meanings in popular discourse. In one sense it refers to the sale of government assets (e.g. corporate assets and local authority housing) to individuals. In a second, wider, sense (used by Swann, 1988, and Pirie, 1988), it refers to the introduction of conditions which typify private-sector, commercial behaviour into the public sector (including 'contracting-out' and 'load-shedding' of previous public responsibilities.

On either definition, the record of the Reagan Administration(s) in the arena of privatisation is not strong. Substantial asset sales of government-owned property were proposed by the Reagan Administration in 1982, but little emerged in reality from this.[12] Deregulation could have been a bigger target for Reaganomics: the regulation of industry has been one of the major 'growth industries' of the US over the twentieth century. In 1936, the number of pages devoted to regulatory measures in the Federal Register totalled 2,599. By 1970, it had grown to 424,000 and by 1977, to 742,000. The extent of regulated industry, upon one estimate, accounted for 8.2% of US GNP in 1965, but had grown to 25.7% by 1978.

Deregulation of industry has occurred in the US since the mid-1970s, but mainly under the prior Carter Administration (as with the Airline Deregulation Act of 1978). Although the deregulation of industry was a goal of the Reagan presidencies, according to a sometime member of the US Council of Economic Advisers, '...we ended up with more regulations and more trade restraints than at the beginning of the [Reagan] Administration' (Niskanen, 1988, p.13). Specifically, the percentage of imported products subjected to trade restrictions doubled during the Reagan Administration, resulting in a cost to the US consumer of around an extra $65 billion a year.

Perhaps the assessments of Anderson and Stockman of the 'Reagan Revolution' are in a sense *both* right. The classical liberal foundations and intellectual backup were undoubtedly there. But this did not often get transmuted into policy practice, as Stockman argues. Buchanan (1989, p.15) contends that the failure to convert principle into policy foundered upon an eschewal of *constitutional* reform of the economic policy process:

> It was evident ...even before inauguration in January 1981 that the Reagan leadership was to move primarily if not exclusively along the policy-within-politics route and to relegate to secondary status any attempt to achieve genuine structural change.... The Reagan administration became itself part of the existing structure; it could no longer succeed in generating changes in the structure itself. All it was left with was to play the standard political game

Thus arises the concern of many American classical liberals, including Buchanan, with constitutional routes to free-market economic reform. They cannot see how a classical liberal programme can be implemented within the interest-group-encrusted log-jam of the existing democratic process, unless through constitutional means. On this very matter, it is useful to turn to the experience of the UK in the 1980s.

THATCHERISM IN THE UK

If the Buchanan diagnosis of the problems confronting classical liberal reform programmes were correct – i.e. that it requires constitutional measures to implement them – we might have expected the UK to have seen even less change under Mrs Thatcher since 1979 than happened in the US under Ronald Reagan. The UK has no written constitution, so it is difficult to envisage how it might be 'rewritten' (e.g. in order to effect an Economic Bill of Rights). Given the British constitutional convention that no Parliament can bind its successor, it would be possible for a new government to overturn any policy rules (e.g. adherence to a balanced budget policy). Mrs Thatcher herself eschewed any interest in constitutional reform, and the practice of her successive governments has been, in Buchanan's terminology, that of 'policy-within-politics'.

Yet, whilst not all of the policy developments under Mrs Thatcher have been in a classical liberal direction, and while some reversals have occurred even there, the general impression of most analysts is of considerable change in the free market direction under Mrs Thatcher (e.g. Riddell, 1983; Smith, 1988; Gamble, 1988). Policy developments which highlight this contention include the abolition of all exchange controls, and wage and price controls (1979); the reform of trade unions (under the Acts of 1980, 1982, 1984, and 1988); the cutting of the top rate of income tax (by 1988) to 40%, and the basic rate to 25%; and the fact that the UK has 'now the lowest ratio of government spending to GDP in the European Community' (Congdon, 1990, p.8).

The most important development under Mrs Thatcher's successive governments has been the privatisation of a large amount of previously government-
owned assets. The term 'privatisation' did not even appear in the 1979 Conservative election manifesto. Yet, by 1984, a massive programme of privatisation
had '...emerged by default as the main theme of Conservative supply-side or
structural (industrial) policy' (Brittan, 1984). The devices utilised to achieve this
transformation under Mrs Thatcher have been varied and include:

1. Sale of local authority rental housing to householders (of a typical order of
   £1 billion p.a. over recent years);
2. Public issue of shares *via* the stock exchange (e.g. Cable and Wireless;
   British Aerospace; British Telecom; British Gas; the Water Boards);
3. Management buy-outs (e.g. the National Freight Corporation);
4. Private sale of government corporate assets (e.g. the sale of the Royal
   Ordnance tank plant in Leeds to Vickers Plc);
5. Placing shares with institutional investors (e.g. the sale of the government's
   holding in the British Sugar Corporation);
6. Joint ventures between public and private enterprises (e.g. the subsidiary
   established by British Steel and GKN – Allied Steel and Wire).

The volume of 'special asset sales' under the Thatcher government during its
first term was on quite a small scale compared to those that transpired in
subsequent years; they constituted either portfolio sales of shares of companies
in which the government owned a part stake, or the entire privatisation of
relatively small companies operating in a competitive environment (eg. Britoil,
Cable and Wireless, Associated British Ports, Amersham International, British
Aerospace, Ferranti, ICL). But in the wake of the successful issue of 51% of
British Telecom's equity in 1984 – then the largest share flotation in history – the
second (1983-87) and third (1987-?) Thatcher governments were dramatically
to expand the horizon and scale of its privatisation plans, to include British Gas,
British Airways, the English and Welsh Water Boards and British Steel (all
achieved by 1989), with further plans in the pipeline for the privatisation of
electricity supply, the National Coal Board, British Rail, and other concerns.

There is concern and controversy about how much of this massive programme
of privatisation represents a genuine move in the direction of an open-market
economy, as advocated by classical liberals (Veljanovski, 1989; see also Chapter
11 of this book). British Telecom was given a master licence for 25 years; the
only other licensed telecommunications operators being Mercury, which is
relatively small, and the City of Hull (until November 1990). British Gas retained
its statutory monopoly of supply upon privatisation. British Airways was
privatised with an 'inherited' system of routes granted by the Civil Aviation
Authority so that what was being sold off, in effect, was a combination of airline

assets and regulatory privileges. The British Airports Authority opposed separate ownership of its London airports in order to enhance competition, and the government acceded to this. Moreover, in the case of some privatisations (as with BT, in which the government retains a 49% stake), the workings of the market in corporate control are hampered by the remaining slice of government-owned equity.

The attempt to 'roll back the state' by cutting government spending under Mrs Thatcher exhibits a similar variability of delivery in actual policy. Smith (1988, ch.3) divides the Thatcher record on this matter into three phases over the post-1979 period: a first phase in which there was an attempt to create real (inflation-adjusted) cuts in general government expenditure; a second phase (from around 1983) of 'revisionism' in which the government simply attempted to keep public expenditure steady in real terms, rather than to cut it; and a third phase of 'realism' (from 1986) in which it accepted that both of the previous strategies were too ambitious. Now it was simply hoped that, if the economy grew fast enough, public expenditure as a share of GNP might decline, by around 1990 perhaps back to the levels of the early seventies.

The Thatcher record on deregulation is also something rather less than that which media hype, and the groans of vested interest groups, would have us believe. Road haulage deregulation preceded the Thatcher governments, with loosening up in 1968 and 1978 – under Labour governments – although the dismantling of the regulation of express coaching under the Transport Act 1980 did add to impetus in this industry. There has been some, but by no means total, liberalisation in domestic airline route operation. In the field of broadcasting, the development of cable and satellite operating has been permitted (subject to regulation). In the financial services industry, there was a supposed deregulatory 'Big Bang' in 1986, leading to greater competition between financial enterprises and sectors of the overall industry; however, considerable growth of 'prudential' regulation and formalisation and extension of controls has occurred since that time. Some modest moves have also been taken towards greater competition, and deregulation, in the professions – as with opticians and legal services.

We therefore have to be careful in viewing the Thatcher experience as the 'revolution' that it is sometimes portrayed to be. The pace of change has been far slower than sometimes alleged in the more exaggerated media accounts. Nevertheless, it is valid to conclude that Mrs Thatcher's 'revolutionising' of British economic policy *was far stronger, and more marked, than the actual experience under President Ronald Reagan.* This is despite the fact that she came into office without the massive backup of a classical liberal 'clan' who might have done much of the economic policy spadework for her.[13]

What accounts for this diagnosed difference in the pace and impact of the Thatcher and Reagan 'revolutions'? To this matter we turn in the next section.

THE CONTRASTS BETWEEN THATCHERISM AND REAGANOMICS

Buchanan's (1988, p.13) assessment – widely shared by others – is that '...Mrs Thatcher has been more successful than Ronald Reagan in carrying through on pledges and promises for effective depoliticisation of the economy'. His analysis of why this was so is instructive in that it reflects the constitutionalist perspective in resurgent classical liberalism, a development which Buchanan himself has led. He argues that:

> parliamentary regimes depend relatively more on who is in office and relatively less on the incentive structure facing who is in elective office. Put very simply, a constitutional democracy is constitutional, which means that rules matter (Buchanan, 1988, p. 13-14).

In other words in the US the implementation of Reaganomics was thwarted at the level of policy enactment by the constraining influence of the American Constitution, including such matters as the formal separation of powers between the Executive, the Legislature and the Judiciary; the inability of a US president to veto any specific measure in the Federal Budget Plan;[15] and the formal independence from the Executive of the Federal Reserve Board. Mrs Thatcher suffered no such written constitutional constraints on her executive power and was able to indulge her policy plans without such inhibitions.[16]

Though possibly an element in the matter, this explanation too is not without difficulties, not least for the classical liberal analysis of policy determination in the public choice tradition. How can it be that – as some public choice-based accounts contend – classical liberal policy reforms can be blocked out by an iron triangle imposing a 'tyranny of the status quo', *and* that the ideas of those actually in office are crucial (at least under parliamentary regimes)?

Thatcherism demonstrates the possibility of classical liberal reform, to a degree, *without* recourse to constitutional measures which, according to some classical liberal accounts, would be an essential underpinning. The special character of the Thatcherist reform programme has been its attention to piece-meal, bit-by-bit reform, rather than the holistic vision of a classical liberal 'revolution' as contained in Anderson's *Policy Memorandum No. 1*. Moreover, it is an approach that has often sacrificed classical liberal principles – as witnessed most markedly in the (variable) failure to privatise in a competitive manner, discussed above – to the necessities of practical politics.

Pirie (1988) has coined the term 'micro-politics' to refer to the underlying Thatcherite strategy, which he views as grounded in the insights of public choice analysis, but which then sets about to design and implement policy taking into account the realities of political markets. It is an approach that fundamentally rests upon policy engineering rather than winning the battle of ideas. This is a novel reading of the Thatcher experiment, in that Mrs Thatcher is more typically seen as a classic example of a 'conviction politician' rather than a Machiavellian policy engineer. Nevertheless there is, I shall argue, a firm evidential basis for viewing the Thatcher experiment in this light of 'micro-politics'.

At the inception of Mrs Thatcher's rule, most emphasis was put upon macroeconomic policy in the form of the Medium-Term Financial Strategy (MTFS) announced in 1980. This was seen then as the 'coherent' part of the Thatcherite strategy, with rolling, pre-announced targets over a five-year horizon for growth in the money supply (initially, the M3 aggregate alone), for government spending and the budget deficit. This foundered on the public expenditure side, as recounted above (although, as Congdon argues, British government spending growth *was* slowed *relative* to the rest of Western Europe). It also foundered on the monetary target side in the following ways: with the abandonment of M3 targets by 1985 (in favour of an 'array of indicators'); under the impact of financial deregulation (in 1986), which introduced new uncertainties into monetary policy: and with the implicit pegging of the £ to the D-Mark in 1987 (abandoned, 1989).[17] By late 1989, 'broad' money was growing in the UK at over 18% on a per annum basis, and the rate of price inflation had just topped 8% – the highest amongst Western industrialised countries. Thatcherite macroeconomics has not been a success story, and there is much to the charge that it has degenerated into discretionary fine-tuning of the 'seat of the pants' style (Healey, 1989).

It is on the side of micro-politics that Mrs Thatcher has scored heavily in terms of reform. Three aspects of the adoption of this strategy - increasingly evident since 1983 - are what might be termed as 'salami-slicing tactics', the 'pick 'em off' tactic, and the 'buying-out interest groups' approach.

The *Economist* (1989) has diagnosed Mrs Thatcher's 'salami-slicing' approach to reform in respect of local government, state industries, housing, and state education as follows: adopting a limited reform in her first term, widening it in the second, then moving on to even more policy changes in the third (and fourth?) terms of office:

> This is government by softening-up: by the time the final Thatcherite onslaught opens, those who might resist have been defeated so often that they are tired of the fight (*Economist*, 1989, p. 25).

This was reinforced by the 'pick 'em off (one-by-one)' strategy. Rather than formulate a massive programme of economic reform – as with *Policy Memorandum No. 1* – the Thatcher approach has been to reject a 'Big Bang' of denationalisation, or whatever, in favour of piecemeal privatisation measures over successive terms of office. This meant it did not have to confront all of the potentially-opposed interest groups at one and the same time. By this device, coalitions of opposition were diffused and put in disarray.

The latter strategy was greatly reinforced by the straightforward tactic of 'buying out the vested interests' (where sufficiently powerful). Nowhere is this more starkly revealed than in the privatisation programme for the great state industries – such as British Telecom, British Gas, and the Water Authorities – allowing their retention of considerable monopoly powers; *plus* new managerial autonomy from Treasury financing; *plus* 'light regulation' in place of government control; *plus* highly generous arrangements regarding employee acquisition of equity in the newly-privatised industries.

Is Thatcherism thus an example of a successful revival of classical liberal policy, working through the new tactics and strategy of 'micro-politics'? Or are there some inherent problems with such a strategy, which flow from the very nature of micro-politics as seen from a classical liberal perspective?

First, a programme of piecemeal reform often fails to 'deliver the goods' sufficiently fast, in economic terms, to keep the citizenry happy (as Mr Gorbachev is even now discovering in the USSR). Second, it takes a long time, and voters get fed up with endless 'nagging' from government as the interest groups are 'picked off' one at a time. Third, the strategy of buying out vested interests in the process of reform creates 'new' vested interests, as with the continuation of statutory monopoly power in privatised state concerns. There is also a moral question involved in the latter strategy: why *should* groups privileged (by the state) receive new privileges at the expense of others?

We might test Thatcherism in these regards as a viable classical liberal revival strategy against the needs and concerns of Eastern Europe and the USSR. Piecemeal economic reform in the Soviet Union is quite literally failing to 'deliver the goods'. Nor is there the time politically available to effect a long programme of bit-by-bit reform along market lines. Moreover, 'buying out the obstructers' could mean giving new privileges to State managers, the *Nomenklatura*, and Communist Party officials – something that may not be too well received by the rest of the population of these countries.

Even within the UK – where economic and political matters are less pressing – questions inevitably remain about the long-run viability of Thatcherism, given its decade-long dithering on macroeconomic policy, as well as the underlying problems in its strategy of micro-politics.

CONCLUSION

Has there been a classical liberal revival in economic policy-making, and what are its sources?

Over the last two decades and more, there has undoubtedly been a resurgence in classical liberal analysis and policy prescription, witnessed in a plethora of books about the 'New Right' (e.g. Barry, 1987; Seldon, 1985; King, 1987;

Green, 1987). The more intellectually-inspired of Marxist and socialist economists and philosophers also commonly confide that they find the current edge of
debate being addressed more pertinently, and with more respectable thought
behind it, than they are prone to witness in their own 'camps'.

But an intellectual resurgence is not necessarily the same thing as a policy
revolution. In the United States, the detailed plans of a formidable group of
economists writing the text of the Reagan economic programme were con-
founded in large part by political forces and the necessity of observing the letter
of the Constitution. In the UK, whilst change was much more dramatic under Mrs
Thatcher than under Reaganomics, this was also piecemeal and may have
embedded some inherent flaws within its 'micro-political' strategy.

Yet I would nevertheless suggest that some sort of classical liberal policy
revolution will jostle out of the present melée of world developments, facts and
exigencies. The harsh truth is that much of Eastern Europe, the Soviet Union and
the Republic of China need, in a dire economic sense, to restructure their internal
and external workings on market lines. It is not that capitalism has succeeded, but
rather that communism has just failed decisively, both economically and politically, in a very large part of the world. No doubt the spread of classical liberal
ideas, for instance to Mr Vaclav Klaus in Czechoslovakia, has been important.
But even powerful tides of ideas cannot predominate unless underpinned by
political and economic forces that are working in the same direction. It does in
fact seem that we are at just such a juncture in history. With the disintegration of
communism over much of the East, and with a rapidly globalising world
economy, the stage may indeed be set for the more widespread adoption of
classical liberal policy ideas.

NOTES

1. The founding 'Statement of Aims' of the Mont Pelerin Society explicitly records that 'it seeks to establish no meticulous and hampering orthodoxy'.
2. To quote again from the MPS 'Statement of Aims', the group explicitly rejected the conduct of 'propaganda' in any form, and existed simply to 'facilitate the exchange of views among minds inspired by certain ideals... to contribute to the preservation and improvement of the free society'.
3. See Young (1986).
4. Sachs (1990) p. 23. One could note in this connection that Czechoslovakia's new Minister of Finance of the post-Communist government, Mr Vaclav Klaus, is a self-confessed devotee of the Friedmanite brand of economics and a visitor to Chicago University in the late 1980s.
5. For a number of evaluations of Hayek's 'road to serfdom' thesis, see Burton *et al* (1984).
6. Public choice theory is evaluated in Chapter 9 by Rosalind Levačić.
7. The Friedmans are perhaps overly modest in the latter regard. Their 'Hayek tide' might better be labelled as the 'Hayek-Friedman tide', notably because of the widespread influence of Milton Friedman's popular writings and extensive TV work.
8. The notion of regulation as redistributive taxation was first developed by Posner (1971).
9. As indicated earlier, there are profound differences between classical liberalism and the

conservative tradition, both in their 'old' and 'new' variants (see Barry, 1987). In fact Anderson uses the term 'conservative' here to refer to a free-market economic policy programme.

10. It is reprinted as Ch. 11 of Anderson (1988).

11. Whilst many classical liberals – such as Friedman – are 'monetarists', the two doctrines are in fact separable. A connection lies in the fact that both monetarists and classical liberals assume the market economy to be inherently stable, although subject to shocks. It is, however, possible to be a monetarist but not a classical liberal – and vice versa; an example of the latter would be Hayek, who rejects the Friedman prescription for the control of the money supply.

12. Government-owned enterprises in the USA were, however, of little significance in the 1970s compared to the UK, their output accounting for around 1.5% of GDP compared to around 12.7% in the UK.

13. For example, Professor (later Sir) Alan Walters, a noted 'monetarist' and classical economist, was 'drafted' into 10 Downing Street only in 1981 as a (part-time) personal economic adviser to the Prime Minister – some two years after the start of her first term of office.

14. For an extensive survey of regulatory reform in the UK, see Kay and Vickers (1988).

15. The Constitution constrains the President to accept or reject the budget as a whole; he has no power of 'line-item veto'.

16. The Bill of Rights of 1689, which is taken to be one of the few written components of the British Constitution, did guarantee the independence of the Judiciary from the Executive.

17. The convolutions of British monetary policy over the 1980s are a story in themselves; see, for example, Smith (1987).

3. Financial Change and Macromonetary Control

Tad Podolski

In this chapter Professor Podolski describes the modifications which financial deregulation and technological advance have made to traditional accounts of money creation and methods of monetary control. Money, always a nebulous concept, has become increasingly difficult to pin down. Aggregates which were the centre of attention a few years ago are now downgraded or have been abandoned. Simple faith in the control of inflation by adherence to money supply targets has given way to a broader consideration of monetary conditions and exchange rates in determining action by the monetary authorities.

INTRODUCTION

Monetary Policy Design

Monetary policies in most Western economies changed in the 1970s, an important part of that change relating to the design of monetary control. Monetary authorities were given the task of achieving a predetermined growth rate of a money stock. Such tasks became known as monetary targets, and by the end of the 1970s most market economies had adopted money targeting as the key feature of monetary control.

The design of the control was a two stage process, as sketched below:

```
CONTROL INSTRUMENTS—>INTERMEDIATE TARGET—>ULTIMATE OBJECTIVE
Central bank control     —>Money stock          —>Nominal income
   techniques                                   (or inflation rate)
```

Theoretical and Empirical Foundations

In the mid-1960s, macroeconomic problems, manifested by inflation often accompanied by rising unemployment rates, defied the then accepted principles of macroeconomics and inspired support for new interpretations of the quantity theory of money. Monetarism became the doctrine in vogue. As it embraces a variety of perceptions, for the sake of clarity references to monetarism in this text relate mainly to the contributions of Milton Friedman who, both as a theoretician and publicist, made a critical impact on macroeconomic strategies after the 1960s.

Friedman's version of monetarism contains two vital strands.

1.   The free market is seen as the most efficient allocator of resources and stimulator of economic effort and initiative. Traditional demand management strategies and the use of government regulations are considered to be impediments to the working of the price mechanism and thus rejected. Government failure is feared more than market failure.
2.   The control of money, however, is seen as a key component of economic strategy. Its objective is to provide the market economy with a stable economic climate, interpreted as the stability of the price level.

Two aspects need to be stressed in connection with this latter strand. First, inflation originates from increases in money, which often follow some government mismanagement. It is a disincentive to real economic processes and adversely influences decision-taking and expectations. Otherwise, money supply changes are, with the exception of some transitory short-term phases, neutral in relation to real (output, employment) changes, which are determined by supply-side factors.

In the broad macroeconomic debate, attention shifted from aggregate demand to the nature of the aggregate supply function and the formation of expectations. In the more narrow monetary debate, attention focused on the demand for money function and its stability. The monetarist argument was that the demand for money was stable, that the supply of nominal money was potentially unstable and hence needed to be controlled, and that changes in the nominal money stock would thus have predictable macroeconomic effects.

In the attempt to corroborate the above argument, econometric studies concentrated on the specification and estimation of the demand for money function and, in particular, on the relationship between the money supply and nominal income. The general interpretation of statistical studies was in terms of support for the hypothesis of stable demand and also a close association between money and nominal income, which was thought to indicate causality running from money to income.

Empirical studies contributed to the ascendancy of monetarist policy propositions stressing the need to control money. However, by the time these were reflected in the new policy design, new econometric studies (and methods) began to cast doubt upon the stability of the relationship between money and other macroeconomic variables (Judd and Scadding, 1982; Hendry and Ericsson,

1983; Hendry, 1985; Goodhart, 1989, pp. 311-22). Technically impressive econometric investigations (e.g. Rasche, 1987) have failed to secure a generally agreed position on the stability of monetary relationships.

Predictable influence of money changes on nominal income or inflation refers only to the second stage of the policy design referred to in the previous section, it is only one of the two necessary conditions for the effectiveness of a monetary targeting strategy. The other condition relates to the first stage, namely our ability to control the money supply. Relatively little attention had been paid to this aspect, the supply-side of money, before monetarists won the hearts and minds of the authorities who implemented the money targeting strategy in the 1970s and 1980s. Thus the questions of the nature of money as a macroeconomic control variable, of its measurement, and of the adequacy of the instruments of its control were relatively neglected.

When the new monetary strategy was being introduced, a concomitant change occurred in the financial systems of Western economies, especially in the US and UK. The change, often referred to as the 'financial revolution', has had a profound impact upon financial behaviour and monetary relationships. We confine ourselves to an examination of the impact of financial change mainly on the first stage of monetary policy, that is the supply-side of money. This includes the identification and measurement of money, the generation of money, and problems of its control.

The Structure of this Discussion

In the following section I sketch the model of money creation underlying the money control scheme outlined earlier. After discussing the nature of financial change, I evaluate its impact on the model and on the efficacy of control instruments respectively. Concluding comments are made in the final section.

THE SUPPLY SIDE OF MONEY: MONETARIST ORTHODOXY

Intermediate Targeting

Monetary targeting demands a quantification of the abstract concept of money, the identification and measurement of which have always posed problems. Prior to money targeting, monetarists were aware of these problems, but in general perceived money as a sum of currency and bank deposits. The existence of a variety of deposits and of other potential money substitutes did not give undue concern. Friedman (1978, p. 373) stated that 'a monetary total is the best currently available immediate guide or criterion for monetary policy – and I believe that it matters much less which particular total is chosen than that one be chosen'.

Other aspects of monetarist prescription for successful monetary control include the following.

1. The intermediate targeting of money was preferable to the targeting of an ultimate objective because the link between monetary policy and the price level was indirect, and the effect of monetary change took longer to manifest itself on prices than on a monetary quantity. A stable relation between the quantity and the price level made the former a clear and early signal of future price changes.

2. Once the monetary total had been selected, its growth rate was to be determined on the basis of some preferred growth rate of prices or nominal income, and was to remain steady for a long period. Monetary authorities were not thought to have adequate information or sufficiently precise instruments to be able to make short-term 'fine tuning' adjustments.

3. The targeted money supply was to be controlled by controlling the money base.

It is important to stress that the money of the quantity theory is essentially an exogenous entity capable of being controlled. Below we present a simplified model which, abstracting from many institutional complications, conveys the key monetarist perceptions relating to money creation and control processes.

A Money Creation Model

(a) The monetary system

Money is a product of the monetary system consisting of the central bank – which supplies the base money (which we also refer to as 'currency') – and the banking system which is seen as a monopolist supplying claims (deposits) possessing macroeconomic properties. The 'banking habit' is well developed, and thus payments from one economic unit to another are in effect transfers from one bank account to another without a leakage to different financial sectors (whose role in the economy is virtually ignored). Bank deposits were traditionally thought of as transactions-related, non-interest-bearing deposits held by customers willing to trade off interest for safety and transaction services associated with such holdings.

(b) Stable financial behaviour: asset management

The steady operations of banks can be represented by a stable fractional reserve ratio ß of (say) currency C to total deposits D (hence ß = C/D. Here we assume that the ratio has a behavioural content, though in many cases it has been prescribed by the central bank.

Banks receive new deposits (currency) and utilise them to make loans. To simplify matters we assume that banks have a choice of only two sets of assets: currency and loans (direct lending or purchases of securities) which bear interest. They maximise profits by being on the minimum reserve ration ß. They only lend more if there is an inflow of new reserves (currency); a steady demand for loans is assumed.

Let us also assume that the banking system consists of three banks a, b, c (the number of banks is not central to the argument) and is in equilibrium in the sense that all banks are on their minimum reserve ratio, assumed to be 0.1 or 10%. Let us now visualise an increase in the banking system of currency of 100 units, first flowing into Bank a. In its initial position (see below), the bank will not maximise its profits as it will be forgoing interest on 90 units and ß >0.1. To do so, it will

Table 3.1 Injecting 100 units of currency into a banking system

Bank a (initial position: ß>0.1)

Liabilities (deposits D)		Assets (A)	
ΔDa	100	ΔCa	100
ΔDa	100	ΔAa	100

Bank a (adjusted position: ß = 0.1)

ΔDa	100	ΔCa	10
		Loans(L)	90
ΔDa	100	ΔAa	100

Bank b (adjusted position: ß = 0.1)

ΔDb	90	ΔCb	9
		ΔLb	81
ΔDb	90	ΔAb	90

Bank c (adjusted position: ß = 0.1)

ΔDc	81	ΔCc	8
		ΔLc	73
ΔDc	81	ΔAc	81

adjust its position by retaining 0.1 of its extra deposits in currency and lending 0.9 (see Bank a, adjusted position).

Given the self-contained banking system we have assumed, the 90 units of lending, will find its way to (say) Bank b as additional deposits. The bank will go through the analogous process to that just pursued by Bank a. Having provided for the necessary increase in reserves ($\Delta C = 9$), it will lend 81 units (see Bank b, adjusted position) which will find their way to (say) Bank c, which will repeat the same pattern of behaviour. The process will go on indefinitely, the order in which banks participate not being vital to the argument.

(c) Inverted pyramid on a money base

From the above, the expansion of total deposits in the banking system can be summed up in various ways:

$$
\begin{aligned}
\Delta D &= \Delta Da &+& \quad \Delta Db &+& \quad \Delta Dc &+& \quad .... \\
\Delta D &= 100 &+& \quad 90 &+& \quad 81 &+& \quad .... \\
\Delta D &= 100 &+& 100(1\text{-}0.1) &+& 100(1\text{-}0.1)^2 &+& \quad .... \\
\Delta D &= \Delta C &+& \Delta C\ (1\text{-}\text{ß}) &+& \Delta C(1\text{-}\text{ß})^2 &+& \quad .... \quad = \Delta C/_\text{ß}
\end{aligned}
$$

The expressions are geometrical progressions which, as shown in the last line, sum to $\Delta C/\text{ß}$ (given the process to infinity and ß being a fraction). This last expression yields the simplest form of the bank multiplier $1/_\text{ß}$ with which readers may be familiar. In our example, with $\text{ß} = 0.1$, the multiplier is 10 and hence (in the limit) the increase in the total bank deposits is 1000. At that point the banking system would return to equilibrium at which $D = C/_\text{ß}$.

So far we have concentrated simply on bank deposits. We now recognise that currency C is held by banks (Cb) as well as elsewhere, say the public (Cp), and that the money supply (M) consists of deposits and currency in circulation with the public (hence $M = D + Cp$). The public's financial behaviour is also regarded as stable and is conveyed by a steady ratio α of Cp to D. With these extensions it can be shown that $M = kC$ where k is the familiar 'money multiplier' equal to $[(1 + \alpha)/(\text{ß} + \alpha)]$. k remains stable for as long as ß and α are stable.[1]

The representation of the money supply as a multiple of currency inspired the vision of the financial system as a symmetric structure akin to an inverted pyramid, based on and conditioned by the tip C of central bank liabilities. It also inspired the belief that a strategic monetary quantity could be controlled simply by controlling the base money.

The assumptions made in the derivation of this money-creation model may well have reflected the institutions and financial behaviour of the past. Various stages in the construction of the model are utilised below as an organising scheme to analyse the impact of recent financial change on our perception of the monetary system today and on the efficacy of the present monetary control design.

THE PROCESS OF FINANCIAL CHANGE

Financial Innovations

Much has been written in recent years about financial innovation and change, and their impact on monetary theory and policy.[2] Only a basic outline of the process of financial change can be undertaken here. The explosion of literature on this subject may have given an impression that, in the last two decades, we have witnessed unusual financial phenomena. This is not so. Financial innovations, like technological innovations, are a constituent process of evolution which has been with us for centuries. The process, though continuous, is subject to periodic surges. Some of the origins of the current 'financial revolution' are to be found in the changes of the late 1950s and the early 1960s, such as the internationalisation of financial markets, and the development of wholesale (parallel) markets and instruments (e.g. certificates of deposits). It is mainly the impact of modern computer and telecommunications technology which has accelerated and nurtured the change.

Though we may not yet fully understand the process of financial innovation, it is generally accepted to be motivated by profit expectations. These are often induced not by a single factor, but by a combination of elements on the demand-side (needs of the corporate sector, constraints of public finance, desire to hedge against risks), as well as the supply-side (availability of appropriate technology, willingness of financial institutions to undertake set-up costs). Few innovations have been predicted; indeed few have been noticed before they exerted an impact through diffusion (Hester, 1981). Many have taken place to circumvent government restrictions, and in that sense they are inimical to monetary control when it restricts profit opportunities.

Technology and Transactions Costs

As already stated, new technology has exerted a profound effect on payments and finance. Its influence can perhaps be best understood through its impact on transactions costs. In monetary theory transactions costs have been stressed in the explanation of the existence of money (e.g. Brunner and Meltzer, 1971; Goodhart, 1975, ch. 1; Niehans, 1978) and have been brought in explicitly as a variable determining the holding of transactions balances, initially by Baumol (1952). Though rarely precisely defined, they are broader than the direct costs incurred in transferring from one financial or payments medium to another, embracing such information costs (search, processing) as are necessary for making decisions. They also include other costs of intermediation such as those related to transfers of title and those entailed in bundling and unbundling of different financial attributes involved in the design of new financial devices.

On the supply side, modern technology and lower transactions costs have facilitated many structural changes and enhanced the capacity for further change. Some aspects of this are exemplified below.

1. Many new financial processes, instruments and markets could not exist without modern technology (e.g. credit or cash cards, electronic money transfers, financial futures, options or swap markets). Lower transactions costs encourage (make cost-effective) the creation of new devices to meet new profit opportunities or to circumvent regulations.
2. Falling transactions costs contribute to the breaking down of institutional segmentation by lowering the entry and exit costs and thus making markets more contestable (Kane, 1983, p.99). Modern technology also encourages multiproduct operations by permitting economies of scope (Gilligan *et al*, 1984; Mester, 1987).
3. The previous two points can be applied to the international sphere where, by lowering the barriers to international financial activity, modern technology has contributed to the globalisation of financial markets (BIS, 1986).

FINANCIAL CHANGE AND THE ORTHODOX CONCEPT OF MONEY CREATION

We now come to an evaluation of the impact of recent financial change on the creation and control of money (discussed above) and on the effectiveness of monetary control. It is generally known that in most countries the monetary authorities have had difficulties first in selecting their money target and then in hitting it.

The Governor of the Bank of England summed up the UK experience by observing that, though progress had been made towards achieving the ultimate aim of lowering the inflation rate, 'we have been less successful at a more technical level, in achieving our intermediate aims' (Bank of England, 1987, p. 365). Justifying the dropping of the M3 as a targeted aggregate, he remarked that 'frequent redefinition of the targeted aggregate and upward revision of the target range – often missed even so – resulted in public confusion rather than confidence' (ibid., p.366). Rather than describing the experience of money targeting, we concentrate here on the explanation of the difficulties encountered.

Financial System: Interdependence

The monetary system outlined above is defined in terms of a banking system viewed principally as the 'creator' of transactions money and the monopolist in the payments system. In keeping with the tradition of macroeconomic theory, bank money is the only financial asset taken into account; no other financial assets are given any macroeconomic significance. The banking system is well-behaved as it is not subject to competitive intrusions of other financial institutions. These characteristics might well have sufficed in the bygone compartmentalised financial environment where different financial institutions had their spheres of activity demarcated; when they obeyed the rules imposed by the statutes under which they had been set up, or by the associations of which they were members, or by the central banks; and when the circumvention of the rules was not easy (cheap) because of high transactions costs. However, in the last two decades the financial system has changed dramatically (e.g. Lewis and Davis, 1987; Harrington, 1987; Amel *et al*, 1989).

(a) Receding frontiers: competition and deregulation

Traditional frontiers between institutions have been significantly eroded by technological innovations (reducing transactions costs) and by deregulation and greater competition. It should be noted that deregulation has been as much the outcome of the circumvention of old regulations by innovations and of the potential of the market to thwart new regulations, as the product of the fashionable philosophy of laissez-faire (Kane, 1983, 1988; Podolski, 1986, ch. 7).

Though the banks are still important in the payments and money transmission systems, other institutions, particularly building societies, have breached their monopoly position. In the UK this was formally recognised in 1987 by adding new monetary aggregates M4 and M5 (in place of liquidity aggregates PSL1 and PSL2), incorporating non-bank liabilities (Bank of England, 1987a; see also Note 3).

The spheres of bank activities have widened to embrace practically all aspects of financial services, many of which are transacted internationally or in foreign currencies. Mergers between diverse financial institutions ('conglomeration'), often encouraged by deregulation, joined together previously distinct units of commercial banking, merchant banking, broking, market making and fund management (Hall, 1987). Banks are now multiproduct, multimarket organisations prominent in both retail and wholesale markets, in the housing market, and as arrangers, underwriters and marketmakers in securities markets. The usefulness of the simple bank balance sheets deployed in monetary theory (including this essay) has been eroded by these changes and by the new importance of off-balance-sheet activities. In some countries the traditional monetary restrictions, such as reserve requirements (as in the UK) or interest ceilings (as in the US), have been abolished.

Thus banks have become essentially a set of institutions in the financial services industry. A recent review of UK banking concluded that 'banking has moved over the past 10 or 15 years from being in many cases somewhat institutional in character to being totally commercial and businesslike in its structures. Banking is now a totally competitive industry, virtually worldwide, which can be analysed in terms of the same industrial economics as may be applied to the automobile industry or to chemicals' (Wilkinson and Lomax, 1989, p.15). In this new environment, central bankers, used in the past to dealing with well-behaved banking systems, often admitted to facing confused situations presenting dilemmas (e.g. Volcker, 1986, p.239; Bank of England, 1986, p.500).

At the theoretical and more abstract level, economists turned to investigate banks not as 'creators of money', but essentially as intermediaries whose existence was justified by market imperfections. This is another example of the 'new institutionalism' touched on in the introductory chapter. Some emphasized their function in reducing transactions costs (Benston and Smith, 1976); others viewed them as information producers and a market response to the existence of information asymmetries (Leland, Pyle, 1977); still others as specialists in monitoring the performance of borrowers on behalf of lenders (Diamond, 1984; Ramakrishnan and Thakor, 1984; Boyd and Prescott, 1986; Williamson, 1987). Elsewhere economists explored the relation between credit and intermediation services and real processes (Bernanke, 1983; Bernanke and Gertler, 1987). Good surveys of this area are provided by Gertler (1988) and Gertler and Hubbard (1988).

(b) Financial engineering: new financial instruments

The development of new wholesale markets and instruments, which began the the 1960s and continued strongly in the last two decades, has weakened the effectiveness of the traditional central bank control arrangements such as the reserve ratios and interest restrictions (Broaddus, 1985; Podolski, 1986, ch. 5). It is now easy for banks and financial institutions to 'buy money' in national and international financial markets. The surge in such activities has resulted in considerable financial interdependence. Financial institutions can now make better use of liquid resources (base money) and be less dependent on the central bank as the manager of liquidity (Moore, 1986). On the other hand, financial interdependence makes prompt emergency central bank assistance in crisis situations vital. This was demonstrated when the Federal Reserve contained the 1987 stock exchange crash by announcing its readiness to make liquidity available to support the financial system.

Many new financial devices hybridise the characteristics traditionally associated with separate and diverse instruments. To give various examples: credit cards combine settlements with credit and other services; new interest-bearing bank accounts offer transactions and investment opportunities; note insurance facilities assure borrowers of the availability of funds over long periods, but enable them actually to raise funds at short-term interest rates, convertible bonds give investors the option to convert into equity at a fixed price; swaps lower borrowing costs or lessen risk by converting preferential (low-cost) borrowing into funds actually desired; and multiple option facilities give borrowers access to bank lending, securitised instruments and multicurrency facilities.

Institutions have developed 'financial engineering' giving them the potential to produce instruments which cater for diverse and changing preferences of borrowers and lenders. They can thus generate substitutes and redirect financial flows quickly to take advantage of new profit opportunities. Such behaviour militates against the control of money.

(c) International integration

Financial markets are internationally integrated and interdependent. International capital mobility is high and rising, and foreign markets are capable of supplying substitutes for domestic finance (BIS, 1986). Wide experience, for example with the Eurocurrency markets, has shown that business will emigrate from restricted to unrestricted markets. The use of national monetary measures in such an environment is impaired, especially if these result in international misalignments.

Less Stable Behaviour: Liability Management

The behaviour of banks described earlier and symbolised by a stable ß has been affected not only by those broad institutional changes outlined, but also by growing competition for deposits (liabilities). Differentiated new accounts for depositors/savers in banks and in other institutions have created competition and volatility in the sphere of transactions and savings funds. An important manifestation of this is the rising proportion of 'transactions' accounts bearing interest which is often related to money-market rates. In the UK, between the second quarter of 1982 and the second quarter of 1989, the percentage of interest-bearing deposits in M1 rose from 15 to 59, and in M3 from 59 to 81 (from Bank of England data). The abolition of continuous monetary controls such as reserve ratios or interest ceilings in the 1980s has introduced further competition and potential volatility in an increasingly frictionless financial system.

These developments largely explain the appearance of new monetary and credit aggregates and frequent 'redefinitions' of the existing ones (Podolski,

1986, pp. 88-97, 122-27; Bank of England, 1987a; Walter, 1989).[3] Facing the need to choose aggregates for targeting, the authorities proceeded in an increasingly arbitrary way, while acknowledging difficulties in interpreting the information reflected either in the growth rates of the aggregates or in the gap between the targets and outturn (due mainly to the less certain relation between the aggregates and nominal income).

An important aspect of the money-creation system described earlier was the non-competitive behaviour where banks, in a segmented environment, confined their management to liquidity control on the assets side. They passively accepted deposits, adjusting assets with the aim of maintaining the minimum ratio ß. Such behaviour was reinforced by reserve ratio requirements imposed by central banks and the observance of 'club rules' by financial institutions.

Bank management today, when many monetary constraints have been abolished or eroded by innovations, operates on both sides of the balance sheet and in off-balance-sheet spheres previously associated with merchant or investment banking. Banks aggressively market their products and services, seeking custom from businesses and individuals. On the other hand they compete for deposits, taking advantage of developed wholesale markets in order to fund their loan commitments. This 'liabilities management' (Harrington, 1987), coupled with the continued readiness of central banks to supply 'lender of last resort' help, has the effect of making the process of deposit money creation fully endogenous (Moore, 1986, pp. 448-52; 1988, ch.2).

In this scenario, the stability of ß, or for that matter α, which is of key importance in the orthodox money-creation model, can no longer be relied upon, especially under the pressure of restrictive monetary measures calculated to counteract buoyant market conditions.

Doubts about the Inverted Pyramid Concept

The money equation ($M = kC$) derived earlier is a vital basis of monetarist prescription for monetary control. It raises three main sets of problems: (1) the stability of k; (2) the controllability of C; (3) the selection and measurement of M.

1. Much has already been said to cast doubt on the stability of k, that is the ratio of a money aggregate to the money base. While some economists still have faith in the stability of k and the usefulness of the multiplier approach to money creation (e.g. Rasche and Johannes, 1987),[4] scepticism is more common. Friedman accepted that k would be variable, but claimed that the ratio 'would change gradually and only as financial innovations or changes in business and industry altered the proportions in which the public chose to hold various monetary assets' (Friedman, 1987, p.380). His faith in

gradual change was based on the view that major institutional changes occur only at times of crisis. This is difficult to reconcile with major financial innovations which have occurred in the last two decades in relatively crisis-free conditions.

It is essential to bear in mind that the stability of k depends on the stability of the coefficients ß and α and must be guarded by a caveat 'other things being equal'. In particular k is likely to depend on interest rates (r), transactions costs, and institutional variables. Disregarding the last two, the dependence of k on r [that is, $M = k(r) C$] implies that, with a given C, different levels of M are possible. If the authorities were to constrain credit, preferences of banks and/or the public may change, lowering ß and/or α. For instance, if ß were to remain steady, banks could bid C from the public (wholesale markets) by offering higher rates, thus lowering α and increasing k. With C level of base money (see Figure 3.1) M can rise in response to interest and to consequent (unpredictable) preference changes. Money base control can therefore result in interest volatility without any predictable control over M. Bryant (1983, p.7) concluded that: 'The inverted pyramid is a flexible rather than rigid structure, capable of substantial changes in the size and shape that are not directly attributable to changes in the small tip at the bottom controlled by the Fed.'[5]

2. Economists advocating monetary base control claim that the monetary base can easily be both defined and regulated as it consists of central bank liabilities which the bank must be able to control. In practice, neither is straightforward (Foot *et al*, 1979). In particular, to portray the control of the monetary base as painless has been questioned. Its creation must be seen in the context of wider central bank functions including the finance of central government debt (Bank of England, 1984, pp. 488-9), and above all the duty to maintain orderly markets. Thus the ability to control the monetary base is constrained (Goodhart, 1989, pp. 322-6) and, in the longer run, prolonged restraint would induce the financial system to circumvent it (Dow and Saville, 1988, ch. 9). It has also been argued that in modern financial systems the base is endogenous (e.g. Moore, 1988; Bohara *et al*, 1987). Some libertarian theories even contend that in a deregulated world the monetary base, as understood here, would disappear altogether.[6]

3. As already mentioned, the 'definitions' of M in the context of macromonetary stabilisation has proved to be an intractable problem. The difficulties experienced in the identification and control of intermediate targets made Friedman change his mind (1987, p. 368) and advocate direct targeting of a non-interest-bearing base, in spite of its less close relation to nominal income than that of M1. Alternatively, some economists propose an improved way of measuring 'money' by applying aggregation theory to replace the simple summing of liabilities to aggregates. In recent years the

Figure 3.1 Different levels of 'money' with a given monetary base

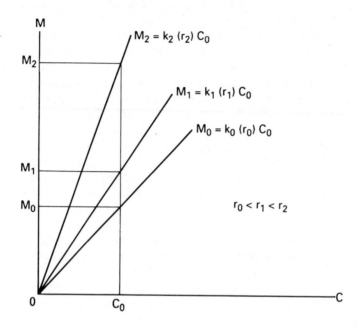

pioneer in this field has been Barnett (1980, 1987) who engineered monetary quantity indices for various Ms, known as Divisia aggregates.

The idea of a weighted aggregate extracting the 'moneyness' or transaction services from financial claims possessing 'monetary' characteristics is not new. However, recent financial innovations and their effects on monetary aggregates revived interest in them. In the UK, an attempt was first made to produce Divisia quantities in the early 1980s (Bailey *et al*, 1982; more recently 'unofficial' monetary services indices have been compiled (Batchelor, 1987; Spencer, 1989).

Thus far monetary quantity indices have not been utilized in monetary policy, though Germany has targeted 'Central Bank Money'. This consists of a simple weighted average of the components of M3, with reserve requirements on various deposits acting as weights in relation to currency which receives the weight of 1 (Trehan, 1988, pp. 30-2).

Simple summing of components which are less than perfect substitutes is not intellectually satisfactory, and in that sense the use of aggregation theory in the measurement of 'money' has merit. Furthermore, such an approach would lessen the need to 'redefine' high level aggregates which have been particularly affected by financial innovation. On the other hand, there are still unanswered questions concerning the nature of the demand, as well as the political acceptance and control of such statistical constructs (Podolski, 1986 pp.79-81).

Improvements in the measurement of money would not suffice for those who question the very foundations of current design of monetary policies, whether based on intermediate or money base targeting. A systematically developed argument along these lines is presented by Moore (1988). Distinguishing sharply between commodity and credit money, he stresses the crucial part played by the borrower in initiating money creation processes, the endogeneity of all financial claims comprising 'money' and the fact that modern financial behaviour does not follow a steady or regular pattern. On empirical grounds, Benjamin Friedman (1988) has challenged the macroeconomic usefulness of any monetary quantity.

CONTROL INSTRUMENTS

Though monetary authorities were inspired by Milton Friedman's policy pre-scriptions, they did not follow them in every detail. Thus multiple rather than single targets have often been used, and growth rates have not been fixed for long periods. Nor has monetary base control been adopted, with the exception of an experiment in the US between 1979 and 1982, abandoned partly because it resulted in wide swings in federal funds rate, and partly because the linkage between the intermediate aggregate M1 and economic activity became unreli-able (e.g. Meulendyke, 1988, pp. 13-14).

In the UK's Medium Term Financial Strategy, fiscal policy and interest rates have been named as the control instruments of money supply. At the beginning, stress was placed on the former and on controlling broad money M3 (then sterling M3). As supply-side control through the money base was not adopted and given the financial behaviour (liability management) described earlier, controlling money became essentially a matter of influencing lending (asset formation) and, because of this, attention focused on the asset counterparts of money changes (see below), derived from the flow of funds accounts (Goodhart, 1984, ch. 4).

$$\Delta M3 = PSBR - DmP - ExF + BSL + ExTR + NDL$$

PSBR : public sector borrowing requirement
DmP : purchases (–) of public sector debt by UK non-bank private sector
ExF : external and foreign currency finance of public sector (increase–)

BSL   :   Bank sterling lending to UK private sector
ExTR   :   External and foreign currency transactions of UK banks
NDL   :   non-deposit liabilities (increase –)

We concentrate here on fiscal control (PSBR – DmP – ExF) and control by interest rates (mainly of BSL).[7] We should, however, note the aversion of the authorities to the use of non-market control instruments. 'The experience in the UK and elsewhere has shown that direct quantitative controls, once thought to be a possible instrument of monetary control, are not only inefficient and distortionary, and so unreliable, but also ineffective in today's sophisticated financial markets. Even a decade ago, markets were learning quickly how to circumvent such controls; their proficiency in doing so would be much greater now' (H.M. Treasury, 1989, p. 11).

Fiscal Policy and Debt Management

The authorities endeavoured to contain money growth by decreasing net public sector expenditure (lower PSBR) and/or funding PSBR by non-bank means such as sales of government securities (higher DmP). Over the years the government, aided by privatisation, has been particularly successful in containing PSBR and has developed innovative methods of raising non-bank finance. PSBR of 5% of GDP in 1979/80 became negative, that is PSDR (public sector debt repayment) of 3% in 1988/89 (H.M. Treasury 1989).

Over-funding, that is selling more debt than necessary to cover PSBR [(PSBR –DmP–ExF) < 0], developed as a means of retarding monetary growth. However in 1985, largely due to distortions in financial flows (including the rise in the stock of commercial bills at the Bank of England, generated to keep the banking system liquid), level-funding policy was adopted, aiming to have a largely neutral fiscal effect on money growth. In practice, the overall impact of public finance on broad money growth was on average negative (col. i in Table 3.2), whereas bank lending to the private sector (col. ii) accounted for more than the overall monetary growth. Thus the control of money has become critically dependent on the efficacy of the demand-side control by interest rates of bank lending in sterling (BSL).

Control by Interest Rates

Central banks can directly influence short-term interest rates through the cost at which liquidity is provided to the discount market and the banking system (Dow and Saville, 1988, ch. 8). The extent to which such action can affect other rates depends on such factors as expectations and cannot be easily predicted. There is some evidence that financial change has altered the relation between short and

Table 3.2 Impact of public and private finance on growth of M3, 1982-89 (£bn.)

Fiscal years	(i) Funded PSBR[1]	(ii) Bank lending[2]	(iii) Other trans.[3]	(iv) £M3	(ii)/(iv)
1982/83	−1.9	14.4	−2.7	9.8	1.5
1983/84	−4.1	15.4	−3.6	7.6	2.0
1984/85	−4.5	18.6	−2.4	11.8	1.6
1985/86	0.4	21.4	−2.7	19.1	1.1
1986/87	0.3	30.4	−5.2	25.5	1.2
1987/88	−0.1	44.8	−11.4	33.3	1.3
1988/89	−0.9	58.7	−17.1	40.7	1.4

Notes:
[1] PSBR–DmP–ExF; overfunding = − (till 1986)
[2] BSL
[3] ExTR + NDL
For symbols see text
Sources: Bank of England Quarterly Bulletin, various issues, Tables 12.1

long rates (Miles, 1989). Here we shall raise only two issues concerning interest rate control: limitations on the use of interest rates and the impact on monetary aggregates.

(a) Limitations on use

Action on interest rates is often constrained by broader economic and political considerations. The following points may be noted.

1. Rates are changed in response to some unanticipated development. They influence economic behaviour in general indirectly and often unpredictably through their effect on costs, expectations and the value of wealth.
2. The setting of rates takes place in a political context. Increases in rates often reflect some policy failure and may be associated with socially adverse effects such as increases in mortgage rates. This makes it difficult to administer large enough increases at the right time.
3. Financial markets today are both resilient and powerful, and it is difficult to counteract a determined course of market behaviour. 'We need always therefore to try to work with the grain of the markets to achieve the required effects' (Bank of England, 1987, p. 369).
4. Interest rates have increasingly been used to influence exchange rates,

though here too their effect is not precise. Conflicts of external and internal policy objectives can arise in this context.

(b) Impact on aggregates

The use of interest rates as a monetary control instrument has always been fraught with problems largely due to difficulties of variable sensitivity of monetary quantities to rate changes. Financial innovation and liberalisation brought further uncertainties in this area. It is generally believed that interest elasticity on narrower aggregates is more predictable (Johnston, 1984) and greater than that on broader aggregates whose sensitivity remains weak and is falling (Dow and Saville, 1988, pp. 139-40; Wenninger, 1988). Increases in interest rates have been known to produce perverse effects by increasing broad aggregates (e.g. M3 in the UK) through switches of financial flows to interest-bearing accounts included in the aggregates (Niehans, 1982, pp. 10-12).

Financial innovations in hedging devices which protect borrowers from the effects of interest-rate changes increase interest insensitivity. High interest rates over a longer term elicit Schumpeterian creative responses, making financial institutions less affected by them (Podolski, 1986, pp. 127-31).

As already stated, to control broad aggregates it is necessary to control lending to the private sector. Such lending has proved rather impervious to interest rate action, which partly explains the difficulty of controlling high-level aggregates. With liability management and rising proportions of interest-bearing deposits related to market rates, changes in interest rates affect both sides of the balance sheet. Though the central bank can influence rates generally, it is less able selectively to affect the formation of monetary assets (Goodhart, 1984, ch. 5; Bank of England, 1987b, pp. 366-7).

To conclude, the central bank has been left with few monetary control instruments – mainly with interest rates. While the raising of the rates has a generally restrictive effect, its direct influence on bank lending and upon monetary quantities is unpredictable and ambiguous. Furthermore, the use of interest rates is circumscribed by wider political and economic considerations. Indeed, interest rate changes may more directly affect other macroeconomic variables and 'money' only indirectly.

CONCLUDING OBSERVATIONS

The first stage of the current design of monetary policy, that is the use of monetary instruments to hit a monetary quantity target, has not worked mainly because the institutional structure in which such a strategy could operate successfully has been eroded by financial change. The enhanced capacity for change (brought about by the application of modern technology and by falling transactions costs) has rendered monetary control difficult and uncertain, and has challenged the theoretical foundations underlying the control of a monetary quantity as a macroeconomic control variable.

The increasingly frictionless financial system and the intractable difficulties of defining money, let alone controlling it with traditional methods, has inspired a variety of theoretical debates, especially by libertarians. The basic question posed has been whether the state can and should have a role in the provision of 'money' or whether this can be left entirely to the market.[8] Radical changes in monetary standards or constitutions, calculated to enhance stability by reducing or eliminating the state from money management, have been proposed. The impact of these absorbing but often abstract debates on practical monetary arrangements has been negligible. One is inclined to agree with Friedman and Schwartz (1987) that particular attention must by paid to historical experience when advocating new models of monetary constitutions.

Meanwhile the issue of monetary control is in a state of some confusion. Of course it is easy to demonstrate that the monetary system and policy do not function in accordance with orthodox theoretical principles, and that control instruments do not operate with textbook precision. However, it is far more difficult to identify a model which does explain financial interrelationships and the relations between the complex and changing financial system and real phenomena. There is a need for a Keynes of the modern monetary or financial economy.

Four broad aspects of the confusion may be distinguished. First, it is now hard to recognise what monetary policy actually is. Though the authorities declare that the original basic framework of the policy has not altered, in practice, policy announcements and operations have changed substantially. For instance, during the ten years of the UK's Medium-Term Financial Strategy, monetary control has changed drastically. The sharp definition of its design and the faith in the macroeconomic power of a monetary quantity, found in the original MTFS declaration (H.M. Treasury, 1980a), have given way – largely under the impact of unanticipated financial change and liberalisation – to a de-emphasis on quantity targeting. Statements about decisions to change interest rates are now vaguer, based on 'a comprehensive assessment of monetary conditions'. These include the behaviour of the wide monetary base M0 in relation to its target, but also take into account (increasingly) the exchange rate as well as broad monetary and liquidity aggregates. In particular, the exchange rate has been recognised as 'a key influence upon, and a key indicator of, monetary conditions' (H.M. Treasury, 1989, pp.13-14). In the present-day financial system, information extraction from all financial and monetary indicators has become difficult.

Secondly, the control of inflation in the UK has been increasingly linked with the need to control the exchange rate. Interest rates have recently been used to stabilise or influence exchange rates in this context. Stabilisation of exchange rates as a prime intermediate objective of economic policy has thus become a key issue. While it is generally recognised that intra-European stabilisation of the sterling exchange rate could be enhanced by the UK joining the Exchange Rate Mechanism of the European Monetary System, this issue, as well as the broader question of the future independence of UK monetary policy, have been further complicated by proposals for European Monetary Union (e.g. Bank of England, 1989b).

Thirdly, theoretical debates do not seem to be leading us to a new 'consensus' and often replay old controversies (e.g. Humphrey, 1988). It should be noted that the monetarist orthodoxy outlined above has not been universally abandoned in spite of the financial changes discussed. Indeed, in his review of monetary policy, Goodhart (1989) justifiably stresses the 'divorce' between macromonetary theory and the practice of monetary policy.

Fourthly, the preoccupation at the theoretical level with informational asymmetries, with difficulties experienced with orthodox monetary control and with the growing risk brought about by rising interdependence in financial markets, has helped to switch emphasis to prudential and supervisory control over financial institutions in general (Baltensperger and Dermine, 1987; Pecchioli, 1987; Bank of England, 1987c, 1988). Particular attention in this context is being paid to the international harmonisation of prudential arrangements and bank supervision (e.g. Dale, 1984; Portes and Swoboda, eds, 1987) and, more generally, to the need for coordination between national macroeconomic policies as a way of checking international financial disturbances (e.g. Bryant and Portes, eds, 1987). Macromonetary policies of the future must recognise the existence of an increasingly internationally-interdependent financial system capable of frustrating uncoordinated national arrangements. This issue (discussed in Chapter 4) will remain regardless of the outcome of the European exchange arrangements and European unification referred to earlier.

NOTES

1. With reference to the text, the money equation is derived below.
    (i) $M = D + Cp$
    (ii) $C = Cb + Cp$
    (iia) $\beta = Cb/D$ or $Cb = \beta D$
    (iib) $\alpha = Cp/D$ or $Cp = \alpha D$
    Substituting (iib) in (i) and rearranging:
    (iii) $M = D(1 + \alpha)$
    Substituting (iia) and (iib) in (ii) and solving for D:
    (iv) $D = C/(\beta + \alpha)$
    Substituting (iv) for D in (iii):
    (v) $M = C [(1 + \alpha)/(\beta + \alpha)]$ or:
    (vi) $M = kC$ where $k = [(1 + \alpha)/(\beta + \alpha)]$

On the evolution of the 'multiplier' approach, see Humphrey (1987). For critical comment see, for example, Goodhart (1975) ch. 6.

2. On financial innovations and their impact see, Podolski (1986); articles in *Oxford Review of Economic Policy*, 2/4, 1986 (esp. by Rose and by Goodhart); BIS (1986); and Spencer (1986).

3. Following the incorporation of the Abbey National in 1989, which produced a large (11%) change in M3, yet another review of published aggregates has taken place, including the cessation of publication of the aggregate and of M1. It seems that M4 has now taken the place of M3 as 'the broad money' measure. For details see Bank of England (1989a).

4. In their statistical investigation, on the basis of which they concluded that the controllability of money had not suffered, the authors took into account institutional and regulatory changes. However, uncertainties about the predictability of future financial changes leave doubts about monetary base control. The need to take into consideration financial innovations in assessing monetary relationships is now generally acknowledged (e.g. Johnston, 1984; Taylor, 1987).

5. In the UK, the ratio M/C (that is, average k) changed, rising for M1 and M3 (between second quarter, 1980 and second quarter, 1989) from 3.1 to 7.7 and 6.3 to 16.5 respectively, and for M4 and M5 (between second quarter, 1983 and second quarter, 1989) from 14.6 to 26.1 and 15.7 to 27.2 respectively (from Bank of England data).

6. Theories, such as the 'legal restrictions theory of money' associated with N. Wallace, or BFH (Black-Fama-Hall) propositions, are part of a broader debate referred to earlier and in Note 8.

7. For a wider discussion on control instruments and issues see, for instance, Cuthbertson (1988) ch. 8.

8. The literature on these debates (encompassing overlapping 'free banking', 'competitive currency systems', 'monetary standards', 'monetary constitutions' and 'new monetary economics' controversies) is voluminous and complex and often harks back to much earlier discussions. Only references to collections of contributions or to review articles (critical or otherwise) on aspects of the literature are listed.

Collections: in *Journal of Monetary Economics*, 12, 1983, and *Journal of Post Keynesian Economics*, Spring, 1989; Siegel, ed, (1984); Salin, ed, (1984); Dorn and Schwartz, eds, (1987).

Reviews: Greenfield and Yeager (1983); Yao (1984); Yeager (1985); Selgin and White (1987); White (1987); Boschen (1988).

4. Open-Economy Macroeconomics

Peter Spencer

It is no longer possible – if it ever was – to ignore the macroeconomic impact of the world economy on domestic policies and performance. From relatively simple open-economy macromodels such as those proposed by Mundell and Fleming, economists have recently built up a more realistic framework which poses the pressing problem of international policy coordination. New models draw heavily on game theory, and Peter Spencer points out that as a consequence, in the international arena as elsewhere, economists are now increasingly concerned with the design of institutions as well as policies.

INTRODUCTION

Macroeconomists have made great progress in understanding the open economy in recent years. A latter-day Rip van Winkle who had fallen asleep during a lecture on the monetary theory of the exchange rate in the mid 1970s would now awake to find himself looking at a much richer and more realistic model, in which trade barriers, price rigidities, and strategic behaviour all played an important part, together with both fiscal and monetary policy. He would see that the macroeconomic framework sketched out on the blackboard closely resembled that of the Mundell-Fleming model of his textbooks, but that the behavioural assumptions used to bring this to life had developed beyond recognition.

This chapter reviews these developments, starting with a look at the relatively simple monetary macromodels of the open economy which were so popular during the 1970s. The Mundell-Fleming distinction between domestic and foreign output is then examined, along with Salter's alternative dichotomy between traded and non-traded goods and services. This establishes the framework for the 'Extended Mundell-Fleming' or exchange rate overshooting model, with its emphasis on price rigidities, capital mobility and rational expectations. The chapter then looks at recent attempts to relax the perfect capital mobility and small country assumptions implicit in these specifications, as well as at the formidable problem of analysing international economic policy coordination in a world of mobile capital and rational expectations.

THE MONETARY THEORY OF THE OPEN ECONOMY

Far from making life more complicated, a high degree of openness can simplify macroeconomic analysis considerably. In an extreme case, without geographical constraints, trade barriers, exchange controls and so on, international arbitrage will equate prices of goods and financial assets in different currencies, at least when measured in terms of a common currency such as the US dollar. This is the famous *'law of one price'*. The small open economy effectively becomes a price-taker, quantity setter in world markets.

The Basic Model

Because relative prices (including real interest rates) are fixed elsewhere, the Hicksian aggregation theorem applies, allowing macroeconomists legitimately to use aggregates such as 'goods and services' and 'bonds'.[1] In this extreme case, the excess domestic demand for goods, services and financial assets only affects the balance of payments. By Walras' law, this is in turn equal to the excess supply of money, the difference between demand and domestic supply. In a fixed exchange rate environment this is reflected in the foreign exchange reserves, giving 'the monetary theory of the balance of payments' (Johnson, 1976). But with no official exchange market intervention, the exchange rate (and hence through international arbitrage, the domestic price level) must adjust to equilibrate the money market, giving 'the monetary theory of the exchange rate' (Mussa, 1976).

Output is determined, on the supply side of such an economy, independently of monetary and fiscal policy. So economic sovereignty is worth very little in the fully open economy, simply allowing the authorities to influence the current account through fiscal policy, and the overall balance of payments (or the domestic price level) through monetary policy. Issues of economic sovereignty are being hotly debated in Western Europe as the 1992 deadline for the Single Market approaches (see e.g. Padoa Schioppa, 1988), but it seems difficult to escape this basic prospect of devalued economic sovereignty. This situation is ideal for a *common currency* as outlined in the seminal paper by Robert Mundell (1961). The central bank would be better off pooling its sovereignty and entering into a fixed currency arrangement with its trading partners, an argument which has become very topical in Europe in the run-up to 1992.[2] All in all, there seems little to distinguish the national from the regional economy if all geographical and political barriers to trade have been removed.

Second Generation Monetary Models of the Open Economy

A non-trivial macroeconomic environment results if not all markets are com-

pletely open. In most economies there are barriers to trade which hamper the law
of one price, at least in the markets for goods and services (Kravis and Lipsey,
1979; Isard, 1977). This means, in turn, that the monetary theory of the open
economy cannot hold in its simple form. Some economists have responded to this
criticism by arguing that published price indices are poor measures of the
appropriate transactions price deflators (Bilson, 1980). The 'true' price indices
should on these grounds be treated as unobservable variables, with a ratio defined
to equal the exchange rate: being the relative price of two currencies, this is
simply related to their relative supplies. This gives the *'equilibrium rational
expectations'* version of the model attributed to Frenkel (1976), Mussa (1979),
and Bilson (1980).

Other monetary theorists, notably Niehans (1975) and Dornbusch (1976),
have instead developed the monetary model by relaxing the assumption that the
law of one price applies to all markets. This complicates the process of exchange-
rate determination considerably. It is then necessary to distinguish between
domestic and foreign-produced goods and to ask how closely substitutable they
are empirically. Since this degree of substitution varies widely between different
types of goods, depending upon their homogeneity, portability, and so on, it is
also useful to disaggregate domestic output. This unfortunately increases the
number of relative prices in the system, making analytical work very difficult.
One simple scheme which avoids this problem (Salter, 1959), is based on a
dichotomy between 'traded' and 'non-traded' goods and services. The latter do
not enter international trade, and residents may only substitute domestically
produced non-traded goods for traded goods. They are indifferent between those
traded goods produced domestically and overseas, equating their domestic
currency prices. This gives the *'law of one price for traded goods'*.

There is no direct arbitrage mechanism for equating the prices of non-traded
goods in this model, so that the cost of living may differ from one country to
another, reflecting differences in these prices. Once differences in prices of non-
traded goods emerge, they will be reflected in the *real exchange rate*, defined as
the cost of living overseas relative to the cost of living at home, both expressed
in a common currency. That these models maintain the assumption that capital
is perfectly mobile helps to keep down the number of markets and relative prices
in the system, since it is not necessary to distinguish between foreign and
domestic bonds.

The model can be kept reasonably simple by ignoring the labour market, or
treating labour as analogous to a non-traded good. If prices are perfectly flexible,
changes in the money supply are offset in inflation and simply act as a tax on the
private sector, without affecting relative prices. There is only one relative price
in this system – the real exchange rate or the relative price of non-traded goods
vis-à-vis the bond and traded goods composite. Even if prices are sticky, this
property extends to the steady-state equilibrium of the system as has been

demonstrated in a domestic/overseas good context by Kingston and Turnovsky (1977), and a traded/non-traded good context by Riley (1982).

A KEYNESIAN PERSPECTIVE

Although models of this type retain many of the monetarist features of the simple open-economy model, they also exhibit many significant closed-economy characteristics. Keynesian demand-deficient unemployment can exist if wages and prices of non-traded goods are sticky, and the former low in relation to the latter, as demonstrated by Dixit (1978). This analysis is similar to the four-regime closed-economy analysis of Muellbauer and Portes (1978)[3] in which there is an important role for fiscal policy – provided it affects the demand for domestic or non-traded goods. Fiscal-policy-induced changes in the demand for traded goods have no effect on activity, simply affecting the current account of the balance of payments (Dornbusch, 1974). Assuming that this is a pure fiscal policy financed by a bond issue, it will be exactly offset in the capital account, so neutralizing the balance of payments and exchange-rate effects. Money is neutral in a long-run, static sense.

Mundell-Fleming

The relative efficacy of monetary and fiscal policy in this essentially Keynesian model was originally established by Mundell (1963) and Fleming (1962). They concluded that in a fixed exchange rate regime, fiscal policy would have a powerful effect on activity, and monetary policy would have no effect, but that these positions would be reversed under a floating exchange rate with a fixed money supply. This stark conclusion follows directly from their assumption that international capital flows equate nominal interest rates, independently of monetary policy and exchange-rate expectations. Under a fixed-money-supply, floating-exchange-rate regime, these assumptions serve to fix the price level and interest rates which (with velocity unchanged) also fixes nominal and real incomes. So fiscal policy is fully crowded out, being offset by net trade flows. The first column of Table 4.1 shows the assumptions, both explicit and implicit, of the model.

Static derivatives of the Mundell-Fleming Model

It is relatively easy to relax the assumptions of the Mundell-Fleming model while keeping within the original comparative static framework. For example, Morris (1988) highlights the role of assumption a(iv) of Table 4.1 by assuming zero capital mobility instead, neatly reversing the standard fiscal-monetary multiplier results. In fact the role of the capital mobility assumption in the static model is most easily seen using a standard IS-LM model. This shows that the MF result (that the fiscal multiplier is greater under a fixed exchange rate) depends upon the relative interest elasticity of international capital flows and the domestic demand for money.[4] Within the same comparative static confines, Argy and Salop (1979) develop a version of the MF model in which prices rather than output are flexible. Further useful modifications are considered by Marston (1985).

In similar vein, Robert Mundell's well-known textbook *International Economics* (1968) offers a simple description of international economic interdependence in terms of a static two-country model, demonstrating that the basic

Table 4.1   *Assumptions of the Mundell-Fleming (MF) model and its derivatives*

	Model feature	(a) MF assumption	(b) Development
(i)	Demand side	Keynesian*	Income and asset-based
(ii)	Supply side	Fix price	Flex price, with lags*
(iii)	Expectations	Static	Rational*
(iv)	Capital mobility	Perfect*	Mean-variance based
(v)	Money	Non-traded*	Currency substitution
(vi)	Global framework	Small country	Multi country
(vii)	Policy framework	Nash optimisation*	Policy cooperation

*Maintained in Extended MF Model

MF results hold providing that the propensity to consume domestic goods exceeds the propensity to import. Similar comparative static results have been obtained in a more complex model by Mussa (1979).

Cooperation in a Static World

Once the small country assumption is dropped, it becomes important to recognise the tendency for policy decisions taken in one country to spill over into other countries through international linkages. This can affect the trade-off faced by other policy-makers and introduce feedback effects working through world trade multipliers and the like. At the very least, rational policy-makers should take these feedbacks into account when attempting to steer their economies.

These interdependences represent a fairly trivial complication in the basic MF framework, where the policy-maker is implicitly assumed to have enough policy instruments to achieve a non-inflationary full-employment equilibrium. But if governments do not have enough independent instruments and so cannot maximise welfare by themselves, policy spillovers allow them to do better through cooperation.

This point has been demonstrated within a comparative static framework by a large number of papers, originally by Hamada (1974, 1976, 1985) and, more recently, Canzoneri and Gray (1985), Corden (1984) and Cooper (1984). In this literature, policy formulation is seen as a game in which each government acts as a player and attempts to minimise a welfare loss function defined over deviations of target variables and policy instruments from their desired values. Governments are defined to be Nash optimisers if they act independently, taking the actions of others as given as in the MF model. This behaviour results in a non-cooperative solution, otherwise known as the Nash equilibrium. This non-cooperative solution is not Pareto efficient,[5] and governments can improve upon it as shown in the Appendix. In the absence of cooperation, a government considering a unilateral expansion has to take account of both domestically-generated inflation and the effects of exchange-rate depreciation. But if countries cooperate and agree to expand together, these latter effects are neutralised and the inflation-output trade-off improves, resulting in a higher level of output and welfare. This is simply the 'Prisoner's Dilemma' argument for cooperation.

Oudiz and Sachs (1984) have emphasised the importance of symmetry in this situation, arguing that independent policy-makers facing similar problems will tend to adopt beggar-my-neighbour exchange rate policies. For example, if inflation is Public Enemy Number One, as it was following the 1979 oil price shock, all countries will be tempted to follow tight monetary policies in order to 'export' inflation, possibly tempering the output effects with a lax fiscal policy. If, on the other hand, the main concern is unemployment, countries will tend to engage in competitive devaluation, as in the 1930s. But since terms of trade effects sum to zero, the resulting Nash equilibrium is suboptimal. Cooperation is potentially very useful in this situation, as a way of eliminating exchange rate competition. Oudiz and Sachs note that a system of fixed exchange rate rules could achieve a similar outcome. This helps to explain why the robustness of common currency areas such as the EMS tends to be increased by 'convergence' or similarity between the member economies. However asymmetry destroys this result. Differences over objectives can lead to squabbles. Also differential shocks can make floating exchange rates a better way of organising the international monetary system than fixed exchange rates, as demonstrated in the work of McKibbin and Sachs (1986), which is reviewed in the final section. These issues are also analysed in the Appendix.

Several authors have noted that asymmetries in policy instruments tend to increase the scope for policy cooperation. For example, Brandsma and Hallett (1984) have noted that monetary policy instruments tend to be more effective in the US than in Europe. On the other hand, US fiscal policy is more difficult to adjust and less influential than in Europe. This can lead to situations in which it is appropriate for Europe to make fiscal and the US to make monetary adjustments, at least on a short term basis.

The argument for cooperation in a static non-stochastic two-player situation is compelling, but the real world is more complex. Some dynamic and stochastic complications are discussed later. Yet even within a certain static world there are likely to be more than two players, making it difficult to secure and monitor agreements. There is, however, one game-theoretic specification which can often be usefully applied to this situation: the leader-follower model. In this case there is one player who is large or important relative to the rest, allowing it to act as the *leader*. Other players take the leader's decisions as given and react accordingly as *followers*. (The private sector has always been classed as a follower in these models.) But the large player takes these reactions into account when designing its policy, thus ensuring an outcome superior to the Nash equilibrium. This model offers a very useful insight into the role of the USA in the immediate post war international economy. Melitz (1988) has also used this model to analyse the role of the Bundesbank within the EMS. The leadership model is further discussed in the Appendix.

A Dynamic Development: The Extended Mundell-Fleming Model

The developments discussed above have largely taken place within a comparative static framework. But the real challenge has been to allow properly for the role of expectational and lagged adjustment effects by developing a dynamic version of the MF specification. In the context of the original model this requires a more realistic treatment of price and wage or supply dynamics, as well as exchange rate expectations (assumptions a(ii) and (iii) in Table 4.1).

Once institutional rigidities impede the adjustment of domestic wages and prices, or output, something else must adjust to offset monetary policy and other shocks. One possibility is the domestic interest rate, but until assumptions a(iii) and a(iv) are relaxed, this is determined in the world market. All that remains is the exchange rate, which affects the cost of living through the price of traded goods. If, for example, output and prices are both fixed in the short run, the exchange rate will react violently, overshooting its new long-run value by a multiple equal to the inverse of the weight of these goods in the cost-of-living index. This basic idea underpinned the exchange rate overshooting models until the late 1970s.

Replacing the static expectations assumption by one of rational expectations, Begg (1981) gives a much more realistic and elegant model of the open economy which, following Dornbusch's (1980) discussion, we will label the Extended Mundell-Fleming (EMF) model. The principle involved is essentially the same: because domestic prices and output do not adjust to shocks in the short term, something else must: in this case it is the exchange rate *and* the interest rate. Under the rational expectations assumption, international investors realise that the exchange rate has overshot its long-run value, and expect it to fall back. But with assumption a(iv) still in place, this must be compensated by an appropriate interest rate differential. So in the case of a sudden monetary contraction, for example, the exchange rate initially 'jumps', cutting the price of traded goods but raising domestic interest rates. The rise in interest rates helps to reduce the demand for money, reducing the degree of the exchange rate overshoot. A fall in domestic output, due to the high exchange rate and interest, also helps the money market to adjust. It further puts downward pressure on domestic wages and prices, progressively taking the strain off interest and exchange rates, until the system returns to the initial real equilibrium point, with all prices reduced in line with the money supply.

This exchange rate overshooting model became the workhorse of the early 1980s and was applied to a wide variety of pressing macroeconomic problems, not all of which were monetary in nature. For example, in the UK, Eastwood and Venables (1980) applied the EMF model with great effect to the analysis of the North Sea oil discoveries which were coming on stream at the time (also see Neary and Van Wijnbergen, 1984; and Spencer, 1984). This model has shaped the thought processes of a generation of macroeconomists. Yet the Keynesian nature of the macro demand and supply functions, in conjunction with the perfect capital mobility assumption, mean that the balance of payments plays very little role in the EMF model, except to maintain equilibrium in the markets for traded goods and bonds. There is no medium-term feedback from the current account into wealth and expenditure, nor from the capital account to the production capital stock and productive potential. Given the short-run anti-inflation policy bias of the early 1980s, however, these features were not seen as a major drawback.

The trade imbalances of the mid 1980s, together with worries about the adverse effect of tight monetary policies on real interest rates and investment, naturally led policy-makers and modellers to re-examine these assumptions. These developments were in fact anticipated in a seminal paper by Dornbusch and Fischer (1980) which explored the connection between wealth, expenditure and the current account in an open economy. In a slightly different vein, a paper by Neary and Purvis (1981) analysed the dynamics of the productive capital stock. But it was found that analytical solutions to rational expectations models could only be obtained by looking at the effect of one type of lag at a time, leading to idiosyncratic theoretical models, tailored to specific problems. The need to analyse more complex dynamic situations spurred the development of numerical methods for solving models under the RE assumption, a task which involved theoreticians as well as applied economists (see, for example, Blanchard and Kahn, 1980; and Taylor, 1979).

NEW CLASSICAL OPEN-ECONOMY MACROECONOMICS

The admission of rational expectations into the financial markets by the architects of the EMF model naturally opens them to the charge of inconsistency: if financial operators are so smart why not agents in the goods and labour markets? This dichotomy can perhaps be justified by informational asymmetry and other real-world imperfections which lead to credit rationing, overlapping contracts and other rigidities. Although we know from everyday experience that these institutional arrangements exist and can be important, it is nevertheless necessary to examine the role which they play by asking how a small open economy would behave in a frictionless new classical world.

Ricardian Equivalence

Perhaps the most original contribution of new classical macroeconomists has been the surprise model of inflation, which we touch on in the next section. Another important contribution has been the resurrection of the Ricardian equivalence theorem by Barro (1974, 1989) and others. In its most simple, closed-economy guise, this notes that government debt represents deferred taxation, and that in a forward-looking world with infinitely-lived individuals without credit constraints or other frictions, debt-financed tax changes should leave permanent incomes and hence private expenditure unaltered.

This infinite-horizon version of the model has been extended to the open economy by Stockman (1980), Lucas (1982) and Frenkel and Razin (1985). The Diamond (1986) finite-horizon overlapping-generation model in which debt-financed tax changes are not neutral has been extended to the open economy by Buiter (1981) and Persson (1985). Similar results have been obtained by Blanchard (1985) using a model in which lifetimes are uncertain. These are essentially single-good single-bond models which therefore preclude interesting exchange and interest rate dynamics. However, Van Wijnbergen (1986) has extended the Diamond model to the traditional two-good two-country development of the MF model. In this specification, deficit-financed tax cuts increase private spending initially, putting upward pressure on the exchange rate (assuming again that preferences are biased towards domestic production) as in the traditional income-expenditure model.

In a development of their earlier model, Frenkel and Razin (1986a) use the Blanchard uncertain lifetime assumption together with Salter's traded/non-traded goods framework. Again, a tax cut temporarily raises domestic spending on non-tradeables and hence their relative international and intertemporal prices (real exchange and interest rates). In all of these models, the government budget constraint means that the steady state spending effects are eventually reversed by debt financing costs, usually leaving interest rates permanently higher. The steady state exchange rate effects are highly ambiguous, depending upon the detailed parameter configuration (Frenkel and Razin, 1986b).

Time Consistency and Reputation

As in any branch of the behavioural sciences, the adoption of the rational expectation assumption inevitably leads to the problem of *time inconsistency*. This problem was first formulated by Kydland and Prescott (1977) who noted that if private sector expectations are forward-looking, then the optimal path for a policy instrument changes over time. This is because the mere passage of time changes the optimality conditions relating to the planned value of future policy variables.

For example, consider the announcement of a *future* monetary contraction. If this were to be believed, inflation would immediately begin to fall. Now suppose for simplicity that including these prior benefits would just make it optimal for the government to plan such a policy. When it came to implementation, the prior benefits would already have been secured, no matter whether the policy was implemented or not, and the remaining benefits would then be less than the cost, so the policy would not be implemented. The private sector recognises this flaw and so ignores the original announcement, believing that the government will do whatever suits it at the time.

Currie and Levine (1985) have shown that in this situation the government forfeits its leadership characteristic and behaves as if its actions do not affect the decision relationships of the private sector. The solution degenerates to a Nash equilibrium, which as we have seen is Pareto inefficient. Reflecting this, Kydland and Prescott showed how this sort of behaviour led to a sub-optimal non-zero rate of inflation at the natural rate of employment within a Lucas-style inflation surprise model (see chapter 6). As a solution they suggested the development of institutional arrangements which make it a 'difficult and time consuming process to change policy rules'.

Another approach is to stand the problem on its head, noting that the time-consistent solution is usually so severely sub-optimal that the policy-maker would have a strong incentive to adhere to some other time-inconsistent policy rule in the hope of developing a reputation for following long-term policies, and beginning to influence expectations accordingly. This is essentially the approach of Barro and Gordon (1983) who showed how *trigger mechanisms* could be used to sustain the standard optimal solution in a surprise inflation model. In their specification, policy-makers begin with a *reputation* for long-termism, and the private sector believes that they will follow the socially optimal (zero inflation) policy as long as it continues to do so. If policy-makers cheat by inflicting surprise inflation on the private sector, then they forfeit their reputation for some *punishment interval* during which the system reverts to the Nash equilibrium. Providing that these long-term costs outweigh the short-term output gains from surprise inflation, policy-makers will resist temptation and the standard optimal control equilibrium will be sustained. Barro and Gordon show that, depending upon the length of the punishment period, a number of alternative efficient equilibria are sustainable, a point which has been elaborated by Rogoff (1987) and Canzoneri and Henderson (1988). Oudiz and Sachs (1985) offer an excellent review of these developments and show how these alternative solution criteria can be applied to large-scale international models. The authors note that the sustainability or credibility of a policy depends upon the property of *subgame perfection* which encompasses both time consistent and reputational equilibria.

The Barro-Gordon paper represents a great step forward in the analysis of informational equilibria, opening up a new avenue of research for macroeconomists. But it has proved quite controversial. The basic problem lies with the trigger mechanism and the punishment period. It is not clear how threats could be coordinated by an atomistic private sector, which is usually modelled as a follower rather than a separate bargaining unit. How, for example, would the length of the punishment period be decided? Continuous learning processes, such as the adaptive expectations model, are arguably more applicable to the private sector than discrete trigger mechanisms of the Barro-Gordon variety, but as yet this option has not been rigorously analysed. Another problem is that a finite-time horizon (implied by an impending parliamentary election, for example) can interrupt the punishment period and lead to an unravelling of the solution, so that the system reverts to the time-consistent solution. These and other problems are analysed by Levine (1988).

Cooperation in a Forward-looking Dynamic Environment

With forward-looking expectations, the time consistency problem can also affect relationships between governments. Given the small number of players, the Barro-Gordon reputational solution seems more relevant as a way of sustaining inter-government agreements than reputations of governments with the private sector. In the absence of some learning process or other way of building credibility with the private sector, this opens up a series of questions about the virtues or otherwise of cooperation without reputation.

The central result in this area, identified by Rogoff (1985), is that in the absence of reputation, cooperation may lower welfare. The reason for this result is that time-consistent or discretionary policies mean a higher rate of inflation than in the optimal reputational equilibrium, and cooperation exaggerates this bias by neutralising the externalities associated with currency depreciation. To complement the Rogoff paradox, Oudiz and Sachs (1985) have shown that reputation without cooperation may lower welfare. In this case, reputation helps an individual government to use the exchange-rate-overshooting effect to combat inflation, resulting in an outcome which is more deflationary than in the optimal reputation-with-cooperation solution. These effects are much less acute without reputation. Both paradoxes are discussed by Canzoneri and Henderson (1988) and Currie and Levine (1989). Oudiz and Sachs also show how in a symmetric situation, policy cooperation (or exchange-rate rule) eliminates the time consistency problem associated with the exchange rate. In this case, the exchange rate is set in line with purchasing power parity (see Appendix), eliminating inconsistency. In a neo-Keynesian model of the Dornbusch type, in which the exchange rate is the only forward-looking variable, this is a very convenient result. However there remain problems of time consistency associated with forward-looking expectations in domestic markets, particularly the labour market which (as the Rogoff example shows) cooperation may exacerbate.

INTRODUCING UNCERTAINTY

Another aspect of international policy coordination which turns out to be related to the sustainability issue – model uncertainty – has cast a shadow over a wide area of applied macroeconomics. How, for example, can one handle rational expectations in the usual model-consistent way when the public and private sectors may start with different models of the economy? In the international context, different governments also tend to use different models, often with very different properties. This point has been emphasised by Frenkel and Rockett (1988) who considered the likelihood of agreement between the USA and the rest of the OECD. Each policy-maker had a choice of one out of ten empirical models upon which to base its discussions, giving a total of 100 combinations *ex ante*. Nature then chooses the true model, giving a total of 1000 outcomes *ex post*. Frenkel and Rockett then used the models to evaluate the total static gains from cooperation and found that these were positive *ex post* in only 62 percent of cases. In other words, 38 percent of these bargains would have been unsustainable, breaking down as time passed and the true model revealed itself.

Holtham and Hallett (1988) have pointed out that many of the original bargains were suspect even before the true model revealed itself: in many cases countries would have expected their partners to have been left worse off (on the basis of their own preferred models) by cooperation. They classify these as *weak bargains*, since they would be expected to disintegrate, distinguishing them from *strong bargains* in which both countries believe that neither of them will be left worse off, with an incentive to renege. These authors provide several plausible reasons why, even in the absence of altruism, no country would knowingly enter into an unsustainable bargain. Re-examining the Frenkel-Rockett details of four models for which full results were published, Holtham and Hallett find that out of the 16 prior combinations of beliefs and 64 possible outcomes, 35 (55 percent) are successful *ex post*, resulting in gains for both parties. However only 9 of the original 16 Nash bargains are strong bargains, resulting in 36 possible outcomes, of which 25 (69 percent) are a success *ex post*. The authors conclude that differences of view are actually helpful because they furnish alternative models and hence robustness checks for international policy trades. But note that this is at the expense of reducing the total number of successes, from 35 to 25 in their example. As in any uncertain situation, there is clearly a trade-off between type 1 and type 2 error,[6] forcing a choice which will depend upon the relative costs of making these errors. All in all, these studies reveal model uncertainty to be a serious obstacle to policy trades, by making it difficult either to secure agreements in the face of asymmetric information, or to sustain agreements as the true model reveals itself.

Portfolio Balance Models

Another aspect of uncertainty is its effect on private sector portfolio behaviour. All the theoretical models of the dynamics discussed so far preserve the assumption of perfect capital mobility and hence exhibit the central MF result that fiscal policy is more expansionary with a fixed exchange rate than with a fixed money supply. Valiant attempts have been made in recent years to relax this assumption, using ideas stemming from the Tobin-Markowitz mean-variance asset market theory (Dooley and Isard, 1980; Sachs and Wyplosz, 1984; and Argy, 1986). These models regard assets denominated in different currencies as imperfect substitutes, asuming that investors demand risk premia for holding securities denominated in foreign currencies. They are naturally difficult to observe, making it very hard to test the degree of international asset substitution. But the difficulty of rejecting the Efficient Markets Hypothesis, which states that the exchange rates simply follow a random walk (Frenkel, 1981), is evidence against the hypothesis of imperfect substitution. Attempts to apply the Tobin-Markowitz capital asset pricing model rigorously to the current markets have not been successful (Frenkel and Engel, 1984). But in view of the difficulty of devising tests to detect risk premia, the degree of capital mobility must remain an open question.

EMPIRICAL EVIDENCE

Which brings us to the broader empirical issues. This section reviews some of the papers which have examined the international linkages; not without shortcomings, their conclusions depend heavily on the model and objective function chosen. Moreover, some results are suspect because they tend to underestimate the long-run adverse consequences of stimulative policies, for example, by ignoring the cumulative effect of government borrowing. Nevertheless, they illustrate some of the more important theoretical points, as well as providing an insight into the workings of the world economy and the scope for policy cooperation.

International Macromodels

The recent Brookings volume *Empirical Macroeconomics for Interdependent Economies* (Bryant *et al*, 1988) provides an invaluable assessment of the current state of international macroeconomic modelling. It reveals major differences between the main empirical world models, not only concerning the scale of interaction effects, but also the direction of these effects. As we have seen, lack of agreement about these linkages could significantly complicate the issue of coordination. Consider for example the theoretically ambiguous effect of fiscal policy on the exchange rate. In the Brookings simulations, most models showed that expansionary fiscal policy in the US (or the rest of the OECD) led to an appreciation (depreciation) of the US dollar, consistent with the MF model result. However, in some models, an expansionary US debt-financed fiscal policy leads to a depreciation of the US dollar, a result explained of course by a relatively low degree of capital mobility. In contrast, the effect of monetary policy on the exchange rate seems to be robust: a monetary expansion always leads to a depreciation in these models, though of varying degree.

The effect of exchange rates on output and income is also ambiguous *a priori*. Several offsetting mechanisms may be involved, including the real balance effect. In the Brookings models a *fiscal* expansion always has a positive spillover effect overseas. *Monetary* expansion leads to a depreciation but in many empirical models is also transmitted positively abroad, contrary to the prediction of the MF model (Helliwell and Padmone, 1985). For example in the Taylor (1985) model the positive international spillover stems from the positive effect of a domestic depreciation on foreign real money balances, powerful enough to offset the decline in price competitiveness of the foreign country.

The Gains from Policy Cooperation

Table 4.2 below describes some of the models which have been used to assess the benefits of policy coordination. The Japanese EPA and Fed's MCM models are empirical structures with backward-looking expectations, while those of Taylor and McKibbin/Sachs are small simulation models with forward-looking expectations and parameters loosely based on a range of empirical estimates. Two basic methods have been used to evaluate the welfare gains from coordination and from various alternative fiscal, monetary and exchange rate regimes. The first approach is to calculate benefits from cooperation as the difference between the outcomes of optimal cooperative and non-cooperative strategies. The second technique is to subject the system to shocks and then measure welfare in terms of the changes in the variability of the target variables which result under cooperation and under competition.

Oudiz and Sachs (1985) analysed coordination between the G3 countries (US, Germany and Japan) over the period 1984–86 using policy multipliers taken from the MCM and EPA models. They found that welfare gains from co-ordination were small and accrued primarily to the benefit of Japan. Using the MCM, an optimally coordinated policy involved a shift to fiscal expansion and monetary expansion in the US, and to fiscal contraction and monetary expansions in Germany and Japan. Using the EPA model, coordination led to fiscal contraction and monetary expansion in all three countries. The main benefits occurred through a simultaneous fall in interest rates and accrued mainly as output growth. But given the low weight attached to output in the revealed-preference objective function that Oudiz and Sachs use, the welfare gains were modest. Gains (expressed in equivalent percentage points of GNP) ranged from 0.03 to 0.17 for the US, 0.03 to 0.34 for Germany, and 0.37 to 0.99 for Japan. Oudiz and Sachs concluded that it was the anti-inflation bias of policy-makers rather than the lack of coordination which prevented a general expansion.

This pioneering study has inevitably proved controversial. Several of those originally involved in policy coordination (Marris, Schultz, Woo) criticised Oudiz and Sachs' use of the revealed-preference method to parameterise the welfare function, arguing that the US policy mix at that time could not be regarded as the outcome of optimising behaviour. Blanchard argued that the methodology was appropriate, but that the set of target variables was too narrow. Moreover, the US had as many instruments as independent targets, which would not be expected to leave much scope for coordination-induced welfare improvements. Despite such qualifications, this approach has spawned a wealth of subsequent studies in a similar mould. Oudiz (1985) for example examines coordination between Germany, France, the UK and Italy. He allows for the exchange rate in the objective function and asks whether welfare gains from coordination are higher among these countries given their stronger financial and trade linkages. Yet the conclusion is the same; welfare gains are found to be small because the major benefits accrue in the form of output, which is not assigned a very high utility weight. Welfare gains are low for Germany and the UK (about 0.2), but higher for France (1.0).

Ishii *et al* (1985) use the MSG model, which includes internal equations for Japan, to examine gains from coordination among the US, the rest of the OECD and Japan. They adopt the Oudiz-Sachs baseline approach but with arbitrary weights, giving a relatively high weight to the output gap. Compared with baseline policies, coordination leads to monetary expansion in all three regions,

Table 4.2   Five models of international linkage

	Model	Description	Basic theory[1]	Time frame[2]	Para-meters[3]	Expect-ations[4]	Asset substituta-bility[5]
1.	EPA (world economic model of Japanese Economic Planning Agency)	Large structural model: full models for 9 countries and 5 other regions covering RoW.	K	Q	E	B	I
2.	MCM (Multi-Country Model of US Federal Reserve Board)	Large structural model: full models for 5 countries & RoW.	K	Q	E	B	I
3.	McKibbin & Sachs	Small model: full models for US and ROECD, and foreign trade model for OPEC and LDCs. Stock-flow relationships and intertemporal budget constraints observed.	NK	A	I	H	P
4.	MSG (McKibbin & Sachs Global model)	Identical to (3) but with full model for Japan.	NK	A	I	H	P
5.	Taylor	Small model: full models for 7 countries. Forward-looking expectations but lapping wage contracts in labour market.	NC	Q	I	F	P

[1] K: Keynesian; NK: Neo Keynesian; NC: New Classical
[2] Q: Quarterly; A: Annual
[3] E: Estimated; I: Largely improved
[4] B: Backward; F: Forward-looking; H: Hybrid
5 P: Perfect; I: Imperfect

References: for Model 1, EPA (1985); for Model 2, Oudiz and Sachs (1984); for Model 3, Sachs and McKibbin (1986); for Model 4, McKibbin & Sachs (1986); and for Model 5, Taylor (1985).

to fiscal contraction in the US, and fiscal expansion in Japan and the ROECD. This is precisely the fiscal policy mix that policy-makers have been attempting to achieve in the last few years (Funabashi, 1988). Not surprisingly, it results in significant reductions in current account imbalances and substantial output gains for the ROECD (around 5 percentage points in 1988). To put the latter into perspective, the Cecchini (1988) report suggested that the Single Market reforms could increase GDP in the EEC by a similar percentage. Inflation rates, however, are notably higher in the ROECD. World interest rates are again reduced.

Other authors have analysed the potential for coordination when policy is based upon rules. For example, Carlozzi and Taylor (1985) examine how the degree of capital mobility affects the extent of policy independence when a non-coordinated rule linking real interest rates to prices is adopted in each country. Simulation results suggest that even when capital mobility is perfect, exchange rate expectations give sufficient flexibility for independent interest rate rules in the two countries. One country's trade-off improves when the other chooses a more accommodating policy, but this effect is slight.

Similarly, Taylor (1985) examines the efficacy of optimal cooperative and non-cooperative monetary rules as a response to random supply shocks. The rule specifies the degree of accommodation to inflation. Unless there is full accommodation, a supply shock produces real output effects and is transmitted abroad. Policy-makers are assumed to minimise the variances of output and inflation in the steady-state equilibrium. His empirical results support the view that cooperative policy rules are more accommodative to inflation than non-cooperative rules. Moreover, a domestic inflation shock, which causes the central bank to tighten monetary policy, generally provokes an expansionary policy overseas when countries cooperate. Hence, the domestic currency appreciated by more and inflation is more easily reduced. Taylor points out that the 'gain from trade' comes from an agreement for the home country to help similarly if the situation reverses. Nevertheless, as a counter example to the Rogoff case, cooperation does lead to an increase in world welfare, despite the forward-looking nature of this model.

Comparing Exchange Rate Regimes

Several studies have attempted to assess the welfare implications of alternative exchange rate regimes. McKibbin and Sachs (1986) compare the results of non-cooperative and cooperative policies with those obtained under a fixed exchange rate regime and under a version of McKinnon's proposals for a symmetric 'paper gold standard' (McKinnon, 1984). They use a method similar to Taylor's, calculating the steady-state variance of the targets in the MSG model when the economies experience various types of shock. The cooperative solution turns out to be the best. As the theory predicts, fixed exchange rate regimes perform poorly in the case of country-specific inflation shocks, but tolerably well in the case of global shocks. For other shocks, such as negatively correlated disturbances to the demand for money, the McKinnon regime works relatively well.

CONCLUSION

We conclude by referring back to Table 4.1, which shows how theoreticians have been able to generalise all of the main assumptions of the original Mundell-Fleming model. As a result we now have a much better understanding of the role which different assumptions play and a much improved theoretical tool kit. The game theoretic approach has yielded great insights in this field. It may not be possible to obtain qualitative results for the most general dynamic open-economy model, but it is possible to build realistic dynamic models capturing salient features of the real world and yet yielding elegant closed solutions, of which the Dornbusch exchange-rate model is the prime example. We can also construct numerical models of more complex situations with a good understanding of the various building blocks and the characteristics which they endow upon the full system.

Theoretical analysis nevertheless leaves many ambiguities for the applied econometrician to resolve. First and foremost is the degree of international capital mobility, and the question that this raises about the basic Mundell-Fleming fiscal policy multiplier results. Despite its great importance, no consensus has emerged on this issue. A second example concerns the effect of exchange rate movements on output. Here, real balance and competitiveness effects work in opposite directions. Again, there is a proliferation of different results, even for a single economy such as the UK. In view of the pernicious implications of model uncertainty for policy cooperation, this lack of consensus is most unfortunate.

The widespread adoption of rational expectations and the recognition of the problem of time inconsistency have raised severe doubts about the optimal control solution to macroeconomic models. This is particularly the case in multi-country specifications where governments find themselves behaving strategically against each other as well as against private agents. Yet notions of 'subgame perfection' and 'reputation' have allowed the rehabilitation of the standard solution in an infinite-horizon repeated game situation. Non-linearities, large stochastic shocks and finite-horizon problems still present difficulties, but these do not appear insuperable.

The exchange rate overshooting effect, associated with backward-looking real and forward-looking financial markets, has highlighted the role of the exchange rate as a 'shared variable' in the bilateral economy. Following the experience of the 1980s, policy-makers have also come to regard exchange rate externalities as important, more so than the international trade linkages and 'locomotive theories' which dominated the thinking of the 1970s. Consciously or unconsciously, they have been groping towards a system of managed exchange rates, both as a way of outlawing damaging terms of trade spillovers, and of providing a more suitable environment for international policy cooperation.

Meanwhile, recent theoretical work has shown that fixed exchange rate agreements are most valuable and sustainable in such a symmetric situation, when countries are trying to deal with a common inflationary or deflationary shock. A fixed exchange rate agreement is a good approximation to full cooperation in this situation. The monetary policy leadership problem is not very relevant in this case, since policy-makers are able to agree a common goal. Unfortunately, independent shocks or asymmetries in economic structure or policy-makers' preferences destroy these comforting results. In this case, exchange rate constraints are likely to frustrate international cooperation and lead to leadership conflict. Indeed, the empirical models suggest that a non-cooperative regime based on floating exchange rates would be more appropriate in this environment.

Despite the absence of a consensus model and the consequent arbitrariness of empirically-based results, the large world econometric models have proved very useful as a way of studying international linkages. Some apparently robust results have emerged from this programme. It seems clear, for example, that in an inflationary environment, autarkic policies generally lead to a sub-optimal policy mix, involving tight money and lax fiscal policy. Cooperation helps correct this, but is fragile because large gains are typically available to the first country to renege. The potential benefits from coordination have typically been small for industrial countries in the 1980s because they accrued largely in the form of extra output, which was not valued by policy-makers. However, gains were potentially more significant for debtor LDCs, which stood to benefit from any consequent reduction in interest rates. Exchange rate regimes cannot be ranked unambiguously – the best regime depends on the pattern and source of shocks. As game theory tells us, symmetric supply side shocks favour fixed exchange rates, while asymmetric shocks favour floating rates.

The new game theoretic approach is also leading economists to become increasingly involved in the design and analysis of institutions as well as policies, in the international arena as elsewhere. This development reflects Hamada's (1976) suggestion that international policy cooperation would best be implemented by securing an agreement to set up the system of rules which works best, without the need for coordination on a day-by-day basis. We are still a long way away from achieving this goal. But recent efforts at cooperation within the G7 and the EMS countries could represent the first tentative steps in that direction.

NOTES

1. Hicks' composite good theorem says that if the relative prices of some items are fixed, then they form a single economic aggregate. This approach to aggregation is extremely useful in an open-economy situation when arbitrage fixes the relative prices of traded goods and assets, but cannot normally be used in the closed-economy situation when relative prices are variable.
2. See in particular the Delors (1989) report which argues that the Single Market would not be complete without a single currency and outlines a three-stage plan for achieving this.
3. Muellbauer and Portes formalise the 'spillover' or 'multiplier' effects which occur when prices and wages do not move fast enough to clear markets, and quantities adjust instead. They use a closed-economy model with goods and labour markets, and show that the Keynesian unemployment case in which real wages are too low (so that firms are constrained by the demand for goods, and consumers are in turn constrained by the demand for labour) is just one of four possible disequilibrium situations.
4. In the IS (goods market), LM (money market) and BB (balance of payments equilibrium) fixed exchange rate model, a bond-financed fiscal expansion initially shifts the system up along the LM curve, causing an incipient rise in interest rates and output. The effect on the balance of payments and on reserves at the initial exchange rate is ambiguous, depending upon the relative slope of LM and BB. If the exchange rate remains unchanged, then the money supply adjusts in response to the change in reserves, so the LM curve will tend to shift until balance of payments equilibrium is achieved. Equilibrium is then determined by the intersection of the IS and BB lines. But if the money supply and the official reserves are fixed instead, the exchange rate must adjust and equilibrium is determined by the IS and LM schedules (after taking into account the effect of the exchange rate change on the former). If the LM curve is steeper than the BB curve, then the exchange rate appreciates and output is lower than in the fixed exchange rate specification (it is of course unchanged in the MF model with its horizontal BB line). Otherwise, the exchange rate depreciates, exaggerating the rise in output. In the extreme case of zero capital mobility analysed by Morris (1988), floating the exchange rate forces the trade balance to zero, meaning that in macroeconomic terms, the economy is effectively closed to trade with the rest of the world. This neutralises the leakage into imports (as well as the associated spillover to other countries), raising the value of the fiscal multiplier.
5. A Pareto-efficient solution is one in which it is not possible to make one player better off without making another worse off.
6. These terms are used in the statistical theory of hypothesis testing. In the context of model uncertainty, the (null) hypothesis is that cooperation will result in a gain from trade; the test criterion is whether the initial model beliefs indicate a gain or loss. A type 1 error is made when the hypothesis is rejected (i.e. prior beliefs indicate a loss), but a gain actually results *ex post* (which happens in 10 out of 28 cases). A type 2 error is made when the hypothesis is accepted (a gain is indicated) but a loss emerges *ex post* (25 out of 36).

APPENDIX: POLICY COOPERATION IN A SIMPLE TWO-COUNTRY WORLD

This annex is designed to illustrate the potential gains to policy cooperation and exchange rate constraints and to show how these depend upon the symmetry of the situation. For simplicity we consider a two-country world in which there is just a single independent policy instrument in each country: the interest rate. International capital mobility is assumed to keep interest rates in line after allowing for expected exchange rate movements. We will initially assume that

the two countries are identical, with similar economies and similar preferences
on the part of policy-makers.

The situation is illustrated in figure A4.1. The curves marked I^A show the
indifference map of policy-maker A, defined over interest rates at home (r^A) and
abroad (r^B). These curves take into account the behaviour of the two economies
and the exchange rates, as well as the effect which this behaviour has on A's
output, inflation, other target instruments and hence A's welfare.

Panel (a) characterises A's indifference map in a high-inflation environment.

Figure A4.1 The symmetric situation

   (a) Inflation

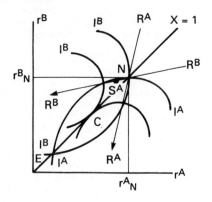

   (b) Unemployment

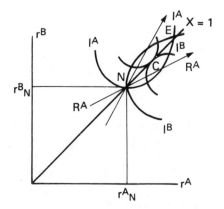

In this situation A benefits from low values of r^B because these mean a high exchange rate and lower inflation. So the lower the indifference curve, the higher A's utility level.

If A acts as a Nash player, he treats r^B as given and sets r^A. For example, if policy-maker B sets his interest rate at r^B_N then A sets his at r^A_N, tangent to I^A, the highest indifference curve or utility level then attainable. Joining up the maxima of these indifference curves gives A's Nash reaction function: R^A. Figure A4.1(b) illustrates the high-unemployment case, in which A tends to prefer high values of r^B, which lower its exchange rate and allow it to export unemployment to B.

The Competitive Solution

The symmetry of the situation means that we can draw a similar set of indifference and reaction curves for B, by rotating through 90°. The intersection of R^A and R^B at point N defines the *Nash equilibrium* or competitive solution in which each policy-maker takes the other's interest rate as parametric. This is Pareto inefficient because the associated indifference curves I^A and I^B are orthogonal rather than tangential. All of the points in the lens-shaped area NE bounded by these curves are Pareto superior, leaving one or both parties better off, without either worse off.

The Cooperative Solution

Point C shows a cooperative solution. This is Pareto optimal because it is a point at which A and B's indifference curves are tangential, so neither can be made better off without leaving the other worse off. There are an infinite number of such points, making the cooperative solution indeterminate, depending upon the structure of the bargaining process adopted and the relative bargaining strength that this endows. However, in a simple symmetric situation it is reasonable to suppose that the gains from cooperation would be divided equally, yielding the solution shown as point C in Figure A4.1. This is a simple example of a *Nash bargaining solution*, which can be justified by the notion of fairness (and other axioms which become relevant when the situation is asymmetric).

Asymmetric Bargaining

The nature of the bargaining game can sometimes lead to asymmetries. For example if one player naturally moves first and the second follows, this results in a Stackelberg leader-follower model. If for some reason A can move first and B follows, then A will do best by moving to the point of tangency with B's reaction function as at S^A. This leaves both players worse off than at C but better off than at N.

The Fixed Exchange Rate Rule

Now let us reconsider the symmetric or fair-game solution C. Because its lies on the 45° line where interest rates are equal, the exchange rate spillover effects are neutralised (purchasing power parity holds). Indeed all solutions lying along the 45° line have this property. So one way to achieve the cooperative equilibrium in this symmetric situation is to secure a credible fixed exchange rate agreement. (For example, in Figure A4.1 countries could agree to maintain purchasing power parity.) There is, however, a potential problem with this sort of agreement, because it also implies an agreement to equalise interest rates internationally, but is consistent with any level of interest rates. So who decided the overall level?

This is the well-known leadership problem associated with fixed exchange rate regimes. However, in this symmetric situation the leadership problem is trivial. Suppose for example that we arbitrarily make A a Stackelberg leader as part of the fixed exchange rate contract. B's reaction function is then the 45° line since B must choose the same interest rate as A. So A will choose the point of tangency with the 45° line, which is the Nash bargaining solution under symmetry. Once the fixed exchange rate bargain is struck, B loses nothing by renouncing leadership to A because his preferences and constraints are identical. So fixed exchange rate regimes are devoid of leadership conflicts in a symmetric situation and assimilate the full cooperative equilibrium.

Asymmetries

Unfortunately this property is destroyed by asymmetries. Take, for example, the situation shown in Figure A4.2. This represents an inflationary situation in country A and an unemployment problem in country B. The competitive solution is at N as before. (For the purpose of exposition this is drawn on the 45° line, but this is immaterial to the argument.) But the set of Pareto superior points, the lens NE, is now to the south-west of the 45° line involving a higher value of r^A and a lower value of r^B. These raise A's exchange rate, allowing it to trade its surplus inflation for B's surplus unemployment. The Nash bargaining point will lie at a bilateral tangency point within this lens, and is illustrated by point B, which both parties prefer to N.

Figure A4.2. The asymmetric situation

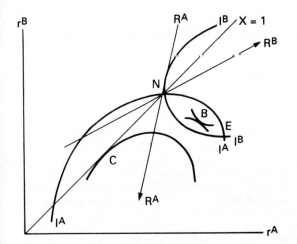

5. Rational Expectations and the New Macroeconomics

David Peel

Professor Peel provides an outline of the rational expectations hypothesis, which has had such a dramatic effect on macroeconomics in the last 20 years. He points to what the hypothesis assumes, and what it does not assume. He explores three applications – the well-known criticism of the long-run Phillips curve, the time-inconsistency problem, and the efficient market hypothesis – each of which are discussed further in other chapters. Finally he reviews the evidence in favour of rational expectations, and argues that this hypothesis is likely to remain at the centre of macromodelling strategies in the future.

INTRODUCTION

Expectations are fundamental in economics. Every economic decision is about the future, given the existing situation. For example, consumption decisions depend in part on expectations concerning current and future income. Investment decisions by firms depend on expected future demand and relative prices. Wage settlements depend in part on firms' and unions' expectations of inflation over the wage contract period. Even decisions apparently only involving the current situation, such as choosing to buy apples rather than pears, implicitly involve a view of the future. In this case it is a view both about future income (which determines how much money one is prepared to allocate to apples and pears) and about future prices (which dictates whether it is worthwhile storing them in place of future purchases).

By definition, the future is unknowable. Economics, the study of economic decision-making, is therefore concerned with how people deal with the unknowable.

In this chapter I wish to outline some of the theoretical implications and empirical evidence in favour of one particularly radical approach to modelling agents' expectations of forecasts of the future, known as the rational expectations hypothesis.

A key hypothesis in macroeconomics – the study of the interaction of aggregate variables in an economy, such as the price level, investment, or national income – is that in the mass, individual decisions exhibit regularity, even though each individual decision may be relatively unpredictable. It turns out that this hypothesis can be supported in part by appeal to a statistical theorem known as the Central Limit Theorem. It states that a distribution of a sample of random variables will tend to normality as the sample gets larger. Though supported by this, the hypothesis still requires that individual decisions are generated in a systematic way. Since economic decisions taken today by agents depend in part on their expectations of future outcomes, the regularity of aggregate behaviour implicitly requires that, given the economic environment, aggregate expectations are formed in a systematic manner.

Some very great and eminent economists, such as Lord Keynes and George Shackle, have argued against this view. Shackle (1958), for instance, suggests that in evaluating future outcomes people will make their own individual assessments; we cannot say what they will do without a complete knowledge of their psychology, even if we have access to exactly the same factors as they have.

Clearly, Shackle's position is destructive of the postulate of regularity in aggregate behaviour by individuals who are faced with regularities in the economic environment. Whether the postulate is true or false can ultimately only be settled empirically by evaluating the success or failure of economics itself in attempting to apply the basis assertion of regularity.

At first sight the performance of macroeconomic models in the 1970s lends support to the scepticism held by some about the regularity of aggregate behaviour. The early hopes of economists that econometrics would enable complex problems or decision-making by government, firms and individuals to be reduced to the mere application of known mathematical techniques, such as optimal control theory, were cruelly dashed as the Western World grappled with a combination of high inflation, low growth and high unemployment. This combination had in general neither been predicted by econometric models, nor had it responded to policy prescription.

However, before accepting that the postulate of regularity of behaviour in aggregates is erroneous, it is important to note that in the macroeconomic models of the 1970s, expectations were typically modelled by a mechanism where changes in agents' expectations reflected previous forecast errors. This type of mechanism, borrowed from agricultural economics, is known as adaptive expectations. Adaptive expectations schemes imply that expectations are formed as a simple, constant weighted average of the past values of a variable. For example, a simple adaptive scheme would be to forecast inflation for the coming year as equal to last year's rate. This scheme is highly mathematically tractable as a method of modelling expectations and seems reasonable *a priori*. It is however subject to two criticisms. First it implies that agents will make systematic errors if the variable to be forecast has any trend. For example, if the actual path of the percentage inflation rate over a period is 2, 5, 7, 10 then, for the simple adaptive scheme, agents will expect 2 when inflation is 5, 5 when it is 7, and 7 when it is 10. Adaptive expectations relative to the outcome for this scenario would have been systematically too low. Second, the adaptive scheme implies that agents ignore other available information (apart from the past levels of the variable) when forecasting future outcomes. Consequently, relevant policy announcements by ministers; public forecasts of macromodel builders (such as The National Institute, The London Business School or the Liverpool Forecasting Group); the price of oil and past levels of money supply would all be ignored when forecasting inflation.

It was against a background of macroeconomic models which embodies adaptive expectations, producing poor forecasts in the 1970s, that some economists began to search for a reformulation of the models.

Rational expectations is a particular radical reformulation. The essential idea of Muth, who first proposed the concept (1961) is that expectations are informed predictions of future events, and are the same as the predictions of the relevant and correct economic theory. In other words, expectations are formed as if agents understood economic theory and processed all available information within the structure of the correct economic model.

Before discussing the *a priori* criticisms of the rational expectations hypothesis and the empirical evidence for and against it, it is useful first to set out some of the properties possessed by expectations if they are rational, and some of the implications which flow from assuming it.

PROPERTIES OF RATIONAL EXPECTATIONS

The first property of rational expectations is that they are unbiased.[2] This means that the actual outcome (Y_t) minus the forecast outcome (EY_t) is equal to a random variable (u_t) so that

$$Y_t - EY_t = u_t$$

Notice that the property of being unbiased does not mean that rational expectations are perfectly correct forecasts. In general this will not be the case due to the unpredictable element (u_t). However, it does mean that expectations are correct on average (since u_t has an average value of zero) and therefore are not systematically, and hence predictably, wrong in any particular direction.

The second characteristic is known as the orthogonality property and simply means that the forecast error is uncorrelated with any relevant information known at the time expectations are formed. If this were not the case, agents could exploit the correlation to improve their forecast (expectation) of the future outcome. Consider the regression:

$$Y_t - EY_t = \alpha + \text{\ss}Z + \varepsilon_t$$

(where Z is a variable known at the time expectations are formed, α and ß are constants and ε_t is the error term). If expectations are formed rationally, α and ß should be insignificantly different from zero and the error term random in estimates of this equation.

The third property possessed by rational expectations is their consistency. This means that expectations of a future outcome formed at different times should be consistent with one another, which implies that they should only differ by new information. Since new information is by definition unpredictable, they only differ by a random error.

Consider, for example, the forecast made on Tuesday (formulated in terms of the probabilities of a home, away and draw) of the outcome of a soccer game to be played on Saturday compared with a forecast made on Monday. Unless new information has accrued between Monday and Tuesday (injuries to players in training, etc), the forecast made on Tuesday must be the same as that on Monday. If this were not the case, information available on Monday cannot have been processed efficiently.

Another implication of this is that if expectations are rational, today's expectation of your future expectation of an outcome is today's expectation of that outcome. In other words, the best guess on Monday of what your forecast will be on Tuesday of Saturday's game is Monday's forecast.

It is useful at this point to mention an important characteristic that economic models will in general possess when expectations are formed rationally. This is that the evolution of endogenous variables (i.e. those determined within the model, such as output, inflation or unemployment) can in general be shown to depend on expectations of all future values of exogenous variables (those determined outside the model, including policy-determined parameters such as government expenditure or tax rates). Intuitively the rationale for this is that the value taken by current endogenous variables depends in part on expectations of future variables, as well as current policy-determined variables. The value a variable will take in the future will depend in part on government policy at that time. Consequently, current behaviour implicitly depends on the current behaviour of government policy variables, as well as expectations of their future values (see the Appendix to this chapter).

This general property of models which embody rational expectations – that outcomes today depend on expectations formed today of the value of government expenditures, taxes, etc. into the indefinite future – has the key implication that credible announcements of future changes in policy act as an additional policy tool since, *ceteris paribus*, they change outcomes today. The responsiveness of current outcomes to expected future outcomes might explain, in part, a number of phenomena including the response of the Hong Kong Stock Market to announced changes in policy in 1998. Or the constant gripe of industrialists that more stable government policies are required to stimulate investment. Because in the rational expectations model, government policy into the indefinite future determines current investment behaviour, an expectation of radically different government policies in the future will impact on investment today.

Having examined some of the properties rational expectations possess as well as the property of models if they embody rational expectations, we now examine some of the economic implications which flow from assuming expectations are formed rationally relative to some alternative mechanisms.

The number of applications of this hypothesis has increased dramatically in the last few years. Current journals, for instance, consider applications in agricultural economics, industrial economics, voting behaviour and arms races. I have chosen three applications which I hope illustrate some of the dramatic insights which the Rational Expectations hypothesis can offer.

The first, perhaps most striking and certainly best-known application of the hypothesis is its potential implication for the relationship between inflation and unemployment in an economy.

APPLICATION I: INFLATION AND UNEMPLOYMENT

Keynesian-orientated economists relied for many of their policy prognostications upon the belief in the existence of a stable inverse relationship between inflation and the rate of unemployment. This relationship is known as the Phillips curve. Phillips (1958) provided empirical evidence for the UK (using data over the period 1861–1957) that percentage change in money wages and unemployment were stably and inversely related. Because wages are a high proportion of unit costs, without loss of generality we can relate price inflation to the rate of unemployment. The Phillips curve is depicted in Figure 5.1. The idea underpinning the relationship is straightforward. When the demand for labour is low relative to supply, unemployment will be high and this will moderate wage and hence price inflation. Conversely, when labour is in short supply relative to demand, unemployment will be low, and this will result in high wage and price increases. Unemployment is assumed to be proxy for the excess demand or supply of labour, and this is assumed to influence wage and price inflation.

The existence of the Phillips curve appeared to offer policy-makers a simple policy prescription. They could choose the desired rate of inflation and manipulative aggregate demand to ensure the appropriate rate of unemployment to deliver this. Interestingly enough, many eminent Keynesian economists, such as Paish (1968), suggested in the 1960s that a pool of unemployment must be maintained in order to ensure a low rate of inflation.

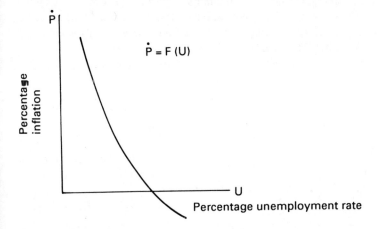

Figure 5.1 The Phillips curve

The standard Phillips curve appeared to be breaking down in the late 1960s and early 1970s. The UK economy was simultaneously experiencing both rising inflation and rising unemployment, not the inverse relationship suggested by the Phillips curve.

Nobel Laureate Milton Friedman (1968), in his address to the American Economics Association, presented an explanation for this. Friedman denied the existence of a permanent trade-off between inflation and unemployment. He suggested that the trade-off was only temporary and occurred when inflation was unstable (in other words, accelerating or decelerating), not from the rate of inflation *per se*.

Friedman argued as follows: participants in the labour market, either as suppliers of labour or demanders, are interested in the real wages which are paid to them, not in money wages. For instance, a wage offer of $3,000 a week seems a lot, but is not if a basket full of ordinary goods costs $4,000. The suppliers of labour evaluate wage offers in terms of the prevailing price level. Similarly, the demand for labour is formulated on the basis of the money wage in terms of the price of the product produced. Given this, Friedman hypothesises that a given set of real circumstances in the labour market, as proxied by the unemployment rate, will be associated with a given rate of change of real wages. Trade unions or employees bargain for a given money wage, but since they are interested in real wages, allowance will be made for the expected rate of inflation. In Figure 5.2 we depict the implication this has for the Phillips curve.

There is now a different Phillips curve corresponding to different expectations of inflation. This relationship has been called the expectations-augmented Phillips curve. For any given rate of unemployment, say U_0, inflation can be any number, corresponding to firms' and unions' expectations of inflation. Only if expected inflation were zero would we have the old-fashioned Phillips curve. Note further that the trade-off is now between unemployment and *unanticipated* inflation ($\dot{P}$-$E\dot{P}$ and U), not inflation itself.

If expectations are formed adaptively, as Friedman implicitly assumed, then the current Phillips curve is dependent on previous inflation. Since expected

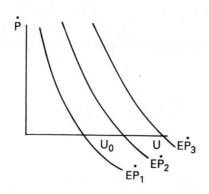

$$\dot{P} = F(U) + E\dot{P}$$

$$\text{or } \dot{P} - E\dot{P} = F(U)$$

$$E\dot{P} = \text{expected inflation}$$

$$E\dot{P}_3 > E\dot{P}_2 > E\dot{P}_1$$

Figure 5.2 Expectations-augmented Phillips curve

inflation is a function of past inflation, the trade-off is between accelerations and decelerations of inflation and the rate of u (i.e. in the simplest adaptive case $\dot{p} - \dot{p}_{-1} = F(u)$).

If expectations are formed rationally, then because of their unbiased and orthogonal properties, actual and expected inflation only differ by a random unpredictable error. Consequently, there is *no* trade-off between inflation and unemployment. The Phillips curve becomes vertical, as depicted in Figure 5.3. The (expected) unemployment rate which occurs when the actual and expected inflation rates are equal is independent of the rate of inflation and defined by the structure of the labour market. This rate has been called the natural or equilibrium rate of unemployment. At this rate of unemployment, inflation can be any number. Most economists would assume that this will essentially correspond to the rate of monetary growth net of real output change. Consequently, two otherwise identical economies could have precisely the same unemployment rate but different rates of inflation corresponding to different monetary growth rates. The policy implications of the Phillips curve, if expectations are formed rationally, are radically different from those envisaged by early Keynesian economists. In their analysis, changes in monetary policy would not directly influence price expectations (since they are based on past inflation) and consequently could have a strong influence on aggregate demand, and hence unem-

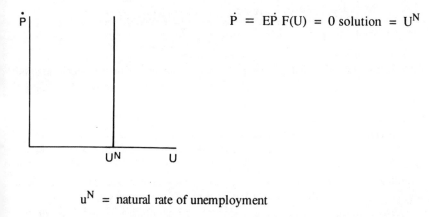

$$\dot{P} = E\dot{P} \quad F(U) = 0 \text{ solution} = U^N$$

u^N = natural rate of unemployment

Figure 5.3 Vertical Phillips curve

ployment. However, in the augmented Phillips curve model, changes in monetary policy anticipated by agents will only influence expected inflation and the rate of inflation. Only unanticipated changes in inflation influence unemployment and, because people are informed, the government cannot systematically achieve unanticipated inflation in a particular direction. In the rational expectations model, lower unemployment can be achieved without higher inflation but not through monetary policy. In order to bring unemployment down, it is necessary to introduce policies which change the real structure of the labour market. These might involve, for instance, policies which relate to the reform of social security benefits, the structure of the unions and the nature of the housing market (see, e.g. Minford, 1983).

To reiterate, in an economy embodying an augmented Phillips curve the rational expectations hypothesis implies that anticipated monetary policies have no influence on unemployment.[3] Unemployment and the rate of inflation are independent. A society can choose low unemployment and low inflation or high unemployment and high inflation. This will simply depend on the structure of the labour market and the rate of monetary growth in an economy.

This result is now widely known. Less attention has been focused on a second application of the RE hypothesis, that optimal plans of policy-makers will generally be time-inconsistent.

APPLICATION II: OPTIMAL PLANS ARE TIME-INCONSISTENT

We showed earlier that a crucial feature of an economy in which agents' expectations are rational is that expected future policy actions will influence current behaviour. This is not the case in models in which expectations are backward-looking or adaptive, since current outcomes will then depend only on current and past policy decisions. When expectations are backward-looking it is in principle relatively straightforward to calculate optimal policies for an economy, using mathematical techniques such as *optimal control theory*. This involves specifying the objective of the policy-maker and maximising this function subject to the postulated behaviour of the economy.

When attempts were made to compute optimal plans for models involving rational expectations, a curious fact became apparent (see Kydland and Prescott, 1977). Optimal policies were invariably time-inconsistent. The term inconsistent in this context has a precise meaning. At time zero, policy-makers formulate their plans for policy variables over the planning horizon. The optimal policy is that plan known by agents which delivers the best performance of the economy over the planning period. The inconsistency problem arises because in general, during the actual execution of the plan, policy-makers were found to be able to improve performance by reneging on their original plan and carrying out a new one, even in an unchanged environment. In essence, policy-makers had an incentive to cheat. This is defined as the time inconsistency of optimal policies. One way to understand the problem of inconsistency (borrowed from Sheffrin, 1984) is to begin with what seems a truism: 'Whatever situation policy-makers inherit they should use their policy tools to pick the best current course of action.' Whilst seemingly innocuous, in many situations this truism may lead to peculiar policy advice.

Consider, for example, patent policy. In order to encourage research and spur invention, a government offers patent protection and monopoly rights to the inventor, for a period of time. After the product has been invented, policy considerations change. The truism suggests abolishing the patents for the product. After all, the policy-maker has inherited a situation in which the product has been invented, and if the policy-maker's aim is to maximise social welfare, it is optimal to allow free competition in the provision of the good.

In this example, the time-consistent policy would recognise that patents should be withdrawn. In general, however, such time-consistent policies will be unattractive. If scientists know that patent policy will be stripped away immediately following an invention, inventive activity will drop sharply. This poses an unhappy dilemma. Either policy-makers choose bad policies which they have no incentive to cheat on, or they choose good policies which they will have incentives to cheat on. The difficulty is, of course, that if they do cheat, they will create severe problems of future credibility and thus probably of later policy effectiveness.

For these reasons *credibility* and *reputation* are now key concepts in every economic policy-maker's lexicon, and a tremendous amount of interesting work has been done on these issues (see, e.g. the survey by Blackburn and Christenson, 1989). It is clear that a policy-maker's announcements should be as credible as possible. Lack of credibility causes agents to insure against backsliding or cheating which, in turn, limits policy options. The overall result is then likely to be inferior to that of choosing consistent policies, even if these appear sub-optimal. To summarize, the time-inconsistency of optimal policies and its associated problems arise as follows:

When expectations are forward-looking, policy announcements, if they are credible, act as an additional instrument of policy. Once these announcements have had the desired effect on behaviour, their influence erodes until it is time to implement them.

Bygones being bygones, the policy-maker will then be tempted to act in whatever way seems best. Quite likely the policy-maker will want to 'cheat', to do something different from what was announced. The problem is that agents realise that the policy-maker will face this temptation. If the policy-maker cannot find a way to make a credible commitment that he will not cheat (even though at a later date it will appear rational to so do), then the original announcement will not be believed. Achieving credibility therefore means that policy-makers must consciously and visibly restrict their own future freedom of action, their ability to renege on earlier commitments. In Japan, I believe, regional lords added credibility to their declaration of loyalty to the Shogun by leaving a relative as hostage in the Shogun's castle. Politicians – and, dare I say it, university heads of departments – often find it hard to come up with plausible hostages for good behaviour.

The third implication of the rational expectations hypothesis I would like to outline relates to the functioning of asset markets.

APPLICATION III: RATIONAL EXPECTATIONS AND THE FUNCTIONING OF ASSET MARKETS

A particular feature of financial markets, such as the bond, foreign exchange or stock markets, is that trading can occur, in principle, almost continuously, and the market price is free to move in order to eradicate any imbalance between demand and supply. Furthermore, since the assets traded can be resold or traded in future periods, it follows that financial markets are, more obviously than others, speculative in the technical sense that expectations of future asset prices affect current asset prices. In a seminal paper, Fama (1970) has defined three types of market efficiency, according to the extent of information reflected in market prices.

A market is defined as *weak-form efficient* if it is not possible for a trader to make abnormal returns by developing a trading rule based on the past history of prices or returns. A market is defined as *semi-strong efficient* if a trader cannot make abnormal returns using a trading rule based on publicly available information (such as past inflation figures, company financial accounts, or reports in the financial pages of periodicals). A market is defined as *strong-form efficient* if a trader cannot make abnormal returns using a trading rule based on any information source, whether public or private.

These three forms of efficiency represent a crude partitioning of all possible information systems into three broad categories – the perceived boundaries of which are not easily defined. However, they have proved useful for classifying empirical work on market efficiency. As their names suggest, strong-form efficiency implies semi-strong efficiency which, in turn, implies weak-form efficiency while, of course, the reverse implications do not hold. Because all definitions of market efficiency invoke the concept of abnormal returns, we are required for empirical work to have a theory of the normal or equilibrium-expected rate of return for assets. This is a central topic in modern portfolio theory (see, e.g. Copeland and Weston, 1979). One model of the equilibrium return is based on the Capital Asset Pricing Model, whereby the normal return on an asset will reflect both the risk-free rate of interest and the covariation of the asset with a diversified market portfolio of assets. Tests of market efficiency are conducted after allowance for the normal rate of return.

The semi-strong efficient markets model, which is based on publicly available information, is an application of the concept of rational expectations. On reflection, it seems clear that if expectations are non-rational, then publicly available information will not be reflected in asset prices, and systematic abnormal opportunities will be available. It is of some interest for economists to note, from a defensive viewpoint, that if assets markets are semi-strong efficient, this nicely explains away the constant jibe that 'how come if economists know so much about financial markets then they are not rich?' The answer, of course, is that much (all?) of the economist's knowledge is publicly available and therefore already reflected in asset prices. It follows that if asset markets are semi-strong efficient, then asset prices (given movements in the normal return) should change, essentially, only in response to new information, which is random and unpredictable. The rational expectations hypothesis thus has the strong implication for asset markets that, given the normal rate of return, changes in asset prices should be non-predictable, so that systematic abnormal returns cannot be obtained on the basis of publicly available information.

CRITICISM OF THE HYPOTHESIS

Having set out three implications of the rational expectations hypothesis, I would now like briefly to consider some of the *a priori* criticisms of the hypothesis and also briefly review some of the empirical evidence in its favour.

One criticism often advanced against the rational expectations hypothesis concerns its informational requirements. Agents are assumed in aggregate to form expectations as if they knew the correct model of the economy and solved it appropriately. It is difficult to see how this can literally be true, though from a methodological perspective it is arguably unimportant (see, e.g. Friedman and Savage, 1948, p. 298). As Shiller (1978) writes: 'While it may sometimes be useful as an expositional device to assume that agents have this much information, the assumption cannot be taken seriously. If economists are only now discovering these models, we cannot seriously propose that everyone else knew them all along.'

Given that Shiller's point appears formally correct, one issue we must address is how far from an *a priori* viewpoint the assumption of rational expectations might depart in aggregate from a useful description of how agents form their expectations. In this regard it is important to note:

1. First, that the hypothesis does not require that all individuals have the same beliefs, only that they are distributed around the true value, so that any idiosyncratic behaviour will average out to give an informed aggregate expectation.

2. Second, that in many markets, such as asset markets, it is technically feasible that a few individuals can arbitrage the market so that it may behave 'as if' rational even though many individuals in the market are passive (however, see also Figlewski, 1980). From this perspective we should also note that many decisions are delegated in a representative democracy, so that experts (such as trades union negotiators in labour markets or financial experts in asset markets) take decisions on people's behalf about wage goals or savings strategies. Just as we do not have to assume that all agents understand and can practice medicine in order to have efficient medical care, similarly it is not necessary to assume that everyone is an economic theoretician in order to obtain informed expectations about the economy.

3. Third, that in a modern economy much informed economic opinion is available at very low marginal cost. For the price of a daily newspaper one can obtain major public forecasts of inflation, output, etc., from reputable agencies such as the National Institute or Liverpool (or their equivalents in other countries).

Given that *a priori* arguments do not rule out aggregate expectations being well approximated by the rational expectations hypothesis, is the rational hypothesis supported by the empirical evidence? I briefly consider three aspects of it.

First, numerous surveys of expectations of consumers, businessmen and financial market participants have been conducted for a large number of countries and the properties of the expectations analysed (see, e.g. Holden, Peel and Thompson, 1985). For instance, in the UK, surveys of consumer expectations of inflation have been conducted by Gallup; producer expectations of inflation by the Confederation of British Industry; and brokers' expectations of the money supply by Money Market Services.

The empirical evidence, based on surveys, provides some support of the rational expectations hypothesis for 'experts', but is less supporting for consumer surveys. However, since the latter represent the views of the person in the street, this empirical evidence is not necessarily destructive of the rational expectations hypothesis. In particular it is not clear from a marginal cost/benefit perspective that these persons have strong incentives to be informed, in general, about the questions asked of them. In addition, with all survey work there will always be doubts about whether respondents have the incentive to answer honestly, or whether they correspond to the marginal traders in a market.

Second, there has been a tremendous amount of empirical work on the efficient markets hypothesis.[4] Numerous empirical tests have been conducted of the various definitions of market efficiency (see, e.g. Guimaraes *et al*, 1989, and references). Amongst the vast number of empirical studies so far conducted, there do appear to be some findings which are not readily reconciled with the semi-strong efficient markets hypothesis. For instance the finding that stock returns are, apparently significantly lower on Monday or in January than other days or months (see, e.g. Connolly, 1989; Ikenberry and Lakonishok, 1989). Much current research is endeavouring either to explain these inconsistencies and/or replicate them on new data sets. In spite of these anomalous findings, it is perhaps surprising (given one's propensity to be surprised!) to persons who have not previously considered in detail the theoretical and empirical work on asset markets, to find so few apparent departures from the efficient markets/ rational expectations paradigm.

Third, in many empirical studies of, for instance, wages, prices and interest rates, proxies for expectation (which meet the rational expectations requirements) have been constructed and the statistical properties of such equations contrasted with those which embody numerous alternative ways of forming expectations (see, e.g. Holden, Peel and Thompson, 1985). On balance, this empirical work is highly supportive of the rational expectations hypothesis. Overall, the empirical evidence conducted to date is perhaps suggestive that aggregate expectations may well not depart too greatly from rational expectations.

CONCLUSIONS

The purpose in this chapter has been to set out some of the theoretical implications and empirical evidence in favour of the hypothesis that expectations are formed rationally.

Although it is difficult to see how the hypothesis can be literally true, given its stylized information requirements, there is sufficient empirical evidence which accords with the hypothesis to suggest that it will remain a most important method of modelling expectations in both theoretical and applied analysis.

NOTES

1.   This chapter is based on open lectures given at Aberystwyth and the Polytechnic of Central London, as well as borrowings from Minford and Peel (1983).
2.   Strictly we are assuming that the decision-maker's cost function for forecast errors is quadratic, so that positive and negative forecast errors are penalised equally. See Granger (1969) for some analysis of the implications of relaxing this assumption.
3.   It should be noted that this result is peculiar to this model. In a variety of other models (see, e.g. Minford and Peel, 1983), systematic monetary policies can influence output or unemployment when expectations are formed rationally. However, the nature of the impact if expectations are rational is radically different than if they are formed adaptively.
4.   We should also note some of the important theoretical research. For instance, Stiglitz and Grossman (1980), Beaver (1981) and Rubenstein (1975) have all examined the ability of markets fully and instantaneously to reflect all available information.

APPENDIX

Consider, for example, the following simple model:

$$Y_t = C_t + I_t + G_t \tag{A5.1}$$

$$C_t = a + bY_t + \varepsilon_t \tag{A5.2}$$

$$I_t = v[E_t Y_{t+1} - Y_t] \tag{A5.3}$$

where Y_t, C_t, I_t and G_t are, respectively, real income, consumption, investment and government expenditure at time t; a, b and v are positive constants. $E_t Y_{t+1}$

is the expected value of real income at time t+1 formed at time t, and ε_t is a random disturbance term.

The model consists of an identity, equation (A5.1); a simple consumption function, equation (A5.2); and an investment function of the accelerator type, equation (A5.3), whereby investment depends on the expected change in income.

By substitution of equations (A5.3) and (A5.2) into (A5.1), and rearranging, we obtain:

$$Y_t = A + B_t \, EY_{t+1} + CG_t + C\varepsilon_t \tag{A5.4}$$

where $A = a/1-b+v$, $B = v/1-b+v$, $C = 1/1-b+v$

Leading equation (A5.4) one period we obtain:

$$Y_{t+1} = A + B \, E_{t+1} \, Y_{t+2} + C \, G_{t+1} + C\varepsilon_{t+1} \tag{A5.5}$$

Taking rational expectations of (A5.5) at time t we obtain:

$$E_t \, Y_{t+1} = A + BE_t \, (E_{t+1} \, Y_{t+2}) + C \, E_t \, G_{t+1} \tag{A5.6}$$

Now the consistency property of rational expectations implies that

$$E_t \, (E_{t+1} \, Y_{t+2}) = E_t \, Y_{t+2} \tag{A5.7}$$

so that equation (A5.6) becomes:

$$E_t \, Y_{t+1} = A + B \, E_t \, Y_{t+2} + C \, E_t \, G_{t+1} \tag{A5.8}$$

Substituting (A5.8) into (A5.4), and rearranging:

$$Y_t = A + BA + B^2 \, E_t \, Y_{t+2} + BC \, E_t \, G_{t+1} + C \, G_t + C \, \varepsilon_t \tag{A5.9}$$

Now leading equation (A5.4) two periods, and taking rational expectations, we obtain:

$$E_t \, Y_{t+2} = A + B \, E_t \, Y_{t+3} + C \, E_t \, G_{t+2} \tag{A5.10}$$

We can substitute (A5.10) into (A5.9). Repeating this process an infinite number of times, we will obtain:

$$Y_t = \frac{A}{1-B} + CG_t + BC\,E_tG_{t+1} + B^2C\,E_tG_{t+2} + B^3C\,E_tG_{t+3}$$

$$+ \ldots + C\varepsilon_t) \qquad (A5.11)$$

(recall that $\dfrac{A}{1-B} = A(1 + B + B^2 + B^3 + \ldots)$ for $B < 1$)

6. The Ups and Downs of Business Cycle Theory

Brian Morgan and J R Shackleton

During the period when 'Keynesian' thinking dominated macroeconomics, the business cycle was largely ignored in the belief that governments possessed the power to smooth cyclical fluctuations. In the 1970s and 1980s, however, increased macroeconomic instability led economists to think again. The authors make the case for putting the business cycle at the centre of macroeconomic analysis, and outline the models put forward by leading protagonists in the renewed debate, particularly New Classical, Real Business Cycle and neo-Keynesian approaches. Discussion of these models is linked to pre-Keynesian contributions by Austrians and others.

INTRODUCTION

Economists' interest in business cycles has had its ups and downs. Nineteenth-century theorists were mainly concerned with the analysis of long-run static equilibrium, though exceptions as diverse as Marx, Jevons and Juglar made pioneering contributions to the study of cyclical movements. In the first half of this century interest quickened. The interwar years were a particularly fruitful period for business cycle theory, as huge fluctuations in output and employment made the subject impossible to ignore.[1]

With the advent of the Keynesian revolution, though, interest declined. Economists and politicians came for a while to believe that governments could manage aggregate demand in such a way as to eliminate macroeconomic instability.

However, the erratic behaviour of Western economies since the early 1970s has led to a revival of interest in cyclical fluctuations and to an explosion of academic writing. Our intention here is to provide a brief account of the main strands of this literature, and to compare it with earlier contributions.

THE BUSINESS CYCLE

Business cycles are sequences of economic expansion and contraction which produce significant and persistent changes in GDP. Although recurrent and pervasive, these fluctuations do not occur at fixed and regular intervals: consequently, business cycles exhibit important differences in both duration and amplitude.[2] However, cyclical fluctuations in output consistently exhibit strong serial correlation. That is, output in the current period is closely related to its value in the previous period – the economy does not move randomly from expansion to contraction. Instead the expansionary phase builds up over a number of years and this may be followed by a similar period of recession.

Another key feature of the business cycle is that it is a macroeconomic phenomenon – the aggregate response of the economy to a large number of individual economic processes. The major quantity variables – employment, investment and consumption – show a high degree of serial correlation and covariation,[3] both with output and with each other. These variables are procyclical (they vary directly with GDP) but the relationships are not exact: some variables 'lead' and others 'lag', though some are coincident.[4]

Defining the Problem

Other 'stylised facts' about business cycles involve such nominal magnitudes as the price level and short-term interest rates which, along with the money supply and financial activity, also tend to be procyclical. Some real variables, such as the real wage and real interest rates, show less pronounced cyclical behaviour. The main task of business cycle theory is to develop models consistent with these basic characteristics. A more difficult task is to develop models which make inferences about future economic developments. 'We want a model that fits historical data and that can be simulated to give reliable estimates of the effects of various policies on future behaviour' (Lucas, 1987, p. 7).

Modelling the Cycle

Theorists in the interwar years produced some sophisticated analyses of the dynamics of cycles (e.g. Hayek, 1933). Despite the importance of these early contributions, this work was soon superseded by the Keynesian revolution where cyclical fluctuations played but a minor role. It concentrated instead on static macromodels such as the IS/LM model. However, before business cycle theory became a mere footnote in macroeconomic texts, some early Keynesians were quick to point out that observed cyclical movements in GDP could be captured by a dynamised Keynesian model, where time lags and the accelerator were explicitly introduced (e.g. Hicks, 1950).

It can be shown that a hybrid Keynesian/accelerator model yields:

$$Y_t = (v/v\text{-}s)Y_{t\text{-}1} - (1/v\text{-}s)A_t \tag{6.1}$$

where Y represents GDP, A is autonomous expenditure, v is the accelerator coefficient, and s the marginal propensity to save.[5] In this simple difference equation the current level of output depends on previous levels of output. Using appropriate values for the parameters and introducing various constraints into the model, Hicks showed that, despite its simplicity, it could account for the stylised facts of business cycles.

The accelerator is, to use Wicksell's term, a 'propagation' mechanism. The 'impulse' or driving force of this type of model was usually taken to be an autonomous shift in private sector investment spending. In justification, Keynesians could point to the remarks in the *General Theory* about sudden collapses in the marginal efficiency of capital as a result of expectational changes (Keynes 1936/1973, ch. 22).

Equation (6.1) can be generalised:

$$Y_t = a_o + a_1 Y_{t\text{-}1} + e_t \tag{6.2}$$

This is a stochastic difference equation where e represents an exogenous random disturbance. It says that GDP is determined partly by its value in the previous year and partly by a random element. Such a model is called a *random walk with drift* (the drift being a_o). With a_o positive, Y_t will exhibit a tendency to drift upwards through time, a characteristic of many macroeconomic time series. This equation can be used to generate a path for GDP by randomly setting values for e. It is remarkable how closely this (random) path resembles the observed cyclical fluctuations in GDP and exhibits significant serial correlation.

Recent Cycles in United Kingdom GDP

In Figure 6.1 the logarithm of real GDP is plotted together with two different trend rates of output growth. Cyclical fluctuations in output are shown to have coincided with an upward trend in the underlying rate of growth in GDP. The higher of the two lines (TREND 1) is based on data from the first quarter of 1955 to the third quarter of 1973 and then extrapolated to the second quarter of 1989. The lower of the two trends (TREND 2) is based on data for the whole period. The difference between the two reflects the higher average growth in GDP in the earlier period, prior to the oil price shocks. Deviations between real GDP and the trend growth line can be used to represent the cyclical component of GDP. These are shown in Figure 6.2 as DTREND 1 & 2. DTREND 1 tracks output fluctuations quite well up to 1973 but not in the later period. Overall DTREND 2 is the better

Figure 6.1   The time path of real UK GDP and trend growth

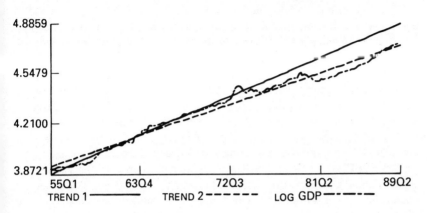

Figure 6.2   The cycle: percentage deviations of GDP from trend

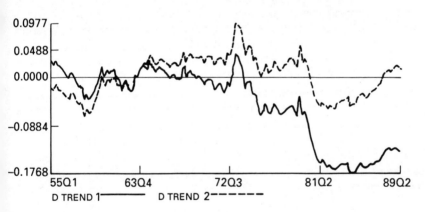

Ordinary Least Squares Estimation:

TREND 1 = 3.87+ 0.00739T $R^2 = 0.988$
                    (76.29)

TREND 2 = 3.91 + 0.00595T $R^2 = 0.977$
                    (76.27)

t-ratios in brackets

fit. However, both sets of deviations illustrate the sharp fall in output in 1973 and 1979 following the oil price shocks and the severity of the 1980 recession.

This approach is useful in highlighting fluctuations in GDP growth and in dating peaks and troughs of the business cycle. However, it fails to take into account the interdependence between the trend and cyclical components of GDP. For example, Figures 6.1 and 6.2 illustrate that the sharp downturn in the cycle in 1973/74 coincided with a reduction in the trend rate of growth.

Some new theories of the business cycle stress this interrelationship between trend and cycle. For example, in real business cycle theory, 'shocks' have an impact on the economy's production technology and cause important, permanent, changes to the underlying trend rate of growth. Another view is that trend output itself is simply the sum of permanent, or near permanent, shocks to output: Nelson and Plosser (1982) argue that 'a major proportion of the variance in output' should be assigned to innovations in the trend component. These theories undermine the conventional view that output fluctuations are primarily due to transitory deviations from a smoothly evolving natural rate. They suggest that GDP has a stochastic trend rather than the deterministic trends produced in Figure 6.1. There is said to be a unit root in the stochastic process driving GDP.[6]

The new econometric technique of cointegration is of some importance in explaining trend/cycle relationships.[7] For example, macroeconomic variables may be drifting upwards through time due to the presence of either a stochastic trend or a simple deterministic time trend. However, stochastic and deterministic trends imply different types of behaviour for Y_t: stochastic trends generate much smaller cyclical components. So in this view we need to discriminate between these types of mechanisms in order to conduct any valid inference about the underlying trend/cycle relationship. Much cointegration evidence suggests that GDP has a unit root. Therefore a deterministic time trend may not be a valid characterisation of the underlying relationship. However, Evans (1989) provides evidence which suggests that the traditional measure of the cyclical component produced in Figure 6.2 remains a good approximation. The issue cannot be considered closed.

EQUILIBRIUM BUSINESS CYCLES

We now turn to review some important business cycle theories, beginning with those which can be classified as 'equilibrium' models, in the sense explored by Leon Walras in the late nineteenth century: markets clear and individuals display optimising behaviour. The idea of an equilibrium cycle may seem almost a contradiction in terms. However, it is a very powerful idea, for it fits the business cycle into the corpus of microeconomic theory accepted by practically all professional economists. Far from being an irrational phenomenon, to be explained by *ad hoc* deviations from the optimising behaviour we assume elsewhere, the business cycle results from rational individuals doing the best they can in circumstances of imperfect information. Such an analysis usually carries the anti-Keynesian corollary that government intervention to counteract the business cycle is misguided.

The Austrians

We begin with the oldest fully-developed approach of this kind, but one which has undergone a remarkable resuscitation lately. The Austrian analysis, as developed by Hayek (1933, 1935), links equilibrium theorising with the formation of expectations. Hayek noted in particular that full market-clearing over time can occur only if people's expectations are mutually compatible. He argued that we must make very definite assumptions about the attitude of individuals towards the future. This insistence that macroeconomic analysis must rest on microeconomic assumptions and be compatible with standard value theory anticipates the theoretical concerns of recent macroeconomists. The Austrian emphasis on consistent expectations is a clear forerunner of the rational expectations hypothesis.

For Hayek, business cycles result from expectational errors. Entrepreneurs are misled by following indicators which normally serve as a good guide to behaviour but are currently distorted. Money or credit is seen as the causative factor. An expansion of bank credit can cause the market interest to fall below its long-run, 'natural', level. (This analysis, drawing on the earlier work of Wicksell, is outlined in Leijonhufvud, 1987.) As a result, savings and investment plans are then out of balance. If entrepreneurs expect this (lower) interest rate to continue in the future, they increase investment. However, when the interest rate eventually readjusts to its natural level, the intentions of consumers and entrepreneurs are no longer compatible. The extra investment turns out to be unprofitable: liquidation of these redundant capital assets will then cause the economy to contract.[8]

In Hayek's view, a recession is the necessary and unavoidable consequence of the initial 'malinvestment'. Governments should not attempt to interfere with the market's healing processes. They only make matters worse if they try to retard the economy's downturn by pumping extra spending power into the system on what have now come to be seen as 'Keynesian' lines.

Hayek's analysis concentrated on interest rate disturbances and other distortions to relative prices which cause the expectations of consumers and entrepreneurs to be incompatible. He also emphasised the information problems inherent in decentralised economies where knowledge is dispersed and fragmented. These ideas were taken up by the monetarists and later extended by the New Classicals, who are indeed sometimes referred to (in our view, somewhat misleadingly) as neo-Austrians. For an interesting historical acount of the link between Austrians and later writers, see Kim (1988).

Monetarism and the Business Cycle

Hayek and his followers reasoned from first principles to provide a monetary theory of the business cycle. By contrast modern monetarists such as Milton Friedman claimed to follow the principles of 'positive economics', using evidence on the time paths of money and GDP to show that the rate of money supply growth conforms closely to the business cycle. Monetarists infer from this evidence that changes in the money supply are the main cause of cyclical fluctuations. For example, Friedman insists that 'money is all that matters' for changes in nominal income and short-run changes in real income. If monetary shocks could be eliminated, the economy would be reasonably stable. Keynesians, of course, dispute this. The two schools of thought also disagree strongly over the conduct of economic policy, for monetarists reject the need for activist policies to offset cyclical fluctuations, and are more sceptical about the ability of the authorities to undertake successful stabilisation policies (see 'Rules versus Discretion', below).

Despite some theoretical elaboration and the use of econometric evidence, the foundation of the monetarist platform continues to be the simple Quantity Theory of Money.[9] Thus Friedman and Schwartz (1963) applied this theory to short-run fluctuations in economic activity to produce some early evidence that changes in monetary growth cause fluctuations in nominal and real income. In later work (1982) this simple framework was again used to analyse longer-term trends in money and GDP. They concluded that money is non-neutral in the short run, even though neutrality exists in the long run (the money supply only influences prices).

However, this single-equation approach to the business cycle compelled Friedman and Schwartz to rely heavily on 'reduced form' evidence rather than to use a structural model of the economy. Such an approach is unable to identify ths transmission mechanism, i.e. the channels of influence through which money affects GDP. It has been dubbed 'black box' monetarism and has been heavily criticised, for correlation does not necessarily imply causation (see Tobin, 1970). Although no detailed transmission mechanism was put forward to explain their results, a plausible portfolio mechanism was sketched by Friedman and Schwartz (1963) based on interest rates (subsequently broadened to include additional channels of monetary influence).

The main thrust of the argument is that during the transmission process, adjustments to monetary shocks by both investors and consumers may produce systematic overshooting and generate cycles in economic activity. If expectations are formed adaptively (by an error learning process), the inflation rate is initially misperceived and real interest rates will take time to adjust to the new money stock. In the meantime real money balances are under- or over-estimated leading to changes in expenditure on goods and services. This will cause some overshooting of output and interest rates, creating cyclical reactions to the exogenous monetary shock. Eventually, these reactions work themselves out, expectations fully adjust and real rates of interest and output growth are left back at their original, equilibrium, levels. Thus money is neutral in the long run, but is non-neutral over the cycle.

Despite early criticisms, the monetarist theory of the business cycle gained in influence in the early 1970s, largely because of the collapse of the Phillips curve. This collapse appeared to result from the impact of monetary shocks on inflationary expectations. These policy-induced shocks seemed to give empirical support to the monetarist version of events and, together with Friedman's famous presidential address to the American Economics Association (1968), effectively turned the tide in favour of monetarism.

As David Peel points out in Chapter 5, Friedman's address developed his analysis in the context of the labour market. He added price expectations to the natural rate of unemployment to produce the expectations-augmented Phillips curve. Only unanticipated inflation, in this approach, can affect output and employment. Workers misperceive real wages and alter their labour supply decisions. They choose to work more when unanticipated inflation fools them into thinking that real, rather than nominal, wage rates have risen. There is a short-run trade-off between unemployment and inflation, but this disappears as expectations are adjusted. Again money is neutral in the long run, but non-neutral over the cycle.

Monetarist influence on economic policy now grew rapidly and Friedman's long-held preference for monetary rules, in particular the Constant Monetary Growth Rule,[10] rather than discretionary policy, was soon in vogue. Accordingly, monetary targets were adopted by most Western governments during the seventies and early eighties (including the UK's Medium Term Financial Strategy). However, as Friedman's political influence reached its peak, his influence on economists was beginning to decline as new approaches were developed in reaction to his work. Increasingly he came to be seen not as the monetarist Messiah, but as a John the Baptist figure preparing the way for Robert Lucas and the New Classicals.

Friedman's case for the CMGR was based on three contentious propositions, each of which now looks very shaky indeed. They were: (i) velocity is stable; (ii) the money stock is exogenous (and easily controlled); and (iii) changes in monetary growth are the main cause of fluctuations in nominal income. The first two propositions have largely been discredited by the events of the 1980s, when velocity showed great instability and governments found it increasingly difficult to control (or even appropriately define) monetary aggregates. Chapter 3 is concerned with these issues and we pass over them here. But it is worth noting recent developments in thinking about causality in the relationship between money supply and income changes.

Friedman originally placed a great deal of emphasis on evidence about the timing of money and nominal income changes, arguing that this was evidence of money's causative role in the cycle. This was initially challenged by Tobin, who offered an explanation of the timing pattern in terms of an endogenous money supply responding to planned changes in spending (Tobin, 1970). More recently Sims (1983), drawing on new statistical tests for causality (Sims 1972, 1977), has rescinded his earlier support for Friedman to declare that the volatility of money and output are so unrelated that reducing the former will not stabilise the latter. The evidence is said to be 'incompatible with any version of monetarism which ... focuses on stabilising annual growth rates of the money stock' (Sims, 1983, p. 233).

So it is not certain that a stable money supply (even if achievable) would significantly reduce business cycle fluctuations. However, this long-running debate had one important result: it initiated a revival in business cycle theory and led directly to New Classical and further developments, to which we now turn.

New Classical Business Cycle Theory

Friedman's theoretical ascendancy was, as we have seen, soon over, his place being taken by the New Classical school associated with Robert Lucas.[11] The New Classicals see themselves as developing a line of thought begun by the Austrians and interrupted by the Keynesian interlude. However, although Lucas praises Hayek's contribution, the New Classical approach is rather different. For one thing, the Austrians always eschewed empirical work in economics. By contrast New Classicals have made considerable use of econometrics in their attempts to distinguish their explanation of economic phenomena from that of the Keynesians (they are also very critical of the econometric methodology underlying Keynesian macromodels). In their emphasis on empirical work and in their use of a revamped version of the expectations-augmented Phillips curve, they are in fact closer to Friedman than to Hayek (hence the alternative term 'Monetarist Mark II'). Friedman's idea of 'misperceptions' plays a particularly crucial role. In fact there are three distinguishing characteristics in New Classical theory.

1. *The Rational Expectations Hypothesis* According to the REH (discussed in Chapter 5), the size of expectational errors should be unrelated to any information available when the expectation was formed. People's expectations should, on average, be right. Any errors will be random and will quickly average out to zero: there are no systematic errors.

2. *Full Market Clearing*   This does not mean a static situation in which demand always equals supply, but simply that all observed prices and quantities are the outcome of optimising decisions by market participants.
3. *The Lucas Supply Function*   This can be derived by restating the Phillips curve in terms of output and making inflation the independent variable. Output will then deviate from its natural rate only if inflationary expectations differ from the actual inflation rate. However, inflation forecasts are compounded by the difficulties individuals face in differentiating between relative and absolute price changes: traders are apt to confuse aggregate (nominal) price changes for local (real) disturbances.

The New Classical model has serious implications for Keynesian stabilisation policies because, according to the LSF, for the government to have any systematic influence on output it must be able to cause unexpected movements in inflation. Lucas and others saw cycles as arising from 'shocks' which disturbed people's perceptions of the price level and caused output to deviate from its 'natural' level. These shocks were assumed to result mainly from unanticipated changes in the money supply. In a rational expectations world, agents will anticipate the effects of systematic policy actions so the government can only influence output by being unpredictable – hardly a recipe for stabilising the economy (for further discussion on this point, see section below, 'Government and Business Cycles').

To produce a plausible theory of the business cycle, the New Classicals must explain the persistence of deviations of output from their natural level. For will not random fluctuations quickly be rectified? In fact, in order to explain the observed serial correlation in output and unemployment over the cycle, some fairly arbitrary assumptions are introduced; for example, lagged output and durable capital are given a prominent role.

It now seems that the New Classicals rely for their explanation of business cycles on the belief that random forecast errors (misperceptions) plus some propagation mechanism (lags or durable capital) can convert monetary 'impulses' into serially correlated movements in output. However, according to neo-Keynesians, most propagation mechanisms either violate the equilibrium assumptions or fail to fit the facts.

In any case, recent work has undermined much of the apparent promise of the New Classical approach (see Barro, 1989, Introduction). For example, the microeconomic parable used by Lucas (1975) – involving an economy consisting of a series of islands where isolated worker-producers (not capitalist firms!) can only communicate very ineffectively – has seemed less and less believable. It is now realised that Lucas' results depend on the assumption that buyers and sellers react asymmetrically to price changes (Barro and King, 1984). Moreover, in the real world, investment by firms is procyclical whereas Lucas' model appears to suggest the opposite.

Perhaps most importantly, doubt has been cast on the centrality of unexpected money changes as an explanation of business cycles (Dotsey and King, 1988). Although early work by Barro (1977) claimed that the Lucas hypothesis had 'considerable explanatory power' for the USA from 1941–1973, recent work has been more critical. For instance, Rush (1986) found that the New Classical hypothesis provided some insight into 'normal' business cycles in the USA, but could not satisfactorily explain the depression of the 1930s. It is also unlikely that the experience of the later 1970s and 1980s can be adequately captured by Lucas-style models.

Real Business Cycles

In the last decade a variant of the equilibrium business cycle approach has emerged, one still committed to a modelling strategy based on utility-maximising, full market clearing and rational expectations. However, the models produced rely on real rather than monetary shocks to set off the cycle (Rush, 1987). Disturbances are caused by random shocks to tastes or technology – things taken as given in standard Walrasian general equilibrium analysis.

An analysis which makes some general points about real business cycle theories is provided by Long and Plosser (1983). Here economic agents respond to random productivity changes by temporarily altering their behaviour: they supply more labour as productivity (and wages) increase and thus generate more output. Such a (Pareto-optimal) response is shown to generate many of the stylised features of real world business cycles discussed by Lucas (1981) and, more recently, by Greenwald and Stiglitz (1988).

A range of different models can be constructed on this scaffolding. For example, Kydland and Prescott (1982) specify a model incorporating 'time to build'. New capital goods take many periods to complete, and their full impact on capacity and output is accordingly delayed (there are echoes here of Hayek's pre-war work).

Blinder and Fischer (1981) have a model emphasising another aspect of investment: the accumulation of stocks or inventories. When output rises in one period, inventories tend to fall. Restocking of inventories means that output continues at a higher level in subsequent periods, even if the original expansionary impulse has abated.

Models such as this are richer than their predecessors of the 1970s. However, real business cycle models are less convincing in their explanation of the nature of the impulses which set cycles off. In a formal sense such models usually involve a production function with a 'technology factor' which is subject to random shocks. These shocks are often constrained to operate only in a positive direction, in which case they can be interpreted as unexpected technological discoveries. A negative shock to technology is difficult to rationalise – knowledge only accumulates. Yet without negative shocks it is difficult to explain massive downturns such as the world depression of the 1930s, which went far beyond any plausible reversal of a previous positive shock.

A possible example of negative shocks might be thought to be the oil price increases of the 1970s and early 1980s. By dramatically altering the terms of trade between oil producers and the rest of the world, these episodes might be said to have altered the feasible set of efficient technologies available. There have been attempts to make real effects of oil price shocks compatible with equilibrium business cycle models, but they have involved *ad hoc* assumptions and have carried little conviction. For example Hamilton (1988) postulates a technology where energy-intensive goods cannot easily be substituted by energy-saving goods. Thus, even on market-clearing assumptions and with rational expectations, oil price shocks can generate ('voluntary') unemployment and excess capacity in some parts of the economy. However, such models seem against the grain of EBC theorising, and are rather closer in spirit to neo-Keynesian ideas.

Rather than seeking specific examples of technological shocks, some writers (e.g. Prescott, 1986; Mankiw, 1989) have looked for general evidence on the importance of technological shocks by correlating output fluctuations with variations in the 'Solow residual' (a measure of the state of technology; the percentage change in output less the weighted percentage change in factor inputs). There seems to be some evidence of a systematic relationship. This could be used to support the hypothesis that technological shocks drive business cycles. However, an equally plausible and more widely accepted hypothesis holds that productivity fluctuations are themselves caused by variations in capacity utilisation over the cycle.

Note that 'technology' is used in a broad sense and includes 'financial technology'. For example, King and Plosser (1984) incorporate accounting services as a factor of production. Williamson (1987a) models an economy where financial intermediation plays an essential role in spreading risks and assisting flows of information: he claims to show that when shocks affect the riskiness of investment projects, this can lead to changes in output and price which mimic the behaviour of the real world.

A sub-species of the real business cycle literature explores another aspect of finance: the possibility of speculative bubbles, panics and crashes. Recent writers such as Blanchard and Watson (1982) have argued that bubbles can occur in otherwise efficient markets, and can have potentially strong real effects on asset prices, wealth and thus on aggregate demand. Financial markets may have a multiplicity of rational expectations equilibria, depending on the beliefs of market participants. As Zarnowitz (1985, p. 562) says, 'If the belief that sunspots predict future prices were widely held, many individuals would act on it so as to bear out their expectations'.

Two points emerge from the real business cycle analysis. First, the link between technology shocks and the cycle raises the question of the link between economic growth and cyclical fluctuations. Rather than treating the trend rate of growth separately from cyclical fluctuations, we should recognise (as suggested in the section on recent cycles in UK GDP) that the two are interdependent. This point it taken up by a number of recent writers, for example Romer (1989).

Second, although the real business cycle literature falls within the equilibrium framework, it nevertheless seems to leave room for considerable scepticism about the optimality of output and employment fluctuations. Indeed, it is not a million miles from earlier Keynesian beliefs in the importance of fluctuations in 'animal spirits' as a proximate cause of the business cycle.

THE NEO-KEYNESIANS

We now turn to developments which have drawn on and extended Keynesian insights into the workings of the economy. As with equilibrium theories, the augmented Phillips curve again plays an important role. However, neo-Keynesian analysis is not based on Friedman's misperceptions approach, which is regarded as implausible: after all, information on actual inflation rates is readily available. Most neo-Keynesians accept the rational expectations critique of Friedman's work. Instead, they have built on Phelps' independent explanation of the shifting Phillips curve (Phelps, 1968). This emphasised that adjustment costs in imperfectly competitive markets might prevent the immediate restoration of labour market equilibrium.

For neo-Keynesians the economy consists of two types of market: auction (or flexprice) markets, where prices move swiftly to equate supply and demand; and customer (or fixprice) markets, where prices move much more slowly, causing quantities to adjust in the short run. Auction markets dominate the financial sector, but fixprice markets are more common elsewhere. An economy dominated by fixprice markets displays Keynesian characteristics: output and employment initially respond to demand shocks and only eventually do prices and wages adjust. However neo-Keynesians still need to explain price and (especially) wage rigidity. It is not sufficient simply to assume such inflexibility (as early Keynesian theorists were often content to do): it has to be rationalised in terms of utility-maximisation by individuals and profit-maximisation by firms.

One relevant body of literature concerns the existence of implicit contracts. The key insight here is that 'in the process of exchanging labour, an incomplete insurance policy is traded as well' (Azariadis, 1982, p. 222). Risk-averse workers dislike the substantial variations in income which occur if pay is linked to marginal productivity at every stage of the business cycle. They prefer to be paid less than the value of their marginal productivity in periods of high labour demand (the difference between the wage and MRP being an insurance premium) in return for being paid more than their MRP (an insurance payment) in periods of recession. Employers provide this insurance and thus smooth workers' incomes over the cycle. In return they take a normal rate of profit on the sums advanced, so that workers receive less on average than the expected value of their marginal product. We then have the phenomenon of wage stickiness plus (*ex post*) involuntary unemployment over the recessionary phase of the business cycle.

In another approach, developed by Okun (1981), a sharp distinction is made between experienced employees and job seekers (the unemployed). The former will possess firm-specific skills achieved through on-the-job training which make them more valuable to the firm than job seekers. This explains why firms are willing to continue paying higher wages to experienced 'insiders' even if the unemployed are prepared to work for less. Analysis of this sort lies behind the insider-outsider theory of persistent unemployment (see Chapter 7). It attempts to explain why the rise in unemployment in the early 1980s lasted so long.

Then there is the efficiency wage hypothesis. The claim here is that labour productivity depends directly on the real wages paid by firms. The employer thus has a rather different choice problem from that modelled in the traditional approach. The aim must be to minimise labour cost per unit of output or 'efficiency unit' (Yellen, 1984). Optimal choice on these lines can be shown to be compatible with involuntary unemployment over the business cycle: workers would be willing to work at or below the existing wage and yet cannot find jobs. Employers are unwilling to lower wages because this would lower the productivity of all workers already on the job.

The point to emerge from these theories (discussed further in Chapter 7) is that wage stickiness may be a rational outcome of a bargaining process in which it is in the interests of both sides of industry to reduce the transactions costs of labour turnover and job search. Risks and hiring costs are reduced via contracts, and a rational response to a decline in product demand will be temporary layoffs, over-staffing and part-time work rather than wage cuts (i.e. procyclical quantity adjustments rather than the price flexibility displayed in auction markets).

Of course these hypotheses are not without their critics. For one thing they involve real wage rigidity when the important phenomenon to be explained is *nominal* wage stickiness. Criticisms like this have undermined the explanatory power of this idea, and contracts have not yet been shown to be the optimal outcome of market forces.

However, although not strictly compatible with optimising behaviour, wage and price stickiness may impose only small menu costs on firms. Akerlof and

Yellen (1985) point out that failure to follow profit maximising rules of behaviour in response to small nominal shocks only leads to second-order losses even though this behaviour generates a macro response with first-order welfare consequences.

The cost to price-setters of nominal rigidities can be much smaller than their macro-effects – as long as the pre-determined price is close to the profit-maximising price. If the cost of price rigidity to the firm is negligible, then the private incentives to alter behaviour are correspondingly small. There is in effect an aggregate demand externality because the rigidity in the firm's price contributes to rigidity in the aggregate price level. Adjustment of all prices would prevent a fall in real aggregate demand, but each firm is a small part of the economy and thus ignores this macro benefit.

The combination of small menu costs and imperfect competition produces 'near rationality'. Nominal price rigidity is near rational because it involves only a small departure from full optimisation. However, whatever the reason for these nominal rigidities, the macroeconomic consequences can be highly significant.

Given the existence of wage and price rigidities, policy changes and other demand shocks can induce cycles even if expectations are rational. A simple but highly effective illustration is provided by Fischer's (1977) model, where wage contracts overlap and are set for two years. Half of the firms in the economy renegotiate contracts this year; for the rest, contracts remain fixed until next year. Under these conditions not even the rational expectations assumption can prevent systematic and anticipated policy actions from having an effect. Only part of the economy will be able to respond this year to current money supply figures: we thus have changes in relative prices leading to changes in real variables over the cycle.

The essence of all neo-Keynesian models, then, is the attempt to provide a microeconomic rationale for price rigidities, which means that nominal demand has an important role in the business cycle. Equilibrium business cycle theorists see this as 'adhocery', but we have seen that their own models are not entirely free from this most dreadful of all economists' vices.

GOVERNMENT AND BUSINESS CYCLES

As earlier sections imply, a main theme in the debate on business cycles is the role of government in the economy. Far from being the stabilising influence envisaged by Keynesians, the idea that governments are themselves a major cause of fluctuations has been a recurring theme in economics for many years. Although this was often dismissed in the euphoria of the Keynesian revolution, economists later returned to the view that, by their misguided attempts to stabilise the economy, governments could themselves be the prime cause of business cycles. We now look in more detail at some of the implications of this belief.

Rules versus Discretion

A crucial issue in the debate over stabilisation policies has been uncertainty. Monetarists in particular insist that uncertainty is so pervasive, and policy lags are so long, that governments are impotent to improve on the stabilising elements already in the system. As long ago as the late 1940s, Milton Friedman was cautioning against reliance on counter-cyclical policies because they 'may easily intensify fluctuations rather than mitigate them'. In 1953 he published a classic critique of stabilisation policies under uncertainty. This analysis showed how the lags inherent in the execution of macroeconomic policy could impart instability to the economy.

Friedman showed that the effectiveness of counter-cyclical policy depends on there being a strong negative correlation (i.e. between -0.5 and -1) between discretionary policy changes and the changes in level of economic activity. However, as it took time for governments to recognise the need for action, to take appropriate measures, and then for these measures to take effect, it was possible that the correlation might be much lower. For example, in a recession, by the time the effects of policy changes intended to boost aggregate demand came into effect, the economy might already have recovered so that the extra spending could engender inflation. Discretionary policy would then actually exacerbate fluctuations in economic activity (Friedman, 1953). This analysis led to the conclusion that governments should not manipulate monetary and fiscal policies in an attempt to smooth aggregate demand over the business cycle. To fiscal conservatism, Friedman added the Constant Monetary Growth Rule. Support for this rule increased in the 1960s and 1970s, as we have seen.

One thing which contributed to the CMGR's success as a policy rule was that it sounded simple. But perhaps simplistic is a better word. For a crucial assumption underlying Friedman's analysis is that output fluctuations are random, whereas in reality they are cyclical. Phillips (1954) showed how discretionary policies can improve economic performance by developing feedback rules which take the cyclical nature of output into account. A simple (proportional) feedback rule would be to increase the money supply by say 1% whenever output fell more than 2% below its natural rate. A more sophisticated rule would relate monetary growth to the rate of change of output (derivative control). These are examples of activist rules: they incorporate counter-cyclical responses but eschew discretionary actions.

Fischer and Cooper (1973) surveyed these issues and concluded that cautious feedback rules would be stabilising and would out-perform fixed rules like the CMGR. However, the rational expectations revolution added a caveat to this conclusion: feedback rules reduce output fluctuations only if the parameters of the model are relatively stable. This will not necessarily be the case if the public react to the feedback rule; for instance, prices and wages could be pushed up in anticipation of an expansionary policy. The Phillips curve would then shift even in the short run. Counter-cyclical policies would have no impact on output but simply affect the inflation rate. According to Sargent and Wallace (1976), even activist rules would be neutral because anticipated monetary changes would have no real effect. The rational expectations critique strengthened the case for the CMGR.

The conclusion that the level of output is independent of the level of nominal demand even in the short run depends crucially on the assumptions of equilibrium and full market clearing. For Fischer's two-period contract model (outlined earlier) showed how, in the presence of price stickiness, discretionary monetary policies can influence output even if expectations are rational. Indeed, within this framework rational expectations could lead to even greater fluctuations in output.

The New Classicals counter this by stressing that the structure of contracts can be changed and will eventually respond to activist policies. They also emphasise the importance of policy credibility. Contractionary policies must be made credible by ruling out U-turns. In any case the public's response to discretionary policies will ultimately determine their effectiveness. As soon as these policies become fully anticipated, attempts to expand output simply lead to higher inflation. It is this time dimension that the New Classicals now seek to emphasise: the short-run benefits from discretionary policies quickly disappear and give way to long-run costs. As a result the current debate has centred on policy credibility and time (or dynamic) inconsistency.

Time-Inconsistency and Credibility

This problem, first outlined by Kydland and Prescott (1977), is discussed in an international context in Chapter 4. Take a simple example (adapted from Argy, 1988) where a government faces a trade union movement powerful enough to influence the level of money wage settlements. The government argues that there is no trade-off between unemployment and inflation; as inflation is too high, its optimal strategy is to go for a restrictive monetary policy as a means of controlling it. This is accordingly announced. The unions now have to decide whether to go for high or low money wages. If the government succeeds in establishing its credibility and convinces the unions that it is serious, money wage settlements will be moderated and inflation will be brought down. However, it can obtain a (temporary) reduction in unemployment – which may help it win re-election – by relaxing monetary controls. With wages set on the expectation of low inflation, the unexpectedly rapid increase in the money supply generates a rise in output and a fall in unemployment. Prices rise faster than wages, so real wages fall.

However, if the unions are unconvinced by the government's commitment to its monetary target, they will go for high wage increases to maintain the real value of their pay. If the government then in fact sticks to the target, unemployment rises. As this would clearly be undesirable, a government pursuing its (new) optimal policy will abandon its monetary targets so as to prevent unemployment rising.

This 'time-inconsistent' policy scenario will be recognised by students of game theory as an example of the well-known 'Prisoner's Dilemma'. It suggests that the existence of government discretion over monetary policy leads to poor macroeconomic performance, with inflation higher than its optimal level, yet unemployment no lower. As Blackburn and Christenson put it, the apparent implication of this analysis is the need 'to change the rules or institutional structure...in order to constrain the freedom of the policymaker to alter his decisions' (1989, p. 15). This could be done, for instance, by making the central bank constitutionally independent, or by linking the country's currency to some external target – perhaps a revived gold standard or a strengthened European Exchange Rate Mechanism.

However, more complex strategic models, involving repeated games rather than the one-off scenario outlined above, suggest that informal reputational mechanisms may serve to secure the same result of enforcing commitment to announced targets. A rapidly growing literature on policy credibility explores this possibility (see, for example, Barro, 1986). A government which adopts a longer time-horizon will have an incentive not to engage in short-term policy opportunism, and it may convey its commitment in a number of indirect ways. For example it has been pointed out that Mrs Thatcher's government was able to enhance its credibility in relation to monetary policy by reducing trade union power.

But the literature on credibility, though fascinating in itself, suffers from lack of empirical support. The same lack of evidence undermines analysis of a related topic with which we conclude this survey – the political business cycle hypothesis.

Political Business Cycles

Initially the CMGR and similar rules were discussed in the context of a belief that governments acted from the best of possible motives: that of attempting to maximise social welfare. Discussions were accordingly conducted in a spirit of dispassionate advice-giving. However, the motives of government action soon came to be looked at far more critically (see Chapter 9). Thus in the mid-1970s 'political' theories of the business cycle enjoyed a brief vogue. Here macroeconomic fluctuations were no longer seen by critics as the unintended consequence of well-intentioned policy, but rather as resulting from deliberate manipulation of the economy by governments seeking short-term political advantage.

For example Nordhaus (1975), building on the work of Buchanan and Tullock, saw politicians as operating in a 'political market' where votes were to be won by the appropriate choice of macroeconomic policy. His model assumed that:

1.   governments aim to win elections by pursuing policies which will maxi-
     mise their share of the vote (thought of as distributed along a continuous
     left-right spectrum: in a two-party system, the objective is therefore to win
     over the 'median voter');
2.   electors have a continuous set of preferences between possible macroecon-
     omic outcomes, and these preferences are reflected in their voting behav-
     iour;
3.   governments can manipulate the economy to reach preferred combinations
     of inflation and unemployment.

The last assumption implies the existence of a short-run Phillips curve. Govern-ments seeking to achieve re-election move up the curve, trading a higher rate of inflation for lower unemployment: there is a pre-election boom. After the election, as expectations adjust, the economy reverts to higher unemployment. Repetition of this pattern prior to the next election completes the cycle.

Interesting though this idea is, it has not stood the test of time. For one thing, to account for persistent cycles we would have to assume that the public could be repeatedly 'fooled' into expansionary behaviour by governments. As the 1970s wore on, more and more economists began to accept the logic of rational expectations and were unwilling to accept the assumption of an exploitable trade-off between unemployment and inflation.

For another, writers like Hibbs (1977) pointed out the obvious: that different political parties have different economic preferences. Thus 'conservative' governments might attach more importance to reducing inflation; 'socialists' might worry more about unemployment. No consistent cycle would be discerned as governments changed. Finally, some of the predictions of political business cycle models received little empirical support; for example, the implication that unemployment would rise in the first half of a government's period in office and fall in the second half was not consistently borne out (see Alt and Chrystal, 1983, for a critical review of the evidence).

It would be wrong totally to dismiss the political business cycle approach. Recently, in an interesting restatement, Alesina (1989) has put forward the 'rational partisan' theory. In this view, parties differ in their beliefs and do not pursue a simple vote-maximising strategy aimed at the median voter. In office they will attempt to pursue different policies. Voters know this; they also form rational expectations and cannot be persistently fooled into believing that the economy can deviate permanently from its natural level of output and employment.

However, we live in an uncertain world and thus the public can be 'shocked' by an unexpected election result. In such an event, people will have been expecting a government with one set of macroeconomic policies and thus a predicted inflation rate. Contracts will have been formed accordingly. When an 'unexpected' government is returned, inflation will therefore be higher or lower than anticipated. If contracts cannot be instantly and costlessly renegotiated, there will be nominal wage and/or price rigidities. Output and employment can drift from their 'natural' levels. Partisan behaviour in the presence of uncertainty can therefore have a destabilising effect on the economy.

CONCLUSION

Macroeconomic fluctuations have been with us for a long time and seem unlikely to disappear. Changes in intellectual and political fashion have occurred with great speed in recent years, and readers may be excused some confusion as a result of this rapid survey.

It now appears that monetarist and New Classical theories were too extreme in their assertion that inconsistent monetary policy is the only significant impulse behind business cycles. Nevertheless, these approaches were a useful antidote to earlier faith in the power of governments to manipulate the macroeconomy at will. Furthermore they enabled the debate to move onto a higher technical plane by their emphasis on the importance of formally modelled expectations, the usefulness of the market-clearing assumption, and new approaches to the use of econometrics in the analysis of the cycle. The New Classicals also made a great contribution to the analysis of government-private sector relations by sparking off a continuing debate about the credibility of policy commitments.

However, the more exciting recent work has been produced by the Neo-Keynesians and the Real Business Cycle theorists. Although very different in orientation, their work is to some extent compatible. Both see the private sector's own characteristics as a possible cause of cyclical fluctuations – although it does not follow that discretionary fiscal or monetary policy is desirable.

A particularly interesting area, and one which we think is likely to play an increasing role in the future, is the relationship between the short-run factors influencing the cycle and the long-term factors determining economic growth. An emphasis on this connection is long overdue.

NOTES

1. For an excellent brief summary of the contributions of this period, see Backhouse (1985, ch. 16). For a longer treatment, see Kim (1988).
2. There may, for instance, be considerable variations between countries. Britton (1986) has claimed to find greater regularity in the UK economy than in the US.
3. Serial correlation (or autocorrelation) means that a variable at date (t) is correlated with its own value at date (t-1). Covariation describes the way in which different variables move in relation to each other: a high degree of covariation suggests conformity between the cyclical paths of two variables.
4. For a useful discussion, see Central Statistical Office (1975).
5. If saving is proportional to current income (Y_t), and investment (I_t) is proportional to lagged income, then:

$$Y_t = I_t/s \qquad \text{(the Keynesian multiplier r: s is the} \qquad (A6.1)$$
   average/marginal propensity to save)
$$I_t = v(Y_t - Y_{t-1}) \qquad \text{(the acceleration principle)} \qquad (A6.2)$$

   Substitution yields:

$$Y_t = (v/v\text{-}s)Y_{t-1} \qquad (A6.3)$$

   Adding in autonomous expenditures such as government spending and autonomous consumption (A_t) gives:

$$Y_t = (v/v\text{-}s)Y_{t-1} + (1/v\text{-}s)A_t \qquad (A6.4)$$

6. In a simple autocorrelation (first difference) of the form

$$Y_t = a_o + a_1 Y_{t-1} + e_t \qquad (A6.5)$$

   if $a_1 < 1$ then the series is said to be stationary. Shocks imparted to Y through e have only a transitory effect. However, if $a_1 = 1$ then Y is said to have a unit root in its dynamics and has a stochastic trend. The series is said to be non-stationary. Shocks have a permanent effect. In this case trend GDP should be allowed to change every period. Some econometricians claim that over 50% of the variation of GDP in the long run can be explained by the trend component (Nelson and Plosser, 1982).
7. In equation A6.5, even when $a_1 = 1$ the series can be made stationary by first differencing. A variable which is stationary after differencing once is said to be integrated of order 1: I(1). Similarly, if it is stationary after differencing twice it is I(2). Now consider two variables, x_t and y_t, both I(1). If a linear combination of the two, say z_t ($= y_t + \lambda x_t$) is I(0), then x_t and y_t are cointegrated. (This is also the case if x_t and y_t are I(2) and z_t is I(1) etc.) The beauty of this result is that ($y_t + x_t$) represents the long-run relationship between y_t and x_t, and can be obtained by ordinary least squares regression without consideration of any intervening dynamics. A useful introduction to cointegration is provided in Maddala (1988, pp. 216–18).
8. Hayek's analysis is conducted in terms of Böhm-Bawerk's rather confusing framework of dated capital. Little is lost by ignoring this here.
9. Irving Fisher had developed a broadly similar analysis of the role of money in the business cycle before the First World War.
10. The basic idea of this rule is the expansion of the (appropriately defined) money supply at a constant rate in line with the long-run growth of GDP.
11. Most of Lucas' seminal papers were collected in Lucas (1981). For an informal but very readable introduction to New Classical ideas, see Klamer (1984).

7. Neo-Keynesian Theories of Unemployment

G K Shaw

In this chapter Professor Shaw outlines several new or revived hypotheses which provide an explanation for the wage rigidity associated with the Keynesian concept of involuntary unemployment. These microeconomic explanations of unemployment are compatible with modern developments in macroeconomics, such as the widespread adoption of rational expectations by economic modellers. If some or all of these are valid, the Keynesian view that demand shocks can lead to persistent unemployment may be vindicated.

INTRODUCTION

In his onslaught upon classical employment theory, John Maynard Keynes derived a macroeconomic model which was essentially demand determined, and the fundamental question he posed was simply the following: 'What guarantee is there that the level of demand forthcoming would be such as to absorb the full employment level of national output?' This was a question which the classical economists had largely ignored or had neatly sidestepped by taking refuge in Say's famous Law of Markets; by stipulating that supply creates its own demand, this had effectively dispensed with the demand equation. In the simplest terms, classical employment theory maintained that the employment level would be determined by the natural bargaining process in the labour market. If competition prevailed the outcome would be a full employment economy, in the sense that there would be no one unemployed who was anxious to work at the going wage. If monopoly power or other impediments to the indicated competitive outcome prevailed, the result might be a less-than-full employment economy. In either case, whatever the output, Say's Law guaranteed that demand would be sufficient to absorb it. There was thus no need for detailed concern with the level of aggregate demand as such; attention was focused firmly upon the means of ensuring that a competitive climate would prevail, thus generating the classical full employment solution.

The question posed by Keynes thus shifted the focus of economics away from supply to the side of demand; it led to a detailed analysis of the determinants of consumption and investment spending in keeping with the elementary Keynesian model. Moreover, it naturally led to the posing of a second question, namely: 'In the event of demand proving to be deficient, would there be any natural or inherent tendency operating within the economy to replenish the deficiency?' This issue was to dominate much of the theoretical discussion in the early 'Keynes versus the Classics' debate. The conventional view of the outcome generally sided with the Classicists on the theoretical level by insisting that such automatic tendencies did indeed exist as, for example, those giving rise to the Pigou effect. At the same time, however, with the recognition that such influences were empirically without real significance, there emerged a marked willingness to endorse the policy implications deriving from the Keynesian framework. Thus, the general compromise which was to gain wide acceptance in both Keynesian and classical circles suggested that the classical model was essentially correct but quite irrelevant from the policy point of view, and that for pragmatic reasons there was a need to accept the policy implications stemming from the Keynesian analysis.

Underlying this entire debate was a concept of equilibrium. The classical model postulated equilibrium as a natural consequence of market forces operating in a competitive environment. We can illustrate this situation with the aid of Figure 7.1 where, given the indicated supply and demand curves for labour (both drawn as a function of the real wage), we obtain a determinate volume of employment N_1 associated with the equilibrium real wage $(W/P)_1$. Again, Say's Law guarantees that the output associated with the employment level N_1 will be readily taken up by the market economy. By stressing the role of aggregate demand, Keynes was suggesting an alternative possible outcome. If demand were only sufficient to absorb the output level associated with the employment level N_2, then employment would fall accordingly, with the real wage rising to $(W/P)_2$; the resulting unemployment is indicated as the distance N_2N_3.[1]

The Keynesian position portrayed in Figure 7.1 posed no real dilemma for the classical economist; equilibrium would be restored by the downward pressure upon real wages arising from the very existence of unemployment. As long as competition prevailed, the latter could be viewed as merely a temporary blip in an otherwise Panglossian world.

At this point, it is perhaps necessary to make a distinction between differing groups of economists who would nonetheless regard themselves as Keynesian. On the one hand, there are those usually, although not always, dubbed *post-Keynesians* who, emphasising the importance and non-reversibility of historical time, reject the very notion of equilibrium as being a useful concept; indeed, they display open contempt for much of conventional neo-classical equilibrium economics. This is very much a point of view associated with the Cambridge

Figure 7.1   Keynesian unemployment

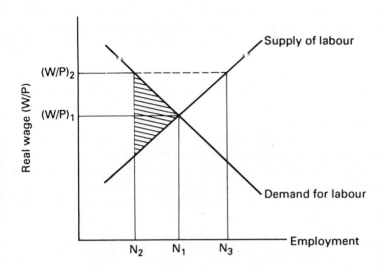

School of Economists led by Nicholas Kaldor, Joan Robinson and Piero Sraffa. These economists were prone to interpret the economics of the *General Theory* as being the economic analysis of the short run, but a short run grounded in historical time. In this view, which is scathing of attempts to reduce Keynesian economics to the short-run equilibria of the comparative static methodology embodied in IS/LM analysis, there is no reason why an unregulated economy should ever achieve equilibrium. Writing of the Keynesian revolution, Joan Robinson stated this in no uncertain terms: 'the revolution lay in the change from the conception of equilibrium to the concept of history.... Once we admit that history goes one way, from the irrevocable past into the unknown future, the conception of equilibrium based upon the mechanical analogy of a pendulum swinging to and fro in space becomes untenable' (Robinson, 1973, pp. 3ff.) The ideas of contemporary post-Keynesians are discussed in more detail by Philip Arestis in Chapter 10.

In stark contrast to this position, there are those economists who, whilst decidedly Keynesian in their policy orientation, also display a general sympathy for the neo-classical framework and for the equilibrium outcome. Indeed, for many of these economists, who would generally be dubbed *neo-Keynesian*, the classical equilibrium solution is but a *special* case of a *General Theory* of Employment. Their concern has been to explain why the classical special case is far from the norm, and why demand deficiency may be maintained for considerable periods of time in the absence of positive discretionary measures. These economists are operating within the framework of internally consistent equilibrium models, but models which confront constraints of one kind or another. They have succeeded in reconciling the concept of unemployment equilibria or persistence in unemployment with rational maximising principles derived from microeconomics. In doing so, they have brought a greater degree of sophistication and conviction to standard Keynesian analysis. In particular, in recent years, these economists have sought to explain why certain markets, and in particular labour markets, may continue to fail to clear even when expectations are formed rationally (in the manner outlined by David Peel in Chapter 5). Whilst accepting the equilibrium framework conceptually, neo-Keynesian economists are thus broadly in keeping with the spirit of Keynes in believing that the automatic adjustment mechanism underlying the classical model is fundamentally flawed and in suggesting that there may be grounds for discretionary stabilisation policies.

Conventionally-trained economists, committed to belief in utility maximising behaviour upon the part of rational and well-informed individuals, have a natural tendency to endorse the principle of market clearance. Stated at its simplest, if a market fails to clear, that is if prices do not adjust so as to equate supply and demand, then implicitly we have a potentially avoidable loss of social welfare. Indeed, as Barro (1979) has emphasised, a situation where supply and demand are not equated implies that some mutually advantageous trading opportunities still remain to be exploited. Referring back to Figure 7.1, for example, at the Keynesian employment level N_2, the shaded area denotes welfare loss in the sense of consumer and producer surplus foregone. On the supply side, there are workers willing to accept less than the existing wage, whilst upon the demand side there are potential employers who would happily take on more labour if only the real wage could be lowered. *A priori*, self-interest would dictate that such a situation must be of short-term duration only.

How does the neo-Keynesian economist respond to the logic of this argument and maintain that unemployment equilibrium may persist for considerable periods of time, thus providing the initial justification for interventionist stabilisation policies? It is to this question that the present chapter is primarily addressed.

IMPLICIT CONTRACT THEORY

Contract theory forms one element – and a very important element – in the neo-Keynesian case for departure from the seemingly inevitable equilibrium solution of conventional supply and demand analysis. Contracts, implicit and otherwise, detail the highly complex agreements reached between workers and management in a two-way bargaining process over the conditions governing the sale of labour services. As such, contracts are determined by bilateral negotiation, implying a radical methodological departure from conventional models which view wage and employment determination as the result of a highly decentralised and instantaneous market process.[2] The motivation for such contracts stems from the fact that both parties perceive potential benefits, the worker in the form of income smoothing and the firm in the form of reduced risk. Moreover, wage negotiations are a costly and time-consuming process, and such costs can be minimised or greatly reduced by extending the period of the contract. In addition, long-term contracts reduce the incidence of strike activity injurious to both parties. Normally, the benefits will be greater the greater the degree of job specificity. That is to say, the more employment involves investment in specialised training upon the part of management, or the more it demands particular qualities and qualifications upon the part of labour, the greater will be the incentive to enter into formal or informal contracts.

The fundamental assumption underlying much of contract theory rests upon the premise that labour is 'risk averse' and is reluctant to tie real wages too closely to its marginal revenue productivity (which may be subject to substantial volatility over the course of the business cycle). In effect, the contract entered into by labour may be seen as a form of insurance which reduces uncertainty and insulates it from unforeseen autonomous shocks. Such insurance renders the wage far less variable than it might otherwise be, thus imparting a certain element of wage and price rigidity. In return, the worker grants to the firm far greater freedom of action by agreeing *ex ante* to behave in a certain way under certain conditions (states of nature). Thus, for example, given an unprecedented shortfall in demand, overtime working may be eliminated or the workers' normal hours reduced (in exceptional cases even to zero), or its conditions of employment may be changed in line with the prior agreement. *Ex post*, of course, labour may be unhappy with the final outcome, especially if this involves unemployment, but since such an outcome was part of the agreed contract pertaining to a certain state of nature, no renegotiation is possible.[3] In terms of conventional supply and demand analysis, what is implied is the abandonment of the traditional labour supply curve. Instead of the worker responding to changes in the real wage by altering the amount of labour he or she is willing to offer, the contract specifies precisely how much labour will be supplied and at what rate of remuneration etc., in each and every feasible situation. In extreme cases, the informal contract may not even delineate the precise hours and conditions of work, but may instead grant them to the discretion of the employer.

It should be emphasised that implicit contract theory does not necessarily imply rigidity of real wages. Indeed, the real wage may well fluctuate according to the state of nature as laid down in the initial agreement. And certainly there is no implication of nominal wage rigidity since index linking, wholly or in part to the retail price index, will often be a feature of the contract itself. Nonetheless, it suggests reasons why wages and prices might exhibit greater stability than would otherwise be the case and, in particular, why real wages may not equate supply and demand in the labour market for considerable periods of time.

Contract theory has developed extensively over the past decade and has provided useful insights into the workings of the labour market in conditions of demand uncertainty. In doing so, it has provided Keynesian unemployment theory with a certain microeconomic rationale which has often been lacking in earlier Keynesian expositions. It is not, of course, without its critics, and it still leaves considerable questions unanswered. What, for example, determines the period of the contract? Why should parties to the agreement decide upon a limited term of contract with a view to renegotiating at a later date, as opposed to entering into a single contract for the entire period of their relationship? This is an important question recently posed by Hart (1987) which has still to be effectively answered.

Again, one difficulty with the theory is that so much of the agreement is essentially implicit and not formally binding, and therefore subject to break-down. Indeed, in recent years the design of self-enforcing contracts has become a major research target in attempting to deal with the observed fact that, in an upswing of the business cycle, workers are more prone to quit their jobs and seek employment elsewhere. In this case, the contract fails as workers, having benefited from the insurance of higher wages in the downswing, now renege on their part of the bargain.

Again, most contracts are notoriously incomplete partly because of the difficulties inherent in making provision for all possible contingencies, and partly because of the costs involved in making complex agreements. Consequently, implicit contract theory often needs to be supplemented by additional rules or conventions which are very seldom specified. Here a possible role emerges for custom or social mores as to what is fair and equitable, and for considerations as to the reputation of the principal contractor. Needless to say, such factors cannot be quantified with any precision and tend to give contract theory a certain uneasy incompleteness. Nonetheless, contract theory has extended our understanding of the labour market and, in particular, has provided a view of how such a market may behave. This is in stark contrast to the machinations of the competitive market so central to New Classical macroeconomics.

EFFICIENCY WAGE MODELS

A second major theoretical development to buttress the Keynesian assumption of persistent involuntary unemployment has been derived from the so-called efficiency wage models. Stated simply, these models stem from the premise that some firms find it advantageous to pay in excess of the market clearing wage since the marginal productivity of labour is held to be positively related to the wage paid.[4] Although the underlying rationale is clear, various alternative efficiency wage models have been developed in recent years. Amongst the most important are the following:

1. *Shirking Models* Such models rest upon the premise that individual workers normally possess some element of discretion over how well they perform their specified job owing to the difficulties and costs involved in monitoring worker performance. In such cases, workers may chose to diminish their work effort to the detriment of the firm. However, shirking involves a risk (namely that of detection and dismissal), and the potential cost of job loss will be greater the greater the wage paid. In a full employment economy, the deterrent cost of shirking would be minimal, for then the dismissed worker could readily find similar employment elsewhere. By raising wages above the market clearing level, firms make it costly for workers to be dismissed as a consequence of shirking activity and hence raise worker productivity. Higher than market clearing wages thus act as a disciplinary device, whilst at the same time permitting firms to decrease their outlays upon monitoring activity. In passing, it may be noted that the existence of unemployment benefits reduces the potential cost of job loss, a consideration which may be relevant to long-term productivity trends.

2. *Reduced Turnover Models* A second efficiency wage model emphasises the importance of the costs of labour turnover to the business firm. By paying wages in excess of the market clearing rate, the firm will diminish the incentive of existing workers to quit their employment. Likewise, in a general equilibrium context, the existence of unemployment (due to wages being in excess of market clearing levels) will provide a similar disincentive. Incremental wage payments play a similar role in helping to retain more senior and more experienced staff members.

3. *Selectivity Models* Since the workforce will generally exhibit substantial heterogeneity in respect of ability and all round performance, the payment of wages in excess of the market clearing rate will permit the firm to be selective in its hiring policy. The higher wage level will enlarge the field of job applications by progressively overcoming reservation wage barriers and thus allow the firm the widest scope in choosing workers who conform

to its perception of superior quality. Needless to say, the same consideration will allow greater discrimination in the firm's employment policy, whether upon grounds of race, age or sex; to the extent that such considerations enter into the firm's objective function, they provide an additional reason for higher than necessary wage levels.

4. *Loyalty Models*   In contrast to the shirking models which emphasise the possible punitive consequences of non-performance, loyalty models highlight workers' sense of identity with their firm and their willingness to cooperate fruitfully providing they feel fairly compensated. Raising the level of wage payment will increase the number of cooperative employees, thus raising productivity. A 'fair' wage cannot easily be determined, but clearly it bears some relation to wages elsewhere as well as to the firm's perceived profitability.

Perhaps it should be emphasised that efficiency wage models are perfectly consistent with assumptions of profit maximisation on the part of business firms. Indeed, they provide yet another example of macroeconomic unemployment being explained by reference to rational microeconomic behaviour. Having determined the efficiency wage, the profit maximising firm will hire labour up to the point where it is equated to marginal revenue product. Secondly, there is nothing invariant about the efficiency wage which one presumes would be positively related to the business cycle. Of course, the efficiency wage need not be uniform throughout the economy. Indeed, the implication is that if monitoring and turnover costs differ between firms, then so too will the optimum efficiency wage. Nonetheless, the optimal efficiency wage paid by any one firm will depend upon the wage paid by competing firms elsewhere. This element of wage interdependence, together with uncertainty as to the response of competing firms, perhaps suggest an additional reason for comparative wage rigidities.

It may be objected that efficiency wage models will only have relevance to those occupations where monitoring or turnover costs tend to be disproportionately high. However, efficiency wage models may have wider application, especially if horizontal equity considerations impinge upon a firm's behaviour. For example, if efficiency wages are paid to minimise shirking and turnover costs in certain of a firm's occupational activities, then similar wage demands may arise in other departments on the grounds of horizontal equity (even though no wage efficiency considerations are involved). Likewise, efficiency wages paid by one firm may influence wage levels paid by a second firm even though, again, no efficiency considerations are involved. Akerlof and Yellen (1987) provide evidence pointing to the importance of such equity considerations in determining wage payments as a whole. The development of efficiency wage models has done much to account for the persistence of wage rates in excess of market clearing levels, despite the existence of substantial unemployment in the 1970s and 1980s. As such, they have brought a new credibility to the idea of Keynesian unemployment equilibria, even though their policy implications initially appear anti-Keynesian. For example, they would suggest that taxes imposed upon the firm's wage bill might be beneficial in inducing the firm to lower wages towards the market clearing level – a decidedly un-Keynesian notion. Similar considerations have led to the call for taxation to be imposed upon the firms whose annual pay awards exceed some pre-determined income policy norm.

INSIDER-OUTSIDER ANALYSIS

One of the questions which puzzled economists in the 1970s and 1980s was why growing unemployment levels seemed to exert no restraint upon increasing wage rates. Indeed, one witnessed substantial increases in unemployment combined with substantial real wage gains for those fortunate enough to remain in full-time work. The persistence of this phenomenon seriously called into question the relevance of the conventional competitive model as applied to labour markets, and led ultimately to the development of the insider-outsider dichotomy. According to this thesis, we may distinguish between *insiders* (employed) and *outsiders* (unemployed); various hypotheses are then advanced to justify the claim that outsiders have no real influence upon actual wages paid. Growing unemployment, therefore, does not in any sense weaken the power of the employed involved in wage negotiations. A similar thesis has been advanced with respect to the growing numbers of the long-term unemployed – people who have been out of work for a year or more. From the employers' perspective, such people are no longer looked upon as being employable and are thus in no position to compete with their more fortunate brethren. Consequently, they can exert no influence in national wage negotiations.

Insider-outsider models, therefore, see wages being set essentially as a result of negotiation between employers and insiders only. What is it that gives insiders such power that they may effectively ignore the existence of outsiders? The answer is seen to lie in the costs of hiring, training and dismissing workers. Hiring and training costs have already been expended upon insiders. Dismissal and replacement by lower paid outsiders would imply incurring such costs again, as well as meeting firing expenses which may included severance pay. Such costs effectively confer on insiders a certain monopoly power which they may exploit in their dealings with employers (Okun, 1981), especially if they are effectively unionised. In addition, the bargaining position of insiders is reinforced by the fact that they will normally possess considerable discretion over the extent to which they choose to cooperate with new entrants, thus directly affecting the latter's productivity (Lindbeck and Snower, 1988). Cooperation amongst insiders is sufficient to explain their superior productivity *vis-à-vis* new entrants or outsiders, and thus accounts for the willingness of firms to negotiate directly with trades unions as opposed to turning to non-unionised labour. Unlike efficiency wage models, where the existence of high wages stems from their perceived benefits to the firm, insider-outsider models explain high wages in terms of the power of employees. Also, unlike efficiency wage models, there are no productivity implications stemming from the higher wage levels.

Various models exist of insider-outsider analysis, some detailing the means and consequences of outsiders gaining insider status and vice-versa. In some cases, workers temporarily laid off retain insider status; in others, loss of employment entails loss of such status, allowing the reduced number of insiders to force an increase in the existing wage (Blanchard and Summers, 1987). Models of this nature are thus able to reconcile the apparently contradictory experience of simultaneous growth in both unemployment and real wages. They also serve to explain why growing unemployment amongst school-leavers has exercised virtually no impact upon national labour markets. The persistence of unemployment is explained in terms of the ability and willingness of insiders to translate increases in aggregate demand into higher wages rather than into increased employment. Outsiders are effectively priced outside the market by the wage bargains struck by insiders.

Insider-outsider models would also appear to possess relevance to the duration of search unemployment. The latter refers to the situation where an unemployed worker turns down offers of employment and continues seeking work elsewhere because the wages preferred fall below expectations. Models of this nature then rely upon some form of adaptive expectations mechanism whereby the unemployed worker revises his or her expectation downwards in the light of experience. Clearly, the duration of such unemployment depends upon how quickly expectations are adapted to reality in the wake of unanticipated demand shocks. However, if outsiders seeking work perceive similarly qualified insiders enjoying comparatively high wage levels, it is likely that the adaptive adjustment process will be muted accordingly and the duration of their unemployment extended.

HYSTERESIS IN UNEMPLOYMENT

One daunting feature of employment experience in the 1980s was the sharp rise in unemployment levels in the short term, followed by their comparatively long-term persistence. Little evidence has emerged of employment returning to its former equilibrium level, the consequence being a growing ratio of the long-term unemployed. In the United Kingdom, for example, the numbers of unemployed rose sharply between 1979 and 1981 under the combined impact of the OPEC oil shocks and the adoption of a highly restrictive fiscal and monetary stance on the part of a government committed to controlling inflation. Only recently and under much less stringent budgetary policies has there been any significant improvement in the employment figures. Attempts to account for this phenomenon have led to the formulation of *hysteresis* models in which the equilibrium rate of unemployment (the non-accelerating inflation rate) is not independent of the level of actual employment. That is to say the equilibrium rate of unemployment is actually *path dependent*; it follows that any autonomous shock raising the actual unemployment rate may also raise the long-term equilibrium rate. In this way economists have attempted to explain the observed rise and persistence of European unemployment levels, in doing so drawing upon the economics of insider-outsider models (Blanchard and Summers, 1987).

One example of such a model is the following. Suppose insiders are sufficiently powerful to dictate the actual wage paid and they set it so as to equate the expected employment level with the size of their membership – the actual employment level being determined by the firm in the light of realised demand conditions. If an adverse demand shock now generates unemployment, the size of the membership shrinks but those remaining as insiders have no incentive to reduce their nominal wage. In any future wage negotiation, they would act in a similar manner and determine wage payments in the light of their reduced membership. In this way, for any given labour force, the equilibrium unemployment level is equal to the former period's actual unemployment level. It follows at once that the economy will exhibit no tendency to return to any fixed equilibrium value.

The model is altogether too stringent to conform with reality; for example, recently laid-off workers may still be counted amongst the insiders for a given period of time and taken into consideration in future wage negotiations. In a similar vein, following upon a favourable demand shock, the newly employed outsiders may not immediately gain insider status but may have to serve a probationary period as new entrants. Nonetheless, by stressing the comparative lack of influence of outsiders on wage negotiations, the model emphasises that the tendency to gain former equilibrium unemployment levels is in no way automatic. Similar arguments have been advanced with respect to the growing numbers of long-term unemployed. Again the contention is that these people will exert little or no influence on the labour market and that, accordingly, demand shocks raising their numbers will not be inherently self-reversing. Their lack of influence stems partly from a decline in their level of skills. As their skills atrophy their productivity may fall below their reservation wage or, more pertinently, below the wage rate determined upon by insiders. Again, discouragement may lead to a decline in the amount and intensity of their search activity, enhancing the power of insiders. Finally, potential employers may view the long-term unemployed in a decidedly unfavourable light and may not include them in their potential recruitment net. If the long-term unemployed exert no impact upon national wage levels, it follows that any increase in their number will only serve to raise the long-term equilibrium unemployment level.

SECTORAL SHIFT MODELS

Finally, mention may be made of the *Sectoral Shift Hypothesis* which many economists see as a necessary antidote to models which are too aggregative in their structure. The weakness of the standard aggregate model of national income determination lies in the fact that it is unable to take account of changes in the composition of demand. Indeed, since most macroeconomic models portray a one-good economy, they implicitly deal with a one-sector economy, so that any discussion of comparative price changes is automatically ruled out.

However, the real world is characterised by differential rates of technical change between sectors, by shifts in the composition of product demand, and by changes occurring in comparative prices partly, perhaps, owing to external shocks (for example, the OPEC crises of 1973 and 1979). Faced with such considerations, firms are constantly being compelled to revise their labour demands, some contracting their workforce whilst others attempt to expand. Unfortunately, however, the labour force tends to be comparatively immobile, especially in the UK where mobility has been impeded by housing policies and the development of the North/South divide, influenced no doubt by the attractions of a united Europe. Workers are faced with the need to change jobs but are unable to match the pace of adjustment demanded by business firms. Frictional or structural unemployment is the inevitable outcome and, in contrast to earlier Keynesian sentiments, may be considerable in scope. For example in an influential article, Lilien (1982) has argued that more than 50 percent of observed cyclical unemployment derives from sectoral demand shifts – a daunting conclusion for Keynesian-oriented economists since by implication it suggests that conventional demand management strategies will be of no avail. Lilien's assertion, which has not gone unchallenged (Abraham and Katz, 1986), rests upon the observed positive relationship between the dispersion of employment growth rates across sectors and the overall unemployment rate.

Sectoral shift theory is not really a theory of unemployment equilibria; nonetheless, in periods of rapid structural change it raises the spectre of frictional/structural unemployment on such a massive scale as to imply that the adjustment process towards full employment could be extremely protracted. The policy conclusion which would appear to emerge from this type of analysis would emphasise microeconomic measures to improve labour mobility. To the extent that demand management strategies are involved, they would appear to lie in the realm of highly selective expenditure programmes as opposed to policies of general tax concessions.

OTHER CONSIDERATIONS

We have advanced several theoretical explanations, which can claim to be based upon rational utility-maximising behaviour, to explain the phenomenon of substantial unemployment being maintained over considerable periods of time. Such neo-Keynesian statements provide a firmer foundation and a more sophisticated rationale to justify the Keynesian intuition that labour markets stubbornly fail to clear. The question we now pose is simply the following: do we need such elaborate theories to account for the relative inflexibility of wages in non-clearing market conditions? Are there not simpler, more plausible, sociological or psychological explanations to account for such observed phenomena? In posing this question we take account of the undeniable fact, emphasised by both Hicks (1974) and Solow (1980), that labour markets differ in many fundamental respects from other markets – for instance, that of mushrooms. In the latter, false trading (exchange at other than supply and demand equating prices) will presumably be speedily eliminated.[5]

In contrast, the labour market is characterised by social conventions, by custom, by a sense of what is fair and just, and by a desire to conform with what is deemed to be socially accepted behaviour. Unemployed workers offer themselves at the going wage. It is simply not true that they approach employers and attempt to undercut existing workers by offering their services for £5 or £10 a week less. In other words, despite possibly being ill-treated by insiders, outsiders do not attempt to damage the latter's interests. On the contrary, they act to protect the insiders' position – the position they themselves aspire to. Equally, a similar argument applies to employers. They do not respond to a situation of general unemployment by sacking the existing workforce and replacing them with cheaper substitutes. There are, as we have seen, sound economic arguments to rule out such behaviour. But even if such action were economic in the strict accounting sense, it would not be deemed an appropriate mode of behaviour. Economic theory too often seems to ignore such considerations; undoubtedly, such social pressures exist and are influential in determining ultimate outcomes. Again, there is a sense in which wage differentials are respected as signalling differences in skills or responsibilities, quite apart from respective supply and demand considerations. Blinder (1988) quotes an interesting empirical study which clearly demonstrated that most firms promptly adjusted their above-minimum wages upwards following a statutory increase in the minimum wage payment. Such action is not readily reconciled with conventional economic theory. Finally, one might mention considerations of status as a possible factor retarding indicated adjustments. If the recently unemployed worker retains the social status associated with his former job, he may opt to remain unemployed rather than accept a lower status job even though the wage offered exceeds his reservation wage. Certainly, such a consideration would suggest a lengthening of the period of search unemployment.

CONCLUSIONS

We began this chapter by asking the question of how Keynesian unemployment models could explain the persistence of unemployment equilibria. What could prevent the normal functioning of competitive markets from quickly reestablishing an equation between supply and demand following some autonomous shock to demand conditions? In confronting this question we have surveyed some important conceptual contributions grounded in microeconomic theory. Essentially, what these models have in common is a willingness to depart from the competitive framework of conventional neo-classical economics. It is not that they dispute the analysis of competitive price theory; rather they do not regard it as relevant to the analysis of the labour market. In this scenario, wages are essentially set by a process of bilateral bargaining between parties who possess certain monopoly powers in a climate of uncertainty surrounding future demand conditions. The context is more properly one of monopolistic competition as opposed to the rarefied abstract of pure competition. In such a world, once the wage rate is determined, employment offers depend upon the profit-maximising behaviour of firms; the extent of take-up of such offers is then best explained in the context of search models of unemployment. This is very much the approach underlying Pissarides' view of recent UK employment experience (Pissarides, 1989).

To the extent that these approaches are more able to account for the observed persistence in unemployment levels over considerable periods of time, they must be considered a superior alternative to the competitive market solution of neo-classical economics, and also to the machinations of the New Classical macroeconomics in which, in the words of Gordon (1976), 'theory proceeds with impeccable logic from unrealistic assumptions to conclusions that contradict the historical record'. In so doing, they reinforce the relevance of the Keynesian message and policy prescription – albeit in a much more sophisticated and complex guise.

NOTES

1. The inverse relationship between employment and the real wage, it may be noted, is perfectly in keeping with the doctrine of wages being equated with marginal productivity in the context of an economy confronted with the Law of Diminishing Returns.
2. Rosen (1985) has summarised the distinction neatly by suggesting that the analysis of the labour market is 'more akin to the marriage market than to the bourse'.

3.   The initial agreement, of course, may include redundancy compensation or lay-off pay.
4.   The underlying idea that productivity is geared to wage payment is by no means new and has figured prominently in the literature of development economics. See, for example, Shoup (1965).
5.   Or perhaps more accurately reversed. Consider traders who bring to market a supply of perishable mushrooms which they expect to sell in the course of an eight-hour trading day. If after four hours they have sold only a quarter of their mushrooms, they will have to reduce their price below the market equilibrium price to exhaust their stock. False trading is the norm and equilibrium trading never obtains.

8. Some Recent Developments in Econometric Modelling

M J Pokorny

The econometric techniques of the 1950s and 1960s proved unequal to the challenge of modelling the macroeconomics of the 1970s and 1980s. In the USA the 'Lucas critique' led to a change of direction in favour of equilibrium business cycle modelling, discussed in Chapter 6. In Britain, much attention was paid to the work of David Hendry and his collaborators, who rejected both the techniques of 'traditional' econometrics and the almost exclusive emphasis on statistical modelling associated with Box and Jenkins. Mike Pokorny brings out many of the key elements in recent econometric debates by concentrating on the specific problem of modelling aggregate consumption behaviour. While sympathising with the approach of Hendry et al, he accepts that their work is an extension of existing 'good practice' rather than a radical break with the past. Still less does it constitute a rigid set of rules and procedures for econometricians; creativity continues to have a central role to play.

INTRODUCTION

The objective of this chapter is to provide a broad overview of one of the current approaches to econometric modelling and estimation. The discussion will be relatively general in nature, and little reliance will be placed on a detailed technical exposition. Readers who require a deeper understanding of these methodologies (and, in particular, who wish to actually apply them) will have to follow up the references provided.

While technical detail will be kept to a minimum, it will be useful nonetheless to place the discussion within the context of a specific application. The estimation of the *consumption function* has been chosen, first, because this application has a long history in economics and econometrics and, secondly, because the economic theory underlying the consumption function is relatively straightforward and well known, making detailed analysis of it unnecessary.

In the first section a brief outline and discussion of what might be termed the 'traditional' approach to econometric modelling and estimation are provided.

The shortcomings of this strategy are then examined, before going on to discuss another approach which has recently been employed.

THE 'TRADITIONAL' APPROACH TO ECONOMETRIC MODELLING

It was in the 1950s and 1960s that econometric modelling became widely accepted as an indispensable tool for the economic policy-maker. This acceptance had its origins in the Keynesian revolution of the 1930s, and the widely shared belief that controlling and fine tuning the behaviour of the economy were legitimate and feasible objectives of government.

In order to derive detailed and specific policy prescriptions from within a general Keynesian framework, it was clearly necessary to adopt a far more rigorous and systematic approach to econometric estimation and inference than had previously been the case. The apparent success of Keynesian-inspired policy initiatives (as pointed out in Chapter 6) had encouraged postwar policy-makers to believe that the potential existed for extensive government intervention in the economy and that now, finally, the business cycle could be tamed and controlled. But for such detailed policy formulation and intervention to take place, a methodology for the precise measuring of a wide range of disaggregated economic relationships was required, and it was within this context that econometrics as a discipline came into its own. A further stimulus to this process of measurement was the rapid development and commercial availability of the computer, thus allowing for the application of a range of econometric techniques that had previously been developed in theory only.

In order to place some of the more recent approaches to econometric methodology within context, we shall first outline briefly the role of econometrics in the early days of model-building and estimation of the 1950s and 1960s. In fact, econometrics is generally considered to have become a distinct and formalised discipline in 1930 with the formation of the Econometric Society and the subsequent publication of the journal *Econometrica* in 1933. Attempts at the systematic application of statistical methods to measurement in economics can be traced back to the early 1900s, and isolated examples of attempts to quantify economic relationships have been found as early as the 17th century.[1]

To the limited extent in which econometric methodology was systematically employed in the 1930s and 1940s, its role was purely one of assisting in the process of discriminating between competing economic theories. Thus, at the time, theoretical analysis and evaluation were the primary means by which economic theory was developed, with econometric methods (essentially rudimentary regression analysis) being employed to provide a limited empirical dimension to this process of evaluating economic theory.

With the growing use of macroeconomic modelling in the 1950s and 1960s for the purposes of government policy formulation, a further justification for econometric analysis was provided. It was now necessary to derive estimates of the behavioural relationships implied by the underlying economic theory so that the relative effectiveness of a range of policy alternatives could be judged precisely. Thus, for example, it was no longer sufficient to be able to deduce that an increase in government expenditure would have a positive effect on aggregate economic activity. Rather, what was required was a precise statement of exactly by how much economic activity would increase from some given or predetermined increase in government expenditure. This then required an estimate of the magnitude of the government expenditure multiplier, which in turn was a function of the marginal propensity to consume.

Thus econometric analysis now had a two-fold function. First, to provide a means for testing economic theory and, in particular, to provide a framework for assessing the consistency between economic theory and available data. And secondly, to estimate the parameters of economic models so that these could be used for policy formulation and forecasting purposes.

However, even though the postwar period saw the widespread adoption and development of econometric methodology, the role of econometric analysis was always well-defined and relatively narrow. Economic theory could only be produced by theoretical analysis; econometric methods would be employed only at a final stage should any testing of the theory be necessary, or should parameter estimates be required in order to apply the theory. In particular, econometric analysis was *not* a vehicle for developing economic theory. Should an econometric evaluation of some economic theory reveal inadequacies (in the sense of some inconsistency between theory and data), then the direct implication was that further theoretical refinement of the model was required. Thus the *theoretical* weaknesses of the model would have to be identified and rectified, and this could only be done using the tools of theoretical analysis.

In other words econometric analysis could not *inform* the process of developing economic theory – at best it might imply that the model suffered from some theoretical weakness, the precise nature of which could only be identified by further theoretical analysis and refinement. Indeed, it was considered poor methodology to test econometrically an inadequately developed economic theory. Econometric testing and estimation were only the very last stage of economic model-building; a well-developed theory should, by definition be consistent with the available data and thus cause no econometric difficulties.

As an example, let us begin by considering the theory and estimation of the consumption function. Stated most simply, the theory that consumer expenditure is a direct function of consumers' disposable income. That is:

$$C = f(Y) \qquad (8.1)$$

Equation (8.1) being very general, the functional form of the relationship must be specified before econometric estimation can proceed. Earlier investigators typically assumed a linear relationship and thus specified:

$$C = \alpha + \beta Y + \varepsilon \qquad (8.2)$$

where α and β are the parameters to be estimated; ε is a disturbance term which accounts for any random variation in C, any imprecision in measurement, and/or the influence of omitted variables. The next step is to obtain a set of sample data on C and Y so as to estimate α and β.

While Equations (8.1) and (8.2) are perfectly general statements in the sense that they could refer equally to a cross-section or time-series relationship, data for the latter are generally far more readily available than for the former. Further, if an estimate of the consumption function is required for forecasting purposes, then a time-series relationship is the appropriate one. Thus the time-series specification of Equation (8.2) would be:

$$C_t = \alpha + \beta Y_t + \varepsilon_t \qquad (8.3)$$

An early study in the United States by Davis (1952), using annual data (in constant prices) from 1929 to 1940, produced the following equation:

$$\hat{C}_t = 11.45 + \underset{(0.02)}{0.78} \ Y_t \qquad R^2 = 0.986 \qquad (8.4)$$

(standard error in parentheses). Using annual data for Great Britain from 1956 to 1980, the following equation is formulated (see Pokorny, 1987, p.109):

$$\hat{C}_t = 8.83 + \underset{(0.01)}{0.76} Y_t \qquad R^2 = 0.993 \qquad (8.5)$$

In both cases very well determined equations are produced, apparently pointing to a close correspondence between the theory and the data.

However, one of the first difficulties encountered with these estimated equations was that they produced very poor forecasts of consumer expenditure. That is, while the equations performed well within the sample period, they performed unsatisfactorily outside it. There are two possible reasons for this poor and inconsistent performance:

1. The theory underlying the estimated equation is incorrect.
2. The statistical methods used to estimate the parameters of the model are inappropriate.

Subsequent developments of the consumption function occurred in both of these areas. Thus in terms of estimation methodology, it was argued that the consumption function is but one formulation within the system of simultaneous equations which make up a macroeconomic model of the economy. By implication it is inappropriate to treat the consumption function as a single and autonomous equation for estimation purposes (that is, it is invalid to use Ordinary Least Squares). Rather, the interrelationships between the consumption function and all the other equations in a macromodel must be explicitly incorporated into the estimation process, thus avoiding the simultaneous equation bias of OLS. Additional estimation difficulties of equations such as (8.4) and (8.5) derived from apparent autocorrelation of the disturbance terms, implying that further refinement of the estimation methodology was required. However, such adjustments were not sufficient to resolve all the forecasting problems of these simple consumption functions.

It was in terms of the theory of the consumption function that most of the developments occurred, and particularly so during the late 1950s and 1960s. Thus, it was argued, consumption function formulations such as Equation (8.2) were far too simplistic an abstraction from the relatively complex process by which consumers reach their consumption decisions. In particular, Equation (8.2) does not possess a *dynamic* structure and therefore cannot distinguish between short-run and long-run (or equilibrium and disequilibrium) behaviour.

Various theoretical refinements were proposed (principally the permanent income and the life-cycle hypotheses), all of which made a distinction between the determinants of short-term and long-term consumption behaviour. Such theories typically produced estimating equations of the form:

$$C_t = \beta_0 + \beta_1 C_{t-1} + \beta_2 Y_t + \varepsilon_t \qquad (8.6)$$

A further rationalisation for equations of this form was that the term C_{t-1} reflected the role of habits, in the sense that consumers do not necessarily respond fully and immediately to changes in income: consumers become used to their current consumption patterns which change only slowly over time.

From Equation (8.6) we can now directly derive the short-run and long-run marginal propensities to consume. Thus the short-run marginal propensity is:

$$MPC_{SR} = \beta_2 \qquad (8.7)$$

while the long-run marginal propensity is obtained by setting $C_{t-1} = C_t$ and solving for C_t. That is:

$$MPC_{LR} = \frac{\beta_2}{1 - \beta_1} \qquad (8.8)$$

Equation (8.6) formed the basis of most empirical work in the 1960s and 1970s. For example, using quarterly, seasonally adjusted data for the United Kingdom, in constant prices from first quarter, 1963 to fourth quarter, 1979, and using expenditure only on non durables (consistent with the argument that expenditure on durables is more akin to an investment decision, thus requiring a different model), the following equation is produced (see Pokorny, 1987, p.250):

$$\hat{C}_t = 1206.614 + 0.666\ C_{t-1} + 0.207\ Y_t \quad R^{-2} = 0.990 \qquad (8.9)$$
$$\quad\ \ (289.356) \quad (0.074) \quad\ (0.047)$$

Thus the MPC_{SR} is 0.207 and the MPC_{LR} is 0.620.

A further theoretical issue with Equation (8.6) concerns the interpretation of the constant (intercept) term, β_0. Theoretically, in static equilibrium (that is, in the long-run), the elasticity of consumption expenditure to income must be one – a necessary condition for static equilibrium to be maintained. In turn, this implies that the MPC must equal the average propensity to consume (the ratio of consumption expenditure to income). These conditions will be satisfied provided that β_0 is zero, thus ensuring that the long-run consumption function passes through the origin. Thus observe from Equation (8.9) that the constant term is significantly different from zero, implying that this estimated equation is theoretically unacceptable.

This result led a number of researchers to estimate consumption functions by constraining these functions to pass through the origin – that is, to estimate these equations by imposing the condition that $\beta_0 = 0$. A typical result is that of Evans (1969), using annual data for US consumer expenditure on non-durables from 1929 to 1962. His estimated equation was as follows:

$$\hat{C}_t = 0.676\ C_{t-1} + 0.280\ Y_t \qquad (8.10)$$
$$\quad\ \ (0.052) \qquad (0.041)$$

This equation produces an estimate of the MPC_{SR} of 0.28 (which arguably is somewhat lower than theory would predict), and an estimate of the MPC_{LR} of 0.86 (which at least is consistent with theoretical expectations – the generally accepted estimate of the APC being about 0.80 to 0.85).

However, this estimated equation suffers from autocorrelation problems. Further, one might question the artificial device of simply suppressing the constant terms, rather than resolving theoretically the inconsistency between the statistical and theoretical results. A further criticism of Equation (8.10) is that, being estimated by OLS, it suffers from simultaneous equation bias. In any event, the forecasting performance of such equations proved to be unsatisfactory.

It was during the 1970s that the whole methodology of macroeconomic modelling and forecasting came in for severest criticism. The latter half of 1970s was a period of considerable economic instability, with most Western economies experiencing recessions of varying degrees of severity. The economic policies of most governments were informed by the results and implications of their respective macroeconomic models, the inability of which to forecast adequately the rapidly changing economic climate brought the entire basis of these models into question. Generally containing hundreds (and sometimes thousands) of behavioural equations, the models were therefore highly disaggregated, theoretically capable of providing very detailed information for policy formulation purposes. That they now appeared to be incapable of providing reliable forecasts and hence robust policy implications was a severe indictment of the whole methodology. Under conditions of economic stability extensive government intervention is unnecessary (and hence the role of economic modelling limited). Only under conditions of instability is intervention required, and when faced with this challenge in the 1970s, the methodology of econometric modelling appeared incapable of meeting it.

CRITICISMS OF THE 'TRADITIONAL' APPROACH

The specific criticisms of macroeconomic modelling which emerged in the light of the failures of the 1970s were twofold. First, the economic theory underlying these models was brought into question. In particular, as virtually all of them were derived from Keynesian theory (and its developments), a school of thought began to argue that the poor performance of macroeconomic models was due to this Keynesian bias, and that a fresh approach to macroeconomic theory was required. This in turn led to models which were much more neo-classical (or 'New Classical') in nature, models which in general reflected much greater faith in the market mechanism (see Lucas, 1981, for a critique of 'Keynesian' econometric practice and an advocacy of 'equilibrium business cycle' modelling).

The second criticism of the macroeconomic models of the 1970s derived from the estimation methodology which was employed. These models had grown to such a size that it was not possible to use theoretically valid simultaneous equation estimation methods to estimate their parameters. Instead, the parameters had to be estimated by biased OLS, thus ignoring the wide range of interrelationships amongst the various equations. It was possible validly to estimate the parameters in some of the smaller sub-models (the money market model, the labour market model, and so on), but not to estimate the whole model validly or as efficiently as possible. Further, these models had become so large and intractable that it was almost impossible analytically to determine their longer-term properties. Indeed, experimental evidence often suggested that some of these models were quite unstable in the long run, but given their complexity it was virtually impossible to identify the sources of this instability. In short, it was argued, these models had become too complex and intractable, with the available estimation methodologies being unable to cope with their complex structures.

One of the major sources of criticism of large-scale simultaneous equation macroeconomic modelling derived from the school of what might be termed 'statistical' modellers, whose approach is probably best reflected in the work of Box and Jenkins (1976). In essence, the argument of the statistical modellers was that it was simply unrealistic to hope to achieve, in any reliable, rigorous and consistent manner, the wide-ranging and complex objectives set by large-scale macroeconomic modellers. The available estimation methodology was unable to cope with the scale of these models, and economic theory was insufficiently developed to provide a reliable and unambiguous basis for constructing them. Far better to set more modest, and hence achievable, objectives.

Thus statistical modellers argued that only short-term forecasts can be produced reliably and accurately. Given this objective, it is unnecessary to construct complex economic models – a rigorous statistical analysis of a given data set will often produce the required forecasts.

For example, if the objective is to produce short-term forecasts of consumer expenditure, all that is required is a set of time-series observations on consumer expenditure. These observations can then be analysed statistically, using a range of integrated (and relatively complex) procedures, to calculate the required forecasts. There is no need to appeal to economic theory in this process: all the information that is required is contained in the past observations on consumer expenditure. Economic theory was not considered irrelevant – the statistical modeller would accept that actual observations on consumer expenditure are the outcome of a variety of (generally complex) economic forces. But isolating each of these economic influences will often be unnecessary if the only objective is to produce short-term forecasts.

Note how this approach contrasts with that of the traditional economic modeller. To the latter, satisfying the requirements of economic theory is of paramount importance. Therefore, even if an estimated economic model is statistically satisfactory, if not consistent with economic theory it must be rejected. The only basis for deriving an economic model is via a process of theoretical deduction, or interpreting the content of the relevant economic theory in a mathematical form. Estimating the economic models so produced is relatively trivial, undertaken merely to render an economic model operational.

For the statistical modeller, the only basis for deriving a forecasting model is via a statistical analysis of the available sample data. Irrespective of the precise nature and characteristics of the underlying process which generated these data (the 'economic theory'), perfectly adequate forecasting models can be derived by statistical analysis alone. No claims are made for interpreting such models in terms of economic theory – they are pure statistical models, the objective being to keep them as simple as possible.

RECENT DEVELOPMENTS IN ECONOMIC MODELLING

While the inadequacies of macroeconomic models were plain to see in the light of their poor performance in the 1970s and early 1980s, the economic modeller refused to accept the limited objectives of his or her statistical counterpart. For to reject the feasibility of causal modelling and to concentrate only on short-term forecasting was essentially to deny that economic analysis had any contribution to make to the process of policy analysis and formulation, whether this be in the public or private sectors.

One lesson learnt from the critiques of the statistical modellers was the need for a far more rigorous approach to the evaluation of the *statistical* properties of an estimated economic model. In general, the statistical modellers had developed a much more sophisticated set of statistical tools for evaluation purposes. Thus the economic modeller began to integrate this rigour and sophistication into the process of economic model-building. Further the economic modeller now accepted that a detailed analysis of the statistical properties of the available sample data could make an important contribution. In short, 'data mining' could be a legitimate input into the model-building process provided that all resulting models could still be interpreted in terms of economic theory. In particular, economic theory provided a basis for developing long-term forecasting models – one area in which the econometric approach to model-building is held to be superior to the purely statistical one.

A further trend that has occurred in econometric modelling is a renewed emphasis on building and estimating single-equation models. In effect, the approach is one of identifying the important relationships in large macroeconometric models, and then of undertaking a detailed examination of each of these relationships in isolation, before incorporating them once again into the macromodel.

For illustrative purposes we will continue with our consumption function example and, in particular, begin by briefly discussing the work of Davidson, Hendry, Srba and Yeo (1978) – hereinafter referred to as DHSY. The basic data set used by DHSY was quarterly, seasonally unadjusted observations of UK consumer expenditure on non-durables and personal disposable income (in 1970 prices) from 1958 to 1975. A forecasting model was derived using the data from 1958 to 1970, keeping the last five years (1971 to 1975) purely for forecasting tests. DHSY derived a formal statistical test of forecasting performance, which essentially examined the consistency between a model's forecasting perform-ance and its estimation performance. That is a model was judged as forecasting satisfactorily if it predicted the data as well as it 'tracked' them, thereby producing an insignificant value of the associated test statistic, denoted by DHSY as z_1.[2]

A useful starting point is a simple graphical analysis of the basic data set, as in Figure 8.1. An obvious feature of this graph is the very regular (and expanding) seasonal pattern in the consumption data, and the relatively more volatile behaviour of the income data – characteristics that would have to be accounted for in any satisfactory model. Indeed, this is precisely what is attempted (at least in part) by Equation (8.6): the term C_{t-1} is included to account for habit persis-tence, and hence the extent to which consumption behaviour does not respond fully to short-term variations in income.

Figure 8.1 Consumer expenditure and personal disposable income, 1958-75

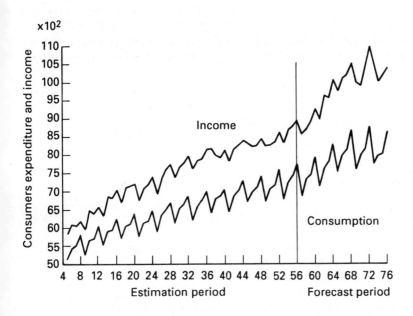

A second feature of the consumption data to be accounted for is their seasonality. The traditional econometric approach is to account for seasonality by the use of dummy variables. In effect, this is equivalent to removing seasonality from the data, rather than explaining it. However, DHSY argue that the regular seasonality in the consumption data is one of their more interesting features and should be explained in the same way as trends or any other features – that is, by a process of causal modelling.

Thus, what is required is a consumption function which, in the long run, collapses to:

$$C_t = kY_t \tag{8.11}$$

thereby ensuring equivalence of the long-run APC and MPC (equal to k). Such a function will therefore be consistent with static equilibrium. But a formulation is required which can also explain short-run behaviour, since the sample data in Figure 8.1 are the outcome of what is predominantly a short-run process.

In a mathematical sense, there are many formulations of a short-run consumption function which can collapse to Equation (8.11) in the long-run. The difficulty is to determine which of these formulations is both *theory consistent* (that is, consistent with economic theory) and *data consistent* (that is, fully accounting for the systematic variation in the sample data). Further, theory and data consistency would also require that the model performs as satisfactorily outside the sample period as it does within it. In other words, a necessary condition for any 'true' model is its ability to forecast data as accurately as it explains them. Thus DHSY use forecasting performance as a central criterion for discriminating between competing models.

We can begin by considering how to explain the seasonality in the quarterly data. Why should consumption expenditure change from one quarter to the next corresponding quarter – that is, from summer quarter to summer quarter, winter quarter to winter quarter, and so on? Explaining this variation in the data would be equivalent to explaining their seasonality. This implies that the appropriate dependent variable is not the level of consumption expenditure, but the fourth difference of consumption expendiure, that is:

$$C_t - C_{t-4} = \Delta_4 C_t \tag{8.12}$$

Therefore a model that satisfactorily explains the variation in $\Delta_4 C_t$ will have effectively elucidated the seasonality in the data, without any need to employ seasonal dummy variables.

An additional aspect of the seasonality of the consumption data in Figure 8.1 (already noted) is the expanding nture of this pattern. One way of dealing with this is simply to take natural logarithms of the data, which would have the effect of reducing the rate of increase in the data variance (logarithmic transformation is a commonly-used variance stabilising technique). Rather than explaining the variation in $\Delta_4 C_t$, we would seek to explain the variation in $\Delta_4 \ln C_t$. Thus if:

$$C_t = f(Y_t) \tag{8.13}$$

it follows that:

$$\Delta_4 \ln C_t = g(\Delta_4 \ln Y_t) \tag{8.14}$$

While Equation (8.13) is a perfectly general statement of the consumption function, Equation (8.14) has been derived with specific reference to explaining quarterly unadjusted consumption data. However, the precise functional form of Equation (8.14) (the nature of 'g') must still be identified before estimation and testing can proceed.

DHSY now refer to a pure time-series (Box-Jenkins) study of the nature of the relationship in Equation (8.13).[3] That is, this study used Equation(8.13) as a starting point, the only economic theory input into the analysis. Identifying the precise nature of the relationship in Equation (8.13) is then achieved by a process of pure statistical analysis, with no further reference to economic theory. The only criteria referred to are statistical ones; these derive essentially from goodness of fit criteria (albeit of a relatively sophisticated form), together with the notion that the resulting model should be kept as simple as possible. The model so derived does not have a strict interpretation in terms of economic theory, being only intended for forecasting purposes. The resulting statistical model is as follows:

$$\Delta_4 \ln C_t = \beta_0 + \beta_1 \Delta_4 \ln Y_t + \beta_2 \Delta_1 \Delta_4 \ln Y_t + \varepsilon_t \tag{8.15}$$

Thus, to stress, Equation (8.15) is the most efficient *statistical* description of the data in Figure 8.1, but does not purport to reflect in any way the nature of the *economic* process which generated the data.

Using the data in Figure 8.1 to estimate Equation (8.15) produces the following equation:[4]

$$\Delta_4 \ln \hat{C}_t = 0.010 + 0.450 \, \Delta_4 \ln Y_t - 0.157 \Delta_1 \Delta_4 \ln Y_t \tag{8.16}$$
$$(0.001) \; (0.040) \qquad\qquad (0.045)$$
$$R^2 = 0.751$$

However, one could still attempt to interpret Equation (8.15) in terms of economic theory and, in particular, to examine the nature of static equilibrium as implied by Equation (8.16). Now, static equilibrium is defined as a state of zero growth, and the properties of logarithms are such that for any variable, X (say), no growth implies that:

$$\ln X_t - \ln X_{t-i} = 0 \tag{8.17}$$

Thus in static equilibrium we have from Equation (8.16):

$$\Delta_4 \ln C_t = \ln_4 Y_t = 0. \tag{8.18}$$

Therefore no solution can be derived from Equation (8.16), and no insights can be offered into the nature of static equilibrium. Of course this is not surprising as Equation (8.15) was derived with reference only to generating short-term forecasts. In fact it can be demonstrated that the short-term forecasting performance of Equation (8.16) is quite impressive, particularly for so simple a model. Therefore a potential way forward is to add some form of longer-term dimension to Equation (8.15).

DHSY simply decide to add to Equation (8.15) the disequilibrium term:

$$\ln C_{t-4} - \ln Y_{t-4} = \ln\left(\frac{C_{t-4}}{Y_{t-4}}\right) = \ln (C/Y)_{t-4} \tag{8.19}$$

The theoretical justification for such a term is that it reflects some notion of a *target* level of consumption expenditure, as derived from the long-term consumption function in Equation (8.11) above. Thus consumers are attempting to achieve some longer-term balance between their consumption expenditure and income: the disequilibrium term in equation (8.19) reflects the extent to which this target is being achieved, and therefore the adjustments which are required to their short-term expenditure. Thus the theoretical model can be written as:

$$\Delta_4 \ln C_t = \beta_0 + \beta_1\Delta_4\ln Y_t + \beta_2 \Delta_1\Delta_4 \ln Y_t$$
$$+ \beta_3 \ln (C/Y)_{t-4} + \varepsilon_t \tag{8.20}$$

Note that in static equilibrium, Equation (8.20) collapses to:

$$0 = \beta_0 + \beta_3 \ln (C/Y)_{t-4} + \varepsilon_t$$

or

$$\ln C_{t-4} = k + \ln Y_{t-4} + u_t \tag{8.21}$$

where:

$$k = \frac{-\beta_0}{\beta_3} \text{ and } u_t = \frac{\varepsilon_t}{-\beta_3}$$

Ignoring the disturbance term in Equation (8.21), this equation can be rewritten as:

$$C_{t-4} = K Y_{t-4} \tag{8.22}$$

or $$C_t = K \, Y_t \qquad\qquad (8.23)$$

where $k = \ln K$. Thus we can interpret Equation (8.23) as the long-term consumption function which is derived from Equation (8.20), and note that by definition (that is, irrespective of the parameter estimates in Equation (8.20)) this long-term function must pass through the origin, as required.

Now, Equation (8.20) is a consumption function which purports to explain both long-term and short-term consumption behaviour. It is the function which should be consistent with the data in Figure 8.1, data which are the outcome of a mixture of short-term and long-term behaviour. There is therefore one further term in Equation (8.20) which requires a theoretical justification, and that is $\Delta_1 \Delta_4 \ln Y_t$ (recall that this term was identified as relevant by the pure statistical analysis of the data in Figure 8.1). An argument which could be made is that while $\Delta 4 \ln C_t$ will certainly be influenced by a corresponding change in income ($\Delta_4 \ln Y_t$), one might expect there to be a differential influence depending on whether income is increasing or decreasing (an influence which is reflected in the $\Delta_1 \Delta_4 \ln Y_t$ term).

Therefore Equation (8.20) is a formulation which can be interpreted as having been derived via a process of both theoretical and statistical evaluation. It is an equation which can be *justified* in terms of economic theory, rather than having been derived rigorously from pure theoretical analysis in the traditional sense. However, Equation (8.20) still has to be tested against the data in Figure 8.1. Estimation of Equation (8.20) produces an equation which still remains unsatisfactory in terms of its forecasting performance.[5] Consequently further refinement of the equation is required.

DHSY observe that the forecast period in Figure 8.1 was one of exceptionally high and volatile inflation rates, particularly relative to those over the estimation period. Figure 8.2 presents a graph of the inflation rate over both the estimation and forecast periods.

A range of theoretical arguments can be developed in order to justify the inclusion of an 'inflation effect' in Equation (8.20). Essentially, these interpret inflation as having the same effect as relative price changes, given that inflation is not fully and immediatley reflected in changed income.[6] However, irrespective of the theoretical arguments which can be used to justify an inflation effect, this can only be estimated using the data over the much more stable estimation period. It must be argued that this effect is a constant one; it is simply more pronounced over the forecast period as compared to the estimation period.

Denoting the inflation rate by P_t, one must decide in what form this rate should enter Equation (8.20). It could be argued that P_t should enter the model in the same way as Y_t – that is, both the change and rate of change of inflation are relevant. Thus Equation (8.20) would be respecified by adding the terms $\Delta_4 \ln \dot{P}_t$ and $\Delta_1 \Delta_4 \ln \dot{P}_t$.

Figure 8.2   Annual rate of inflation in the UK, 1958–75

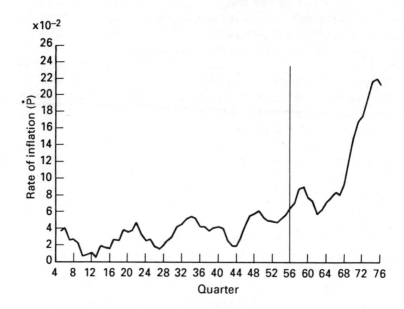

Re-estimating this respecified model, then, finally produces an estimated model which forecasts satisfactorily both the shorter and longer term (the estimated model produces an insignificant z_1 statistic), and is also consistent with economic theory.

The process of developing this model can be interpreted as an interaction between satisfying both data and theory criteria, neither of which is considered in any way superior to the other. The process is very much one of explicit experimentation, with luck even having a role to play. This approach is not to be interpreted as representing any radical development of econometric methodology. Rather, it is an illustration of the benefits which can be derived from a rigorous and careful application of basic econometric methods, resorting also to a certain degree of pragmatism in the process by which economic theory is developed.

It must be emphasised that we have here provided a very broad and general overview of the DHSY approach. There are a range of further statistical testing procedures adopted by Davidson and Hendry which we have not outlined, all of which have contributed to their process of model specification and development.

CONCLUSION

We have examined here only one of a number of recently developed approaches to econometric modelling (see Pagan, 1987, for a brief discussion of this and some alternative approaches). Of necessity, only a very broad outline of this approach has been presented and many of the principles of model-building that DHSY, and particularly Hendry in his later work, have emphasised and advocated[7] have not been discussed.

We should not interpret these approaches as representing some radical development in econometric methodology. Rather, they represent an attempt at formalising and integrating a range of econometric estimation and testing procedures which developed during the 1970s. Indeed, the apparently haphazard development of these techniques was one of the important stimuli for the work of DHSY, spurring their attempts to integrate and place these techniques within some kind of context. Further, the DHSY strategy and its developments certainly do not represent an automated approach to model-building and estimation. Rather, they represent a set of guiding principles which constitute a generalised statement of 'good practice'. In particular, creativity and even luck still have a central role to play, but now within a much more rigorous and coherent framework.

NOTES

1. See Stigler (1954)
2. See Pokorny (1987), pp. 319-22, for a fuller exposition of this forecasting test.
3. See Wall *et al* (1975).
4. Equation (8.15) should in fact contain an additional variable – a dummy variable – to account for the effect of a purchase tax increase in 1968. However we will ignore this complication here. See Pokorny (1987), p.384, for a fuller discussion.
5. Equation (8.20) was actually estimated by omitting the constant term. The justification for this approach is that under conditions of equal growth rates for consumption and income (which would appear to be approximately the case from Figure 8.1) the disequilibrium term ($\ln (C/Y)_{t-4}$) will be a constant and thus collinear with the constant term. Including both terms in the estimating equation would therefore result in imprecise estimation, whereas omitting either variable would hardly affect the estimation performance. However, omitting the disequilibrium term would radically alter the theoretical properties of the model, while omitting the constant term would leave these theoretical properties intact.
6. See Deaton (1977) for a fuller exposition of these arguments.
7. The research strategy of 'Hendrification' has been much discussed in the UK, though less in the USA and elsewhere. Hendry offers six criteria for economic modelling: data coherence (past data should be adequately characterised and thus regression residuals be randomly distributed); parameter constancy outside the sample period; data admissibility (fitted and forecasted values should make sense in terms of measurement definitions); theory - consistency (models should make economic sense); and encompassment (a successful model should be able to account for the results obtained by rival models). See Hendry (1980,1983) and Hendry and Mizon (1985).

9 Public Choice: The Economics of Politics

Rosalind Levačić

Here Rosalind Levačić discusses the public choice literature which, building on the methodological individualism of mainstream economics, seeks to explain the workings of the – highly imperfect – 'political market' on the same basis as the market for private goods and services. Recent developments which are particularly stressed include the analysis of rent-seeking, where groups seek protection or economically valuable privileges from the state, and constitutional reform. Both are highly relevant to the political economy of the 1990s.

> The great desideratum in Government is so to modify the sovereignty that it may be sufficiently neutral between different parts of society to control one part from invading the rights of another and at the same time sufficiently controlled itself from setting up an interest adverse to that of the entire society.
>
> James Madison, letter to Thomas Jefferson, October 1787[1]

THE RESEARCH AGENDA OF PUBLIC CHOICE ECONOMICS

The founding fathers of the American constitution were preoccupied with the problem of designing government institutions so that individuals could reap the benefits of collective action while minimising its costs in terms of reduced liberty. This same problem has informed the work of the public choice school of economists, which rejects the assumption of neo-classical welfare economics that government can be treated as a benign dictator who 'acts in the "public interest" by correcting market failures, adopting tax structures that minimize deadweight losses and engaging in appropriate redistribution'.[2]

The research programme of the public choice school has blended both normative and positive economics. Starting with a few isolated scholars in the late 1940s and early 1950s, it began to attract a wider audience by the early 1960s following the publication of two seminal works, Downs' (1957) *An Economic Theory of Democracy,* and Buchanan and Tullock's (1962) *The Calculus of Consent.* By 1986 public choice was sufficiently recognised for one of its founders, James Buchanan, to be awarded the Nobel prize for economics. In his Nobel lecture, Buchanan recalled the excitement of his discovery of the nine-teenth-century Swedish economist, Knut Wicksell, upon whose insights the public choice theorists have built:

> Stripped to essentials, Wicksell's message was clear, elementary, and self-evident. Economists should cease proferring policy advice as if they were employed by a benevolent despot, and they should look to the structure within which political decisions are made. Armed with Wicksell, I, too, could dare to challenge the still-dominant orthodoxy in public finance and welfare economics . . . . Like Wicksell, my purpose was ultimately normative rather than antiseptically scientific . . . .

Wicksell deserves to be designated as the most important precursor of modern public choice theory because we find, in his 1896 dissertation, all three of the constitutive elements that provide the foundations of this theory: methodologi-cal individualism, *homo economicus,* and politics-as-exchange (Buchanan, 1987, p. 243).

The Calculus of Consent

Wicksell's 'three constitutive elements' were developed by Buchanan and Tullock in *The Calculus of Consent* into a theory of collective choice by utility-maximising individuals who are recognized to have different preferences. From an individualist perspective, the fundamental social problem is how social choice evolves from individual preferences. How this is and should be done for non-market choices in a democratic society is the fundamental problem addressed by public choice. The *Calculus* rejected the welfare economics solution which is to assume either identical linear homogenous utility functions or a social welfare function based on weighting individuals' preferences according to a value judgement about distribution (implicitly made by a policy-making élite). Public choice does not sweep the problem of individuals' and groups' conflicting interests under the carpet, as has much of the mainstream work on economic policy. Instead 'any theory of collective choice must attempt to explain or describe the means through which conflicting interests are reconciled'.[3]

That the purpose of collective action is the furtherance of individual self-interest is both a normative statement and an axiom upon which the positive theory of the economics of politics is erected. Buchanan and Tullock (1962) criticised as inconsistent and implausible the presumption then current that an individual's motivation in the public sphere is different from the self-seeking assumed in the market place. Instead public choice economics is built upon the assumption that self-seeking utility maximising *homo economicus* operates in both the private and public sectors.

The *Calculus* made the important distinction (elaborated in later work such as Brennan and Buchanan, 1985) between two levels of collective decision-making: the *pre-constitutional stage* and the *post-constitutional stage*. In the former one imagines a collection of rational utility-maximising individuals agreeing on decision rules by which resource allocation in society will be determined in the future. The *Calculus* classifies three kinds of decision-making institutions: individual choice or the market, voluntary co-operation (as within firms, clubs or families); and collective choice obtained by setting up a government which coerces individuals into acting as the operation of the collective decision rules has determined. Part of the pre-constitutional settlement is to agree broad rules which assign types of goods and services to the three decision-making institutions. Simply to consider the existence of public goods and externalities (in order to determine which goods are more efficiently provided by the public sector) is insufficient because this ignores the external costs imposed on those who do not get their preferred allocation of public goods and taxes by any collective decision rule which does not require unanimity.

Collective decision-making would not be coercive if unanimous agreement were required. One of the key insights Buchanan obtained from Wicksell is that the Pareto criterion of unanimity is the collective decision-making analogue of voluntary exchange in markets.[4] Unanimity guarantees that politics is a positive sum game because decision outcomes benefit some individuals without harming others. But there are disadvantages to unanimity – the high transactions costs of reaching agreement, including the opportunistic behaviour of those individuals who use their power of veto to extract economic rent from others. The costs of unanimity mean that individuals are prepared to agree to a constitutional arrangement in which post-constitutional decisions are taken by majority vote. Thus the device of pre-constitutional social contracting provides a rational and libertarian justification for non-unanimous collective decision rules. The relative costs and benefits of different rules are the basis for deciding which are the most appropriate for given types of decisions. The most ubiquitous post-constitutional collective decision rule is majority voting. The *Calculus* thereby links up with Downs' *Economic Theory of Democracy* to give an economic analysis of certain key political institutions, in particular majority voting. This is accorded no special status in the *Calculus*. 'At best majority rule is one among many practical expedients made necessary by the costs of securing agreement.'[5]

NEW DEVELOPMENTS SINCE THE *CALCULUS*

The *Calculus*, described as 'the jewel in the crown' of public choice economics,[6] set out a clear rationale for a wide-ranging research agenda for a positive theory of resource allocation in the public sector. Developments in public choice economics up to the present time all reflect lines of thinking presented in the *Calculus*. They cover three interrelated areas, aspects of which will be developed more fully in the subsequent sections of this chapter. These are:

1. the positive economic theory of politics;
2. empirical testing of economic theories of politics;
3. the normative theory of public choice.

The Positive Economic Theory of Politics

The authors of the *Calculus*, written when positive economics was in the bloom of promising youth, justify their application of economic methodology to the territory of political science on the grounds that this aids the understanding and explanation of observable political institutions. The purpose of building models based on individual utility-maximising behaviour is to explain facts of the real world. In this way Buchanan and Tullock use the instrumental methodology popularised by Friedman (1953) to deflect the standard criticism, particularly by non-economists, of rational self-interested utility-maximising behaviour as too simplistic and unrealistic. Buchanan and Tullock do not maintain that all behaviour in political or other contexts is of this type. Rather they contend it is sufficiently so to 'allow us to make some very rudimentary predictions concerning the structural characteristics of group decisions'.[7] On this basis 'the theory of public choice is, or can be, scientific or value free' (Buchanan, 1984).

The first phase of the positive theory of politics focused on the demand by citizens for collective goods. The earliest work, some of which began in the late 1940s,[8] consisted of mathematical models of voting in a direct democracy and then moved on to modelling representative government. Much of this theoretical work extended Downs' model of two-party competition. In the 1970s public choice economists began to consider supply side political institutions, modelling public sector bureaucrats as self-seeking utility maximisers. Pressure groups or organised interests, as both demanders or suppliers of collective goods, are also important in public choice analysis, starting with Olson's (1965) *Logic of Collective Action*. A more recent area of interest is 'rent-seeking', which is the social waste due to resources being used up in economic agents' attempts to get government to change or maintain property rights which permit them to earn economic rent.

Thus contemporary public choice now presents a much more complete picture of the range of key institutions and role players. By treating demanders and suppliers of collective goods as distinct sets of actors, each with different arguments in their utility functions, the relationship between voters, politicians and bureaucrats is analysed as one between principals and agents. This provides a public sector analogue to the analysis of the principal-agent relationship in private sector firms (see ch. 11 and Rowley, 1988, for a discussion). A wide range of positive theories explaining many different aspects of public sector behaviour, mainly in liberal democracies, has now been spawned. Two broad types of theories have emerged. One type relies on tightly specified models in the form of mathematically derived deductions from basic axioms. Median voter theorems and some of the rent-seeking models are of this type. The other group of theories are less rigorously derived from axioms and so are more qualitative. They come within a broad political economy tradition which offers plausible but speculative explanations of historically specific processes, such as the growth of government (generally argued to be excessively large) or differential rates of economic growth amongst the advanced capitalist economies (e.g. Olson, 1982).

Empirical Testing of the Economic Theory of Politics

In the *Calculus* the main justification for the *homo economicus* assumption is that it will produce an empirically verifiable body of knowledge. Although Buchanan has not undertaken empirical work himself, vast numbers of empirical studies of positive economic theories of politics have now been conducted. In contrast to the qualitative empirical methods of political scientists, sociologists or historians studying the same terrain (who use documents, interviews and observation), these studies are econometric. They depend on finding appropriate quantitative measures for political variables and being able to identify stable causal relationships between them. As these econometric studies cover a wide range of topics I shall not consider them in a single section, but rather refer to them within the discussion of selected topics. A good survey of the evidence can be found in Mueller (1989).

Normative Public Choice

While evident in the *Calculus*, the normative basis of public choice theory, which is individualistic and libertarian, has been clarified and elaborated in more recent work, by Brennan and Buchanan (1985) and Buchanan (1986). The fundamental proposition is that judgements of social value can only be derived from individuals' own judgements and preferences, and cannot be defined externally of individuals.

The critical normative presupposition on which the whole contractarian construction stands or falls is the location of value exclusively in the individual human being (Brennan and Buchanan, 1985, p 21).

This proposition has important consequences for Buchanan's conception of social justice and allocative efficiency. Neither can be evaluated with reference to the outcomes of economic process as is normal practice in economics, but can only be judged in relation to decision rules. For Buchanan social justice means adherence to *agreed* rules; it does not refer to judgements about the distributional impact of the outcomes of decision rules.

As for allocative efficiency, the Pareto criterion is far too restrictive as it excludes almost all alternatives to the status quo unless interpersonal comparisons of utility, disallowed by normative public choice, are made. Instead, Buchanan argues for a judgemental criterion for evaluating efficiency:

Do the rules permit individuals to pursue their private ends, in a context where securing those ends involves interdependence, in such a way that each person secures maximal attainment of his goals consistent with equal liberty of others to do the same? (Brennan and Buchanan, 1985, p. 7)

Buchanan's normative and methodological position is not necessarily held by other public choice economists. Many publish in the positive economics tradition (see Mitchell, 1988) and are not so concerned with constitutional reform. The mathematically inclined use standard Pareto optimality expressed in the form of a social welfare function to assess the equilibrium properties of voting rules. Buchanan himself is critical of the mathematisation of economics because it causes economists to focus on end-states that are judged efficient or not, rather than concentrate on decision processes (Buchanan, 1986, pp. 16-17).

Taking Stock

It is important to consider both the normative and positive aspects of public choice together because they are interrelated. A researcher's selection of public choice analysis as the means by which to study political decision-making reflects a particular way of perceiving the world which is not congenial to those who have a more optimistic view of the social benefits of collective action or who do not observe individuals as rational utility maximisers. Research findings emerging from a positive methodology have an impact on policy judgements. Theoretical work showing that majority voting does not have equilibrating or desirable normative properties together with empirical research supporting predictions of theories based on self-seeking political actors (such as bureaucratic inefficiency and vote buying), help to create a climate of opinion in favour of limiting government.

My purpose so far has been to sketch an overview of developments in public choice since the seminal works of the early period. One can only understand recent developments by linking them back to the major issues placed on the research agenda of public choice in the *Calculus*. The remaining sections of this chapter focus on developments in the 1980s to show the interlinkage of positive and normative elements in public choice research and the shift towards a more pessimistic evaluation of government. In the *Calculus* the main function of government is to provide those public goods which could not be efficiently supplied by voluntary cooperation. These mutual efficiency gains make politics a positive sum game.[9] The *Calculus* also contained the seeds of the more pessimistic view of the potential for government to be coercive and redistribute income from a minority to the majority once a non-unanimous decision rule is used.

THE PROBLEM OF ZERO SUM REDISTRIBUTION: PUBLIC GOODS AND MAJORITY VOTING

The libertarian justification for government is the provision of public goods, given that collective provision is more efficient than voluntary cooperation. But collective provision brings with it the attendant problems of how to distribute the gains thereby secured and the costs of the taxes required to finance the public goods. Wicksell and then Samuelson (1954) drew attention to this problem. Samuelson showed that there are a number of Pareto optimal situations, each associated with a different distribution of tax payments among citizens, in which the sum of individuals' marginal rates of substitution of the public for the private good equals the marginal cost of the public good. So even limiting government to the provision of public goods from which all can gain leads to conflicting interests over the distribution of the net gains.

Samuelson also pointed out that a Lindahl equilibrium, in which each citizen makes tax payments for the public good equal to his or her marginal valuation of the good, cannot be attained because there is no mechanism by which a large group of individuals will accurately reveal their preferences for public goods. Self-seeking individuals will not reveal how much they value the public good because each will be required to pay a tax equal to their stated marginal benefit from it. If they understate their valuations they will pay less tax, and individually they will not affect the amount of the public good provided. But if all act in this way, the amount of public good provided will be less than the Pareto optimal amount. Following Samuelson, standard neo-classical welfare economics has separated the determination of the optimal quantity of the public good from the determination of the taxes required to pay for it. It is received neo-classical wisdom that welfare judgements about the tax structure are separated from those about expenditures and hence taxes should not be earmarked for particular public goods or transfers. This means that taxes cannot be used as a way of signalling citizen preferences for public expenditures. In contrast, public choice economists advocate earmarked taxes by which benefits are related to tax payments so that taxpayers can signal their preferences for public goods through their willingness to pay taxes.

Demand Revelation

One of the more esoteric endeavours of public choice has been devising ingenious mechanisms by which self-seeking individuals would reveal their true preferences for public goods. A number of such mechanisms have been proposed, and discussions can be found in Mueller (1989) and Stiglitz (1986). These proposed demand revelation procedures are complex since they have to give individuals the incentive to reveal their true preferences, while at the same time ensuring that they do not demand more of the public good than they would be willing to pay for. The proposed mechanisms have a number of weaknesses: they are too complicated to be practicable, depend on the absence of collusion between individuals, and do not guarantee that the amount paid in tax equals the cost of the public good. One then has to fall back on the ubiquitous decision rule of majority voting.

Majority Voting

Once collective decisions can be sanctioned by majority vote, the distinction between allocative efficiency and redistribution becomes blurred. The winning majority can turn the allocative efficiency issue of public goods provision into a redistributional one by ensuring that most of the costs are met by the minority. As many goods with externalities are also private goods (education, health services, the arts, for instance) and as there are also increasingly large transfer payments, the redistributive nature of collective decision-making is further enhanced.

Downs' median voter theorem was attractive because it produced a determinate result; however, as Hinich (1977) showed, this result depends upon assuming that the political platform can be defined in terms of a single issue. One of the earliest results (reported in Black, 1958) was that voting produces 'cycling'. Given three or more voters with different preferences, there is no dominant outcome that will gain a winning majority unless preferences are single peaked. Once the model is complicated to enable electors to vote for a multidimensional political platform (e.g. government expenditure and unilateral disarmament), even single peaked preferences do not guarantee the absence of cycling. Only restrictions on individuals' utility functions, equivalent to the assumptions required for a social welfare function, will do this (Mueller, 1989). The problem of cycling for economists is that it does not produce determinate outcomes. Another problem is that cycling is not observed to occur much in legislatures and committees, though its absence has been explained away in terms of agenda manipulation (Tullock, 1981) or log-rolling.

The earlier proofs of cycling depend on assuming deterministic voting; that is a voter is certain to vote for the one platform that maximises his or her utility. More recent theoretical work has rescued the equilibrium property of majority voting by specifying models in which there is only a probability that a voter will vote for a particular platform. It has been proved mathematically that when voting is probabilistic and candidates select a platform to maximise their expected votes – taking their rival's platform as given – then the platform will be Pareto optimal (Coughlin, 1982) and one of these will be the winning platform (Ledyard, 1984).

However, rescuing the median voter theorem by assuming probabilistic voting implies features of representative democracy that are not reassuring. Probabilistic voting implies that voters are uncertain about candidates' platforms, and that candidates are uncertain about electors' preferences. Indeed, Downs originally proposed that a rational elector would not find it worthwhile to spend time and resources becoming politically well informed, since the effect of a single vote on the electoral outcome is normally miniscule. This also implies that electors do not have well-formed preferences, and are influenced by impressionistic evidence. Candidates need not stick closely to their electoral platform once elected since deviations will have an attenuated effect on their political support. Furthermore, if candidates are uncertain about how electors will vote, they will advocate policies favoured by interest groups, since this increases the probability that they will secure the votes of citizens with the same interests.

A number of empirical studies have been undertaken of candidate competition, in particular on the effect of campaign expenditures and contributions to political parties. Mueller (1989) reports that studies generally show that money does buy votes in the USA, at least for incumbent politicians. Close contests increase political contributions, and a close relationship between the ideological positions of contributors and candidates is confirmed by Poole and Romer (1985). However, Mueller concludes that the evidence does not support the median voter theorem's explanation of electoral outcomes in representative democracies.

RENT-SEEKING

The rent-seeking literature depicts government as being about redistributive transfers. Interest groups compete against each other for rents, which are payments to them in excess of what they would get if a different assignment of property rights ensured that factor returns reflected opportunity costs in a competitive market. Rent-seeking is wasteful because it uses up resources in the process of redistributing claims to wealth. The end result is not an increased national output as in Schumpeterian competition for monopoly profit by firms. The more recent emphasis on collective action as redistributive rather than efficiency-promoting in part reflects the pessimistic assessment of the median voter theorem. This leads to the conclusion that politicians respond only weakly to the preferences of voters and give greater weight to the interests of pressure groups, in particular those who make political contributions. If politicians have discretion to pursue income, perquisites or group interests, they are motivated to grant favours to rent-seekers.

State provision of public goods itself creates rent-seeking opportunities, since both private and public sector organisations are involved in the production of public goods, such as defence, roads and public health. Public sector bureaucrats may be rent-seekers in their own right or may be the targets of rent-seeking activity when they have the discretion to allocate rents to other groups in the form of licences, laxer regulations or transfer payments (such as grants to firms and other public sector organisations). Public goods producers' ability to benefit from rent-seeking can be limited through monitoring by politicians on behalf of electors. The extent to which this is done depends on politicians' motivations and the amount of pressure exerted by voters in return for electoral support.

The Theory of Rent-Seeking

Though the original insight into the potential welfare losses of rent-seeking is attributed to Tullock (1967) and the term itself to Krueger (1974), the topic became a major focus of interest in the 1980s with the publication of articles such as those in Buchanan, Tollinson and Tullock's (1980) *Toward a Theory of the Rent-Seeking Society*. The well-known example of trade restrictions illustrates the social costs attributed to rent-seeking (see Figure 9.1). The world price of good M is P_w at which domestic consumers would demand Q_{co}; domestic producers would supply Q_{do} and foreign producers $(Q_{co} - Q_{do})$. If a tariff is imposed which raises the domestic price to P_t domestic demand falls to Q_{c1}. Dom-estic producers increase their output to Q_{d1} and imports are cut back to $(Q_{c1} - Q_{d1})$. The deadweight welfare loss in standard analysis is made up of triangles B and D, which are the net loss of consumer surplus. Area A is the trans-fer of additional rent to domestic producers from consumers' surplus. Area C is the increase in tax revenue going to the government as a result of charging a tariff of $P_t - P_w$ on imports; it is thus a transfer from consumers to the government, and hence to those who benefit from this addition to state revenues. Areas A and C represent the rents from import controls which attract rent-seeking efforts which use up resources. A standard monopoly diagram can also be used to illustrate the monopoly profits that attract recipients to seek regulation.

Figure 9.1   Sources of rent-seeking: the example of import controls

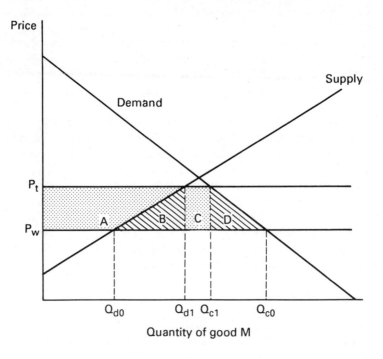

Buchanan *et al* (1980) distinguish three sources of wasteful rent-seeking:

1.   efforts and expenditures of potential rent recipients;
2.   activities by politicians and bureaucrats in response to rent-seekers;
3.   third-party welfare losses due both to rent-seeking efforts and to the trade restrictions which successful rent-seekers obtain.

The last item includes the standard deadweight welfare loss due to restrictions on competition in the net social costs of rent-seeking. The resources used up in rent-seeking can only be classified as a net social cost if they do not give rise to any direct utility; for example, time spent gathering and communicating information, attending meetings and lobbying. Expenditures by rent-seekers on items such as lunches or holidays which give government officials utility are just income transfers and cannot be counted as a net social cost. Brooks and Heijdra (1988) extend the static conception of the costs of rent-seeking by including the higher future return that the resources devoted to rent-seeking could have yielded if invested productively.

A key question which the literature has addressed, through building theoretical models, is the likely size of the investment of resources in rent-seeking in relation to the amount of potential rent. Some models show that rent-seeking expenditures can equal or even exceed the value of the rents being sought. It is suggested that risk-neutral rent-seekers and those whose assets are large in relation to the rent sought will invest more in rent-seeking (Hillman and Katz, 1984). As private sector managers, public sector bureaucrats and pressure group leaders are not risking their own assets in rent-seeking, they are therefore likely to invest considerable resources in it.[10]

Constraints on Rent-Seeking

However, there are a number of models which suggest that political competition will limit welfare losses due to rent-seeking. Pelzman (1976) posits a vote-maximising regulator who limits a regulated industry's monopoly rent to less than its maximum in order to equalise voting support from producers and consumers. Becker's (1985) model of competition among pressure groups specifies two groups, one seeking subsidies and the other composed of taxpayers. Each invests in activities which bring pressure to bear on government. The amount one group spends varies directly with the amount of pressure applied by the other. Because of deadweight welfare losses with respect to both subsidies and taxes, only a proportion of resources taken away from taxpayers gets transferred into utility for the subsidised group. An increase in the deadweight loss of taxation increases taxpayer pressure to resist taxation, while an increase in the deadweight loss of subsidies reduces pressure for subsidies. Hence the costs of rents and rent-seeking act as an equilibrating brake to limit the amount of resources spent on pressure group activities.

Criticisms of Rent-Seeking

A fundamental criticism of rent-seeking, made by Samuels and Mercuro (1984), is that the concept is ill-defined and ideologically biased. They argue that rent-seeking is defined to include the costs of all activities directed at changing the existing distribution of property rights. Yet efforts to change the values and interests given effect by the state's definition and allocation of property rights are both inevitable and, in some cases, beneficial. There is no way of unambiguously determining which property-rights-changing activities are unambiguously zero-sum (rents) and which lead to net social gains (profits). Thus rent-seeking relies on an artificial distinction between rents and profits, and is biased in favour of the existing distribution of property rights. Samuels and Mercuro's stance favours a pluralist and corporatist political system. While rightly pointing to flaws in the attempt to define rent-seeking costs as net social costs, Samuels and Mercuro go too far in asserting that the proponents of rent-seeking favour the status quo, since the latter use the concept to advocate removing property rights which encourage rent-seeking.

North's (1986) criticism is of quite a different order. He does not quarrel with the rent-seeking concept as such but regards it as too *ad hoc* and limited. It fails to take into account the transactions costs of different assignments of property rights by which the 'new institutionalists' rationalise and evaluate the specification of property rights and their associated contracts.

Policy Implications of Rent-Seeking

Rent-seeking is applied to a wide range of policy topics, in particular regulation, international trade and government contracting. It also has some interesting implications for tax policy that contradict received wisdom. For instance, it is usually argued that the excess burden of a direct tax is minimised per unit of tax revenue if it is placed on goods with inelastic demand. But taxes on goods with inelastic demand result in a larger loss of producer surplus and so, argues Tollinson (1987), induce more rent-seeking by organised producers in lobbying against the tax. It would be therefore less socially wasteful to tax goods with elastic demand. Rent-seeking thus makes it more difficult to reach judgements concerning the most efficient tax structure. For example, the imposition of tax costs on tax-paying groups could be beneficial if it causes them to resist pressure by special interests to raise government spending. The rent-seeking (or tax-cost reducing) activities of some groups provide political competition to those seeking higher transfers. This is another example of how public choice questions the efficiency pronouncements of welfare economics.

A crucial implication of rent-seeking analysis is that it questions the value of competition in political settings. Competition is not unambiguously beneficial. It might be the case that rent-seeking – induced by the regulation of a privatised natural monopoly, by the competition for franchises for monopolies (e.g. radio waves), or for procurement contracts for government purchases – outweighs the efficiency gains of removing an activity from the public sector. Rent-seeking considerations reinforce the general message of public choice that policy advocacy means making judgements about the efficiency properties of different decision rules, property rights allocations and institutional arrangements. To minimise rent-seeking, limited modifications have been proposed, such as auctioning licences rather than allocating them according to the judgements of bureaucrats or politicians. More fundamentally, rent-seeking needs to be minimised by appropriate collective decision rules, though obtaining these is likely to require constitutional changes.

CONSTITUTIONAL POLITICAL ECONOMY

'The ultimate aim of limiting the harm that governments do while preserving the range of beneficial-collective activities'[11] is a succinct summary of the normative endeavours of public choice. This has featured strongly in Buchanan's work, particularly in the 1980s (e.g. *Liberty, Market and State* and *The Reason of Rules*) and is reviewed by Reisman (1990). In order to fulfil the 'ultimate aim', a set of agreed rules must be established within which governments operate, and it is this which is referred to as 'constitutional political economy'. It is based on the fundamental premise that social values can be derived only from the stated preferences of individuals; any definition of the 'public good' external to individuals' stated preferences is ruled out of court because it restricts individual liberty.

Constitutions to Limit Negative Sum Politics

The Reason of Rules elaborates the distinction made in the *Calculus* between the outcomes of decision processes and the rules which define the decision processes. The fundamental rule by which a society makes its collective decisions is its constitution. A contractarian constitution is one that can be legitimized 'as if' it emerged from the unanimous agreement of all members of society. Such a constitution grants government limited and specified coercive powers to guarantee and protect the rights of individuals agreed in contract. Brennan and Buchanan proceed to argue that members of society will benefit from rules which pre-commit them collectively. Pre-commitment means that rules limit the decisions that can be taken in the future. Pre-commitment is more desirable in collective choice than in private choice because, in the political sphere, the individual is far more affected by the decisions of others and wishes to diminish uncertainty about others' future choices. Constitutionalists are keen to establish pre-commitment rules which will prevent the zero and negative sum political games caused by government from being used for securing redistributive transfers. Excessively high government spending and taxing; public debt, whereby the current generation consumes at the expense of the unfranchised future generation, and inflation are cited as prime examples of inefficient and coercive economic policies that should be constitutionally outlawed. These ideas are highly germane, for example, to the current debate in the European Community on the constitution of the proposed European central bank. Constitutionalists favour a central bank independent of politicians operating according to known rules, such as a fixed exchange rate and a single currency.

As unanimity is an excessively restrictive requirement, constitutionalists limit the necessity to abide by it to decisions of fundamental importance – in particular, agreeing the constitution itself. The principle that the size of the majority required should depend on the nature of the decision being taken is reflected in the EC constitution. Amending the Treaty of Rome, which defines the rules which members have agreed to abide by, requires unanimity, whereas the Single European Act (1986) lays down areas in which decisions are reached by majority voting of ministers from member-states.

Social Justice

The primacy of the principle of unanimity comes into conflict with personal judgements about the social justice of the existing distribution of property rights. If one thinks that this is unjust, then one would approve coercive measures to bring about a 'better' distribution. Buchanan tackles this problem in two parts. First he coins the term 'distributive' justice for concern with the distribution of the outcomes of market and political processes. Non-libertarians use distributive justice to determine whether rules are 'just'. Contractarians reject this because, in their philosophy, justice cannot be a primary concept. Rules are only just if they have been voluntarily agreed, and conduct is just if it is in accordance with agreed rules. Buchanan's second step is to point out that in the pre-constitutional stage members of society may well wish to agree rules that predispose outcomes that are judged distributionally just. Here Buchanan is prepared to draw upon Rawls' (1971) contractarian approach to justice. Under the veil of ignorance in the pre-constitutional stage, individuals are uncertain of their position in society and so are biased towards agreeing rules that will maximise the welfare of the least well off.

Buchanan maintains that the focus of concern about the justice of the distribution of individual welfare should be the rules and not the outcome of the rules. Buchanan (1986) argues that distributive outcomes are determined by birth, luck, effort and choice. He uses the metaphor of a game to argue that unequal outcomes in playing games are not unjust provided that the players start with equal chances and the rules are fair. In relation to market outcomes, only birth (which causes differences in endowments and capacities) should be compensated for. Hence Buchanan approves of public funding of education. If more equitable outcomes are desired, then this should be ensured through constitutional rules and not left to the mercies of majority voting 'which is a highly imperfect mechanism for securing redistributive justice'.[12] Brennan and Buchanan suggest that a constitutional transfer arrangement with an agreed tax rate and an equal per capita lump-sum benefit would be the best method for securing distributive justice, as it is a redefinition of property rights which gives no incentive for rent-seeking.

Brennan and Buchanan acknowledge the practical difficulties of achieving constitutional reform since – to stick to its principles – this would require non-coercive voluntary agreement. However, if their diagnosis of the current political arrangements is correct, then potential exists for a Pareto improvement in the rules. There is more likely to be general agreement over the rules determining end-states, because they have an imperfectly known impact on individuals, than on the end-states themselves which have a much more predictable impact.

But there is a paradox. Why should self-interested individuals invest effort in negotiating constitutional reform when it is a public good? To answer this conundrum Brennan and Buchanan have to fall back on the notion of a 'shared moral norm', of participating in collective decision-making in order to secure mutual benefits. Thus we finally reach a logical flaw in public choice theory – self-interest cannot explain everything about collective decision-making.

THE LIMITATIONS OF *HOMO ECONOMICUS*

The Voting Paradox

Even within the confines of public choice, the limitations of the *homo economicus* assumption are recognised. The assumption gives rise to an inconsistency in the logical foundations of public choice theory known as the voting paradox. There is no convincing reason why a self-interested utility-maximising individual should vote. The probability that a single vote has any effect on the outcome of an election is so remote that the individual's expected utility from voting must be less than the cost of voting. An attempt to rescue the self-interested explanation for voting is to include satisfaction from the expressive act of voting in an individual's utility function. But, as Mueller (1989) points out, this robs voting theory of any predictive power since the motivation for voting is not related to the outcome.

The alternative explanation is that voters vote for ethical reasons. It is in the interests of the community as a whole for its members to participate in voting, as well as to be concerned for the welfare of others. Margolis (1982) therefore models collective choice using the assumption that individuals behave as if they had two utility functions, a selfish one and an altruistic one. The individual is in equilibrium when the marginal utilities from allocating resources to selfish and altruistic ends are equalised. In Margolis' approach complete selfishness is dropped but rationality is preserved because individuals perceive that altruistic behaviour is in the interests of the community as a whole, even though personal moral acts are not in the immediate self-interest of the individual. However, Mueller prefers to drop rationality and ascribe moral behaviour to social conditioning[13]. This enables him to explain voting in terms of such factors as home environment, educational experience, religion and community stability. He cites empirical evidence that voter participation is positively correlated with years of education and income, and that people do vote for policies which benefit others.

The Behaviour of Bureaucrats and Politicians

The behavioural assumption of self-interested rationality also has deficiencies when applied to politicians and bureaucrats. As van Winden (1988) points out, public choice models fail to explain how the postulate of self-interest is related to the assumed goals of vote and budget maximisation. Nor has there been much development in the utility-maximising model of bureaucracy. Jackson (1982) and Peacock (1983) replace budget maximisation by alternative goals, such as size of staff establishment or an easy life, which imply x-inefficiency rather than excessively large output. As a complete description of the motivations of bureaucrats (defined broadly as public sector professionals), utility maximisation has never received much credence from non-economists who point out that bureaucrats' self-interest is modified by professionally defined conceptions of their clients' interests. Few attempts have been made by economists to study bureaucrats' behaviour *within* the bureaucracy. One such study is provided by Breton and Weintrobe (1982) who construct a model of exchange of services between bureaucrats in a network where the accumulation of trust is vital for efficient exchange to occur and where selfish opportunistic behaviour is very costly to monitor.

The assumption that politicians are vote maximisers implies that they seek votes the way managers maximise profits. The aim is to secure office for its own sake by producing the political outputs which meet the preferences of as many voters as possible. An alternative view of politicians is that they wish to promote specific policies. These may be derived from a particular ideological conception of the best way to organise society or may reflect special group interests. Politicians only seek votes to the extent that these are required in order to obtain the power to implement their favoured policies. This is equivalent to the managers of a monopoly obtaining utility from x-inefficiency rather than maximising profits. The implications of politicians' discretion for the influence of voters' preferences on policy outcomes is discussed in Levačić (1987). A more sanguine view (as in Cullis and Jones, 1987) is that the inefficiency of the public sector is much less than public choice economists maintain, either because of the countervailing bargaining power of different interests, or because political actors are not purely self-seeking.

A common theme linking some of the specifications of political actors' behaviour which offer an alternative to *homo economicus* is the moral dimension in economic and political exchange. If individuals acted only according to their short-term self-interest, general welfare would be reduced. Market exchanges, even though they involve property rights and contractual arrangements which can be enforced by law, would be extremely costly if traders had to resort to the law to enforce every exchange agreement. The mutual advantages of cooperative behaviour among individuals who interact with each other on many occasions are shown by both theoretical and empirical work in game theory. If there are many plays of prisoner's dilemma and chicken games, individuals eventually choose cooperative solutions which give both parties the maximum benefit (see Mueller, 1989, and McLean, 1987). McPherson (1984) emphasises the importance of moral behaviour in enabling society to reap the benefits of economic exchange, and notes the amount of social energy that is expended on inculcating moral behaviour so that it becomes a conditioned response.

It would be incorrect to leave the impression that the public choice constitutionalists deny the crucial role of morality. It is rather that they choose not to emphasise it because they consider that collective choice systems which only function well if political actors are altruistic are likely to fail – as the fate of communist systems in Eastern Europe attests. In *The Reason of Rules* the primary defence of *homo economicus* is methodological rather than empirical. It is an 'appropriate caricature of human behaviour' not because it is empirically valid but because it is 'analytically germane':

> If we want to discover how institutional rules can turn conflict into co-operation, we cannot simply assume that persons who operate within those rules are naturally cooperative.[14]

CONCLUSION

Public choice is proving to be a rich seam for generating positive theories about the political determinants of resource allocation and distribution. However, one must recognise that this is not soundly based 'scientific' knowledge of the kind positive economics claims to be its goal. As in other areas of economics, we are faced with the problem that inductive work lacks theoretical rigour, while deductive work lacks empirical relevance. In particular it is difficult to get good quantitative measures of political variables. In empirical public choice, as elsewhere, few studies test alternative models against each other; rather, they are limited to the less demanding test of showing that observations are consistent with the predictions of the theory being tested. Empirical results have not been consistent and so have failed to reject incompatible public choice explanations. For example, Wellisz (1982) considers that 'our knowledge of the political economy of trade is still in its infancy. The observed pattern of trade restraints is compatible with any number of hypotheses concerning the nature of political processes.'[15]

It is interesting to recall that the prime justification for the *homo economicus* postulate in the *Calculus* is the one mainstream economists also subscribe to – that its use will lead to better explanatory and predictive models. There is no sign yet that economists are abandoning their mono-methodological approach to empirical work, but the problems of coming to grips with how – and with what effect – collective decisions are made in institutional settings may eventually lead to the use of more qualitative methods.

A methodological problem for public choice economics is the extent to which valid explanatory and predictive theories can be built on the assumption of *homo economicus*. While public choice and neo-classical economics share this problem, it is more acute with respect to collective than private choice. Normative public choice is probably even more contentious as it is naturally rejected by those who see collective action and the state as expressions of a moral collective purpose that should override individual preferences.

However, because public choice economics 'provides a logically compelling way to integrate economic and political processes, it has attracted growing attention'.[16] As it is only beginning to have a wide influence, public choice is a major source of new thinking in mainstream economics, even though there has been no *fundamentally* new thinking within the field itself. Instead there has been consolidation, clarification and extension. The public choice perspective enables economics to contribute to the study of economic policy formation and implementation in real-world political contexts, rather than limit itself to welfare economics' normative prescriptions of public policy based on unrealistic and non-operational assumptions of social welfare. The public choice approach still retains the distinctive strength of economics as a 'policy science' – its emphasis on policies which are efficient because they secure mutual gains. Buchanan's stress on evaluating decision rules, rather than outcomes, points the way to economists recognising more openly that making policy recommendations involves assessing how to combine and interpret the complexities of the real world and one's social objectives with a knowledge of economic theory and empirical evidence. One of the main messages of public choice economics is that decision rules do matter:

> The same individual with the same motivations and capacities will interact to generate quite different aggregate outcomes under differing sets of rules with quite different implications for the well-being of every participant (Brennan and Buchanan, 1985, p. 1).

This emphasis on decision rules is of great contemporary relevance to crucial debates about political and economic issues. Examples are the EC negotiations to amend the Treaty of Rome in order to incorporate new rules for establishing monetary union and an EC central bank; the Uruguay round of negotiations to extend the General Agreement on Tariffs and Trade, and the urgent need in Eastern European countries for a new set of collective decision-making rules to replace central planning and Communist party monopoly of government. Judgements have to made as to how different variants of such rules will work. This cannot simply be predicted from rigorous models or from extrapolating experience with past institutional structures. Hence public choice economics has much to contribute to filling in the 'black box' of institutional behaviour which was bequeathed by orthodox neo-classical economics.

Buchanan has provided the best succinct summary of the conclusions of both normative and positive public choice economics: 'good games depend on good rules, more than they depend on good players'.[17]

NOTES

1. Quoted by Wagner and Gwartney (1988).
2. Romer (1988) p. 167.
3. Buchanan and Tullock (1962) p. 4.
4. Wagner (1988).
5. Buchanan and Tullock (1962) p. 96.
6. Rowley (1987).
7. Buchanan and Tullock (1962) p. 5.
8. With, for example, Duncan Black's work on committee voting, culminating in Black (1958).
9. There were zero-sum interpretations of politics coming on stream, in particular that of Riker (1962) whose mathematical theory of coalitions was based on the assumption that the winning coalition gains at the expense of the losers.
10. See Mueller (1989) for a fuller discussion.
11. Brennan and Buchanan (1985) p. 150.
12. Brennan and Buchanan (1985) ch. 8.
13. Mueller (1989) p. 363.
14. Brennan and Buchanan (1985) p. 53.
15. Wellisz (1982) p. 292.
16. Romer (1988) p. 165.
17. Ibid p. 150.

10 Post-Keynesian Economics: Recent Developments and Future Prospects

Philip Arestis

Professor Arestis provides an account of the many strands of modern post-Keynesian theory, which builds on the insights of J. M. Keynes, Michal Kalecki and the Classical economists. He shows in particular how in the last decade or so the influential analysis of the behaviour of the 'megacorp' has had an impact in a number of related areas. The general conclusion he draws from post-Keynesian theory is that capitalist economies are inherently unstable, and thus government intervention may be necessary to socialise investment, at least in part. Perhaps surprisingly in view of economic and political developments in the 1980s, he considers such a radical reversal in policy to be a realistic possibility.

INTRODUCTION[1]

The purpose of this chapter is to attempt to isolate and analyse the major characteristics of post-Keynesian economics and to extract the policy implications that follow from it. In doing so, the emphasis will be on recent developments surrounding this school of thought.

It has been argued recently (Hamouda and Harcourt, 1988) that post-Keynesian economists have not yet managed to be totally persuasive for three reasons: the economic issues they are concerned with are controversial; there is enormous diversity in their theoretical constructs; and the existence of ideological objections emanating from the majority of the economics profession. Another reason is that post-Keynesians sometimes define their programme in a negative way, as a reaction to neo-classical economics (see, for example, Lavoie, 1989). There is yet another dimension to this argument in that the different 'approaches' which comprise post-Keynesian economics sometimes conflict with one another. 'We say "approaches" because we may identify several strands which differ from each other both with regard to method and with regard to the characteristics of the economy which are included in their models' (Hamouda and Harcourt, 1988, p.2).

However, despite all these problems, post-Keynesians are united, not just because of their critical attitude to neo-classical economists, but more importantly because of their attempt to provide a coherent alternative paradigm to orthodox economics. The title of the reference we have just quoted, *Post-Keynesianism: From Criticism to Coherence?*, is very apt from this point of view. It is important to note, however, that the same authors conclude:

> The real difficulty arises when attempts are made to synthesise the strands in order to see whether a coherent whole emerges .... This is a misplaced exercise, that to attempt to do so is mainly to search for what Joan Robinson called 'only another box of tricks' to replace the 'complete theory' of mainstream economics which all strands reject. The important perspective to take away is ... that there is no uniform way of tackling all issues in economics and that the various strands in post-Keynesian economics differ from another, not least because they are concerned with different issues and often different levels of abstraction of analysis. (*op. cit.*, p.25)

Clearly, they argue that coherence does prevail within the strands identified as post-Keynesian. It is a coherent post-Keynesian *vision* that in their view is a futile endeavour.

Whilst I agree with the contention that such a coherent paradigm has not yet been identified, it is nonetheless the case that more recently post-Keynesians have attempted to provide a coherent model (Rowthorn, 1981; Eichner, 1987; Schefold, 1985; Lavoie, 1989). I will be concerned with one post-Keynesian model which, although it may not encompass all the 'approaches' that Hamouda and Harcourt refer to, is eclectic enough to encapsulate many recent developments within the post-Keynesian school of thought. Although very much within the spirit of analysis that Hamouda and Harcourt have appropriately labelled as the 'horses for courses' approach, it is in fact much nearer to the literature referred to above.[2] Were I to hazard a guess about future developments within post-Keynesian literature, I would suggest that it could very well proceed along the lines just propounded. That is to say, there could very well be further attempts by post-Keynesians to provide a more coherent core for theoretical explorations which might not be inconsistent with a 'horses for courses' approach.

I will complement this analysis with the policy implications of post-Keynesian economics. In doing so I am mindful of the proposition that policy prescriptions cannot be generalised to all situations and experiences. Economic policies of the post-Keynesian kind are very much predicated upon concrete situations where historical experiences and sociological characteristics are of profound importance. In this sense, post-Keynesian economics can be thought of as a school of thought that emphasises *realism*, an aspect taken on board in the section that follows. As such, post-Keynesianism can be said to be of particular relevance to *real* economic problems and, consequently, in a good position to analyse and explain current economic problems satisfactorily.

A final section summarises the argument and concludes.

METHODOLOGICAL ASPECTS OF POST-KEYNESIAN ECONOMICS

There are certain methodological premises that all post-Keynesians claim to adhere to. The most important is that a free-market economic process is inherently unstable and generates forces from within the system that are responsible for the instability and fluctuations in economic activity. In this scheme, theories should represent economic reality as accurately as possible. Eichner and Kregel (1975, p.1309) remind us that the purpose of post-Keynesian theory is to explain the real world as observed empirically. Consequently, post-Keynesian theory is context-specific; as such it requires continuous and repeated reappraisal of its uses of theory in the context of current developments (Dow, 1988, p.15), a view which is very much consistent with Hamouda and Harcourt's 'horses for courses' approach. To do so post-Keynesian theory begins with observation (Dow, 1985, p.76) and proceeds to build upon 'realistic abstractions' rather than 'imaginary models' (Rogers, 1989, pp. 189–92).

One important implication of this methodological position is that post-Keynesians emphasise explanation in economics, and not so much predictions (Caldwell, 1989). However, the same author argues that 'In addition, post-Keynesians should consider adding the methodological weapons (of) Friedman's brilliant methodological turnabout....' (*op. cit.*, p.61) which is of course prediction (see, however, Lawson, 1989, for a different view). Similarly, econometric modelling is thought to be another dimension which ought to be taken more seriously since 'post-Keynesians are in an empirical tradition....Econometrics is a tool, and tools do not have ideologies. One suspects it is a tool that could be used to good purpose by post-Keynesians' (*op. cit.*, p.62). The precise form econometrics should take in post-Keynesian analysis is, like theory, 'diverse and context-specific' (Lawson, 1983). And whilst its limited capacity for prediction is recognised, econometrics could be useful in identifying structural changes with the help of models undergoing continuous revision as new evidence emerges.[3] Furthermore post-Keynesians regard 'observations' necessary for the empirical aspects of their work as containing both subjective and objective elements (Dow, 1985, p.77). Observing 'facts' requires a certain degree of objectivity, whereas the grouping of 'facts' to suit a theoretical framework entails subjectivity to some extent.

If realism is the fundamental methodological premise, it is clear that history and institutions have to be an integral part of such methodology. Also of immeasurable methodological importance is the contention that individuals are social rather than atomistic beings. The role of dominant institutions and imperfect markets can thus be introduced into the analysis. This is the more important when we come to consider the central concern of post-Keynesian economics, which is with production and distribution. Post-Keynesians are, of course, concerned with the causes and consequences of structural change, but with respect to production and not so much to exchange. The major concern of the post-Keynesian analysis of production is the causes of the growth of output and resources rather than the allocation of existing resources. In fact the theories of imperfect competition embedded in post-Keynesian analysis predict excess capacity, and hence no scarcity of resources (at least of capital equipment). Furthermore, post-Keynesian analysis takes on board the scarcity of demand rather than scarcity of resources. So 'effective demand' assumes a more important role than supply, although the latter, of course, is not totally ignored.

The role of exchange is such that individual choice is limited, for it is determined essentially by income, class and the technical conditions of production, rather than by relative prices. Consumer choice is based on lexicographic ordering,[4] that is to say on a hierarchy of needs (Robinson, 1956, ch. 34 and Pasinetti, 1981, p.75 are two good examples where this idea is endorsed). This ordering is based on the notion that different goods satisfy different needs, so that goods can be grouped according to the needs they satisfy. Substitution effects may only take place within groups, so that they are neither dominant nor even prevalent. Consequently, the demand for goods depends on the social and income class of consumers. Income and not substitution effects, along with income distribution amongst social classes, are the object of analysis.

Monopolies and oligopolies in product markets assume socio-political as much as economic power in any one market as such, which allows them to administer prices. This capacity relative to the power over input costs, particularly wage costs, determines the surplus which monopolies and oligopolies can master. It is this surplus which, when translated into investment, provides the engine for growth. The extent to which this translation occurs depends on expectations: on long-term expectations about the product market in question, and on short-term expectations which relate to the prices of financial assets. An important parameter in the determination of the latter is social relations which influence the relative power of financial institutions.

It is important to stress here that within the post-Keynesian model, institutional structure and industrial organisation are by no means fixed, making the historical development of economies the main object of analysis. Consequently, they play a vital role in determining income distribution, the level and composition of output, the generation of surplus and its translation into vital investment. In this process individuals are not omniscient. They are assumed to be able to acquire information, but their capacity to do so is limited. Individuals rely on group behaviour; they are not assumed to optimise. Procedures and rules are set by those individuals or groups which possess power (obtained by their place in the social or economic hierarchy) that allows them to impose their values upon the rest who passively accept and follow them. This bounded rationality, though, is the outcome of another important ingredient of post-Keynesian economics, which is uncertainty. These two aspects contribute to the general environment where the systematic processes of production and accumulation must interact and operate (see Eatwell, 1983, p.127, for more details and a fuller analysis of this contention).

It is the case that uncertainty is of paramount importance in the real world and, as such, one of the central elements of post-Keynesian analysis. A clear and robust reassertion of this view has been provided by Davidson (1988) and Roncaglia (1978), who argue that uncertainty is structural in nature; Bharadwaj (1983), who sees uncertainty as endemic in the real world, and others. The type of uncertainty analysed clearly implies that the future is unknowable and unpredictable, and consequently economic agents' expectations can easily be frustrated. Related to this is the notion of irreversible time – production takes time and economic agents enter into commitments well before outcomes can be predicted. The implication here is that economic agents commit themselves to contracts denominated in money, so that money and contracts are intimately and inevitably linked. In this sense, the importance of money is that it is a link between the past and the present, and also between the present and the future (Keynes, 1936, p.294). Post-Keynesian analysis is thus crucially concerned with historical times as distinct from logical time. The essence of recognising the importance of historical time in an economic system is that its past is given and cannot be changed, and its future is totally uncertain and consequently unknown.

The type of uncertainty meant here can be succinctly summarised: since 'knowledge' of the future can only be formed from past events, it is only 'indirect knowledge' that can be held concerning the future. Such knowledge of the future can only ever be ascertained with a probable degree of certainty. Now, the conditions under which such a probability can be calculated are rarely met in everyday life. Consequently in general terms probabilities of this nature cannot be arrived at. And to quote Keynes (1973), 'By uncertain knowledge ... I do not mean merely to distinguish what is known for certain from what is only probable .... About these matters there is no scientific basis to form any calculable probability whatever. We simply do not know' (pp. 113-14).

It is precisely this kind of uncertainty inherent in historical time which is both the necessary and sufficient condition for the existence of money. Money is viewed as essentially endogenous in a credit money economy, responding to changes in the behaviour of private economic units rather than the monetary authorities. Money, in this view, is an output of the system with its endogenous behaviour governed by the borrowing needs of firms, households and the government, as well as by the portfolio behaviour of financial institutions and of the personal sector. The emphasis in post-Keynesian monetary analysis is therefore on credit rather than on money in enabling spending units to bridge any gap between their desired level of discretionary spending and the current rate of cash flow. This endogenous character of money, being demand-determined and credit-driven, is not really surprising given the emphasis on production which requires a continuing flow of money to sustain the growth of output. Money, therefore, is completely integrated within production, so that any attempt to curtail the required flow of money will produce severe cutbacks in production. It is the rate of interest which is the control variable, a rate under the firm grip of the monetary authorities.

The analysis so far indicates that post-Keynesian economics is ultimately concerned with disequilibrium analysis. Furthermore, the emphasis attached to change over time inevitably leads to growth and dynamics becoming central parts of the analysis. Under these circumstances the purpose of analysis is to explain the erratic nature of the expansion path of a capitalist economy. The driving force behind erratic growth is recognised to be *investment*. Of paramount importance in this argument is the explanation that the instability just referred to is endogenous to the operation of economic processes. Also significant is that there is no attempt to associate mathematical determinism of models with causality in the explanation of 'unstable' economic processes. Nor is there a conscious effort to consider whether an economic process would ever reach a Pareto-optimal point. By contrast, the purpose of the analysis is to explain the actual level of economic activity, as well as movements in economic processes. In doing so, post-Keynesian economic analysis places particular emphasis on the endogeneity of the *erratic* expansion path of a free enterprise economy (see Brown, 1981, for a comprehensive comparison of post-Keynesian and neo-classical views on the points just referred to).

The tradition of post-Keynesian economics reflects its focus on the classical economists together with Keynes and Kalecki. Following Hamouda and Harcourt (1988), it is possible to identify three approaches in this tradition. One has its roots in the *Treatise* and the *General Theory* and was, of course, influenced by Marshall. This approach stresses uncertainty, the full integration of money with the rest of the analysis, the centrality of money-wage and the stock/flow interrelationship in capital accumulation. Another approach, essentially Kaleckian, emphasises the role of effective demand failures but begins, nevertheless, from a 'class' rather than an 'individual' level. In this sense it can be said to commence from Marxist principles. It adapts Marx's reproduction schemes to tackle the realisation problem where social relations are essential to the analysis of the dynamic process. This approach includes, of course, the contributions of Joan Robinson and her followers. Whilst these two groups are concerned with the short-term, the third provides an explanation of long-period levels of income and employment. It contains the Sraffian contributions along with Keynes' effective demand in a way that involves rejecting the propositions that supply and demand determine prices and the Keynesian notion of the downward sloping marginal efficiency of capital/investment and the demand for assets (as discussed in Keynes, 1936, ch.17). Yet a further approach within post-Keynesianism can be identified,[5] one with its roots firmly embedded in the institutionalist framework of economic analysis in the tradition of Veblen and others. This approach, which is process-oriented, evolutionary and thus dynamic, demonstrates that economic performance should be judged according to emerging societal values, in which case the economy is a 'valuating mechanism'. At the theoretical level an interdisciplinary approach is propounded, and at the practical level institutionalist theory requires a detailed and painstaking study of institutions and their development.

My purpose in this chapter is not to elucidate these approaches. It is, by contrast, to draw on these contributions in an attempt to provide a coherent post-Keynesian mode of thought by concentrating on recent developments in this area of economics.

MAIN THEORETICAL CONSTRUCTS

We begin this section with Figure 10.1 where the post-Keynesian circular flow model is depicted (adapted from Hollis and Nell, 1975, and Lichtenstein, 1983). This figure accounts explicitly for the existence of social classes and thus social relations. There is, therefore, an interesting and important contrast here between orthodox and post-Keynesian economics, aptly summarised by Nell (1980): 'Orthodox economics tries to show that the markets allocate scarce resources according to relative efficiency'; post-Keynesian economics, by contrast, '....tries to show that markets distribute income according to relative power' (p.26). It is in fact the case that within the post-Keynesian mode of thought, the output produced by one class of society (the wage earners) is planned, directed and managed by another class that does not participate physically in production (the recipients of residual income, profit), so that social relationships are of paramount importance in production. In this power relationship, capital's objectives are in conflict with labour's so that 'class conflict' is at the heart of the analysis. There are a number of theoretical constructs surrounding Figure 10.1. Given the emphasis put on monetary phenomena by post-Keynesian economics, I begin with money and credit.

Money and Credit

Post-Keynesian monetary theory is firmly based on the premise that no general model can tackle all economic problems for all times and situations. After all, 'Money can only be studied in an historical and institutional context' (Davidson,

Figure 10.1   Post-Keynesian circular flow

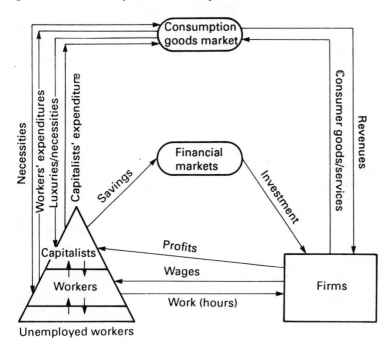

1982, p.241); indeed, 'Monetary theory can never – or at any rate should never – be independent of the state of development of financial institutions' (Moore, 1986, p.443). Institutionalist developments in their turn reflect fundamental characteristics of money since, 'In a modern capitalist economy, the institution of money is inextricably tied to the institution of banking' (Minsky, 1986, p.346). The most important characteristic in this respect is that money is both credit-driven and demand-determined. This results from the emphasis in post-Keynesian theory on credit rather than on money in enabling spending units to bridge any gap between their desired level of spending and the current rate of cash flow. As we have already noted, money is essentially endogenous in a credit money economy, responding to changes in the behaviour of private economic units.

There are three ways money can be introduced into the economic system. The first is due to the fact that production takes time, so that credit is generated to facilitate it. *Productive* credit is, consequently, required for the normal functioning of the dynamic monetary production economy. There does exist, though, the case when the banking sector misallocates credit, for example for speculation due to uncertainty, so that the possibility of non-productive credit arises. The implication here is that in such circumstances firms become unable to repay loans, so that financial crises ensue. This aspect highlights what has come to be known as the 'financial instability hypothesis' propounded by Minsky (1982)[6] The second is via fiscal and monetary operations initiated by the monetary authorities. In this case money is treated as an asset of economic agents, alternative to other financial assets and as such part of portfolio theory (Davidson, 1978, pp.226-7; Lavoie, 1984, p.788). The third way is from overseas flows in the case of open economies. In general terms a balance of payments surplus enhances money creation, while a deficit destroys it. Capital movements are also expected to have similar effects.[7] It ought to be stressed at this stage that of the three ways just discussed, only the first may have any direct effect on the creation of money. For once it is recognised that money is credit-driven and demand-determined, money creation emanating from fiscal or debt management operations or from movements in the balance of payments may be compensated by an equivalent change in commercial bank credit on the part of private economic agents (see, however, Chick, 1986).

Whilst money supply is viewed as endogenously determined, interest rates are assumed to be under the control of the monetary authorities. It is hypothesised that the discount rate, itself under the grip of the Central Bank, influences changes in market interest rates via a markup. It ought to be recognised, though, that events emanating from abroad and pressures on the Central Bank from the domestic banking system could potentially affect the structure of interest rates. The banking sector is seen as oligopolistic in both lending and borrowing behaviour, so that market interest rates are viewed as determined by its degree of monopoly or profit margin. The markup is based on unit variable banking costs, which can be proxied by the discount rate as administered by the Central Bank. Clearly, when the rate of interest is viewed in this way, it becomes a distributional variable that determines the allocation of income between fixed-interest debt holders and the rest of the personal sector. It also becomes an important variable in influencing the exchange rate. To the extent that domestic interest rates relative to overseas interest rates are the dominant determinant of the exchange rate, then it can be argued that the exchange rate, too, is under the firm control of the Central Bank. For while it is true to say that other factors may influence the exchange rate, like the current balance (Arestis and Eichner, 1988), post-Keynesian literature tends to support the contention that it is essentially interest rates relative to overseas interest rates that do so. The clear implication of this analysis is that foreign interest rates, domestic interest rates and exchange rates are necessarily interdependent (see also Moore, 1988).

This analysis clearly indicates that the openness of the economy is taken on board by post-Keynesian economic analysis. What ought to be emphasised, however, is the post-Keynesians' contention that exchange rates are volatile in a 'free' market system, a point which underlines their belief in the instability of free markets. It should also be stressed that, in addition to the exchange rate being influenced by the current and capital accounts, it influences them too. Most importantly, the current account through imports has embedded in it the hypothesis that the marginal propensities to import out of workers' and capitalists' incomes differ (Arestis and Driver, 1987). This is an extension of the post-Keynesian view that marginal propensities to consume out of different categories vary – a point which is further analysed below.

Pricing

The markup hypothesis alluded to above is fundamentally derived from and central to the pricing behaviour of the industrial sector. Modern advanced industrial societies (which form the focus of our analysis) are characterised by the duality of the 'competitive' and the 'oligopolistic' sectors. The 'competitive' sector exhibits the kind of behaviour associated with the neo-classical type of firm. Demand and supply determine price; 'competitive' firms are thus price-takers. However, the 'corporate revolution' (Eichner, 1987) has produced the notion of the 'megacorp' and the 'oligopolistic' sector. As a result there has developed a new class of professionally trained managers and executives now at the centre of decision-making power. It is to this group that the residual income now flows, whereas in the past it was to the capitalist class (Eichner, 1987, elaborates fully on this point). Furthermore, the emergence of the oligopolistic sector has meant that the megacorp has replaced the neo-classical type of firm to become the dominant form of enterprise in modern advanced industrial societies.

The pricing behaviour of the megacorps is simply to add a certain percentage markup on their unit costs of production, as determined by the needs of the megacorps to finance their investment plans (Eichner, 1976). In setting this markup, megacorps' decisions are influenced by a number of factors. Five have been identified in the literature (Eichner, 1976; Reynolds, 1990): the substitution factor, that is to say the possibility of loss of the market to competing goods; the entry factor, which is the potential entry of new firms into the industry; government intervention such as nationalisation, price controls etc.; the uncertainty factor about the response of existing firms in the industry; and trade union pressure, a factor which highlights the 'class conflict' alluded to above.

In this system, a distinction is drawn between short-term and long-term pricing. Short-term pricing occurs when the megacorps set the markup at a level just sufficient to generate the required profit rate to finance their investment plans. Firms operate at their 'standard operating ratio' and justify their short-term expectations. Long-term pricing prevails when investment plans are realised subsequently, that is when long-run expectations are justified. It is obvious now that pricing in post-Keynesian analysis is inevitably linked to the theory of *capital accumulation* and *class conflict*.

Before discussing these aspects there is a comment worth making. This relates to a problem raised by the 'market for corporate control' thesis (see Chapter 11), which if validated could undermine the analysis of pricing behaviour as postulated in this section. Fortunately, though, there is very little empirical evidence to suggest that the post-Keynesian pricing thesis could be undermined. The evidence (for a summary see, for example, Sawyer, 1985a, ch. 13) indicates that it is *size* rather than *profitability* that influences takeovers. This clearly supports post-Keynesian pricing and in particular Eichner's (1976,1987) thesis, as put forward above.

Capital Accumulation

To take capital accumulation first, it is the case that expected profitability is hypothesised to exert a significant influence on investment. But there is a two-way relationship here. Expected profitability induces capital accumulation, with realised investment being viewed as creating the profitability that makes investment possible, partly through internally generated funds. What ought to be considered at this stage, though, are the determinants of expected profitability – the marginal efficiency of investment and the expected growth of sales. The former is thought to be more appropriate as a fundamental determinant of that type of investment expenditure which is directed on equipment designed to reduce costs (research and development being of course the typical item in this respect), and also on equipment which would enable megacorps to create barriers to entry in their sector. Clearly, this type of analysis can give rise to an interest-elastic investment relationship.

This proposition, however, does not find much credence in post-Keynesian analysis for two reasons. First, the volatility of expectations and entrepreneurs' 'animal spirits' renders the ranking of investment projects according to their MEIs inappropriate and thus undermines the interest elasticity of investment propositions. Second, post-Keynesian analysis views the investment undertaken by megacorps on new plant and equipment (to enable them to satisfy the expected demand for their products, as this is proxied by expected sales or income) as by far the most important part of total expenditure. The pervasive nature of expectations under uncertainty which influences the 'animal spirits' of investors plays a vital part in the capital accumulation process, so much so that the volatility of expectations under uncertainty is thought to lead to structural breaks and crises.

Capital accumulation, now, is firmly linked to distribution theory as well as growth and business cycle theories. We deal with distribution theory first.

Distribution Theory

Distribution theory begins by recognising that national income (Y) is the sum of total wage income, that is wages and salaries which workers receive for their labour services (W), and total profits, that is capitalists' income earned through the ownership of the means of production (π). In other words,

$$Y = W + \pi \tag{10.1}$$

We could also write:

$$Y = C_w + C_c + I \tag{10.2}$$

Where C_w = consumption of workers, C_c = consumption of capitalists and I = investment. The following assumptions are made:

$$C_w = c_w W \tag{10.3}$$

$$C_c = c_c \pi \tag{10.4}$$

whereby workers' consumption is proportional to wages, and capitalists' consumption is proportional to profits. We may treat investment as exogenous (only for simplicity) and, with appropriate substitutions, we can arrive at the following two equivalent but alternative expressions:

$$(1 - c_c) Y = (c_w - c_c) W + I \tag{10.5}$$

$$(1 - c_w) Y = (c_c - c_w) \pi + I \tag{10.6}$$

From these we can determine the expressions for the shares in national income as follows:

$$(W/Y) = [(1-c_c) / (c_w - c_c)] - [1/(c_w - c_c)] (I/Y) \tag{10.7}$$

the wage share, and

$$(\pi/Y) = -[(1 - c_w) / (c_w - c_c)] + [1/(c_w - c_c)] (I/Y) \tag{10.8}$$

the profits share. In the latter case, it is clear that the higher the marginal propensity to consume of the capitalist class and the greater the share of investment to income, the higher the share of profits to income. Very obviously, then, the capitalists determine their share of national income through their consumption and, more importantly, through their investment. Similar results emerge if we work with the rate of profit instead. Dividing through equation (10.6) by K, which stands for capital, we may arrive at the following expression fro the rate of profit (π/K):

$$(\pi/K) = [1 - c_w) / (c_w - c_c)] (Y/K) + [1/(c_w - c_c)] (I/K) \tag{10.9}$$

Clearly, the rate of profit depends on c_w and c_c and also on the ratios (Y/K) and (I/K). Pasinetti (1974) is absolutely right to suggest that control over the rate of investment implies control over distribution and the rate of profit.

Growth Dynamics

The central message of the analysis just outlined does not change at all when we turn our attention to growth dynamics. The post-Keynesian concern with this aspect of economics is derived from the fundamental theoretical premise that the main focus of analysis is on an economic system which is expanding over time in the context of history. The dynamic element of post-Keynesian analysis is based on the well-known formula that relates the rate of growth of national income to the ratio of the average propensity to save to the capital/output ratio. This proposition is modified in a significant way to take into account the contention that the average propensity to save is affected by changes in the distribution of income, and differences in the propensity to save out of different types of income. To demonstrate, let us employ equation (10.8) on the assumption that workers do not save, which means $c_w = 1$. We thus have:

$$(\pi/Y) = (1/s_c)\ (I/Y) \tag{10.10}$$

where $s_c = 1 - c_c$, the marginal propensity to save out of profits. Furthermore, simple manipulation of (10.10) can give us:

$$(\pi/Y) = (1/s_c)\ (K/Y)\ (I/K) \tag{10.11}$$

where (K/Y) is the actual capital/output ratio which is equal to the required (K/Y) ratio, or v in more familiar notation, at 'equilibrium' situations. Also, for long-run 'equilibrium' and with the ratio of capital to labour assumed given (determined by technological conditions), the capital stock must grow at the same rate as the supply potential of the economy. The rate of capital stock is then determined by the level of investment in relation to the existing stock, that is (I/K). Consequently, in a situation of steady growth at full employment, we have the ratio (I/K) equal to the natural rate of growth (G_n). Equation (10.11) now becomes:

$$(\pi/Y) = (1/s_c)\ (v)\ (G_n) \tag{10.12}$$

Thus, steady state growth at full employment is linked to distribution and capital accumulation. The distribution of income is determined by the savings propensity of capitalists, the natural growth rate and the required capital/output ratio.

Our analysis so far indicates that post-Keynesian economics is concerned with two types of analysis: short-run and long-run. The former concentrates on the cyclical behaviour, whilst the latter attempts to explain the 'secular' or 'trend' tendencies in the economic system. Post-Keynesian analysis recognises that trend and cycle are interdependent, so that their study comprises what Eichner (1987) referred to as 'the economy's macrodynamic behaviour'. What we still have to elaborate upon, though, is the turning points in the cyclical behaviour of the economy. This particular concern is, of course, the business cycles aspect of post-Keynesianism.

Business Cycles

The fundamental starting point for post-Keynesian business cycle theory is that cycles are viewed as inherent to capitalist economies. Business cycles are thus depicted as being an endogenous phenomenon caused by the normal functioning of the capitalist economic system (Kaldor, 1940; Kalecki, 1971, ch.11; Goodwin, 1967). Exogenous shocks, such as technological innovations, oil price changes etc., can seem to cause instability but they actually accentuate an underlying endogenously embedded instability. This arises from the motive of producers and financial investors alike to accumulate wealth for its own sake. At the heart of post-Keynesian business cycles explanation are investment and expectations. As mentioned above, the latter element is viewed as highly volatile, with long-period expectations being Keynes' 'animal spirits'. Financial markets are also subjected to pronounced cyclical behaviour which is thought of as having profound effects on the production cycle. Thus, the upturn begins as business firms embark on replacement investment and then new investment. As the upturn gets under way, expectations of returns and actual profits become more optimistic, so that the demand for liquidity is low, with commercial banks being more willing to lend than otherwise. Improved profitability, however, carries the seeds of its own destruction by engendering a too-rigorous expansion of output and employment, thus destroying the reserve army of labour and strengthening labour bargaining power. As expansion comes to an end, the process goes into reverse. This is characterised by lower-than-expected returns with concurrent high interest costs, so that profits take a down turn. Markets become less active, commercial banks are less willing to extend credit and, in general terms, credit availability is substantially reduced. Thus the search for profits and the degree of willingness to undertake investment opportunities in an uncertain world by both producers and financial investors are apparently the cause of business cycles in post-Keynesian analysis. In its emphasis on disequilibrium, this contrasts sharply with the main thrust of developments in mainstream business cycle theory (see Chapter 6).

Class Conflict

Returning now to the 'class conflict' aspect of post-Keynesian economics, we begin by highlighting the wage determination theory where labour market bargaining is the fundamental premise of the analysis. The essentials of this theory can be captured aptly in the following expression:

$$\dot{W} = w_1 [(\dot{W}/P)^d - (\dot{W}/P)_{-1}] + w_2\dot{P}^e + w_3\dot{R}R + w_4\dot{U} \qquad (10.13)$$

where $\dot{W}$ is the rate of change in nominal wages, $\dot{P}^e$ is the expected inflation rate, $\dot{U}$ is the rate of change of unemployment and RR is the retention ratio defined as:

$$RR = [(W - DTNIC) / W] \qquad (10.14)$$

where DTNIC is direct taxes including national insurance contributions. In (10.13), w_1 and w_2 are expected to be positive, whilst w_3 and w_4 are expected to be negative.

This wage-formation hypothesis treats the determination of wages as the result of a bargaining process between unions and employers. Unionised and non-unionised workers have goals and aspirations, as well as economic and political power which are described in terms of a *target real wage*. Deviations of actual real wages from the desired level $[(W/P)^d - (W/P)_{-1}]$ affect the level of money wage demands, thus putting an upward pressure on money wages if the desired level is greater than the actual, and a downward pressure when the actual real wage falls short of the target real wage. The target real wage is, of course, net of tax, although negotiations centre around gross money wages. At each negotiation, therefore, trades unions attempt to bargain for a level of money wages which accounts for expected inflation and tax changes (direct taxes including national insurance contributions) since the previous settlement. Furthermore, the rate of change of unemployment is also an important variable which can be thought of as a proxy of the speed at which 'the reserve army of unemployed' changes. As this 'reserve army' expands, the power of the unions is weakened, so reducing their ability to achieve the target real wage and lowering the rate of change of money wages. Similarly, as the 'reserve army' is reduced, unions are more militant and able to push for higher money wages in a way that W would be higher than otherwise.[8]

POLICY IMPLICATIONS

Post-Keynesian economic analysis, as outlined above, contends that the capitalist economic system, based on a free market framework, is inherently cyclical. As such, the system is liable to fluctuations, and left to itself would not achieve, let alone maintain, the full use of existing resources nor their equitable distribution. The cyclical nature of such an economic system is mainly caused by the behaviour of the private sector, especially the insufficiency of private investment which is attributed to volatile expectations and business confidence. Full employment is the exception rather than the rule; even if achieved, it is not likely to be sustainable without government interference. There is, therefore, a potential role for government to initiate, pursue and implement economic policies, central to which is the management of aggregate demand. In doing so, governments are also expected to promote a more equal distribution of market power and, thus, income and wealth. One can argue therefore that a completely 'free' market system does not exist; government and appropriate institutions have evolved to reduce the fluctuations inherent in a 'free' market system.

Post-Keynesian analysis recognises, however, that there are severe obstacles to government action. These are exemplified in Kalecki (1943) and viewed as emanating from objections by 'industrial leaders' to full employment. These objections are based on their dislike (i) of government interference in the area of full employment; (ii) of government spending on public investment projects and subsidies on consumption; and (iii) of the social and political changes resulting from the maintenance of full employment. This dislike is seen to arise from a fear that such extension of governmental activities might threaten to replace capitalism by considerable state activity and socialism. Furthermore, capitalists see employment closely related to the level of investment, which in turn depends on 'profitability' and the 'state of confidence'; government interference would threaten and, indeed, weaken this process and thus destroy the basis of a healthy economic environment. The dislike of public expenditure is based on arguments about 'the need for sound finance' and the like. But in the case of public expenditure in particular, the aversion is essentially based on fears that it would crowd out private expenditure.

Similarly, the dislike of public consumption is couched in terms of its not being wealth-creating and consequently, when the government embarks on such spending, it does so at the expense of the wealth-creating private sector. This is associated with the moral principle that 'fundamentals of capitalist ethics require that "you shall earn your bread in sweat" – unless you happen to have private means' (Kalecki, 1971, p.140). One may also add that another objection to lasting full employment might be that the captains of industry could not tolerate the possibility of workers getting out of hand. Kalecki (1971) argues that rentiers too would wish to see this situation coming to an end since they would be disadvantaged by the inflationary pressures which are inevitable at full employment. What could very well develop in these circumstances is 'a powerful bloc ... between big business and the rentiers' interests, and they would probably find more than one economist to declare that the situation was manifestly unsound. The pressure of all these forces, and in particular of big business, would most probably induce the Government to return to the orthodox policy of cutting down the budget deficit' (p.144). I concur with Sawyer (1985b) that the group of 'more than one economist' referred to in the quote just cited is none other than monetarist!

There are still economic obstacles to lasting full employment. These include insufficient and/or inadequate capacity and lack of a trained and skilled labour force. Perhaps most important is the foreign trade difficulty in that the balance of payments can be a severe constraint in terms of allowing the economy to move to full employment. Expansion of demand is met with balance-of-payments problems, so that the expansionary policy would have to be reversed. This may not be unrelated to the other difficulty just mentioned in that the balance-of-payments constraint could very well arise from the inability of the economy to respond to the increased demand well before full employment is reached, due entirely to capacity problems and shortages in skilled and trained labour.

The implications of this analysis for policy can now be summarised: first, government intervention is necessary in principle to achieve and maintain full employment; second, the increased power of trades unions and workers at full employment would have to be taken on board in the form of involving the workforce in decision-making; third, the inflationary pressures which result from the increased power of workers must be addressed. Planning of incomes along with workers' participation in decision-making would have to be considered seriously. Fourth, there could very well arise a serious balance-of-payments constraint well before full employment is reached. Supply-side policies may be necessary to alleviate this problem. The underlying theme of this scenario is that demand management may very well be able to produce full employment, but alone cannot sustain it.

Beyond the problems enumerated above, one can also mention the mounting deficits and debt accumulation required to keep high levels of investment and employment and thus marginal firms afloat, thereby contributing to poor productivity, inefficiencies and to a declining general rate of profit. Even if sufficient demand were forthcoming, full employment would still be difficult, if not impossible, to maintain because of inadequate or unbalanced supply potential. I have argued elsewhere (Arestis, 1989a, 1989b) that both demand management and substantial supply-side policies are needed. An essential dimension of the latter type of policy is some form of 'direct control' of investment; in the references just cited these policies come under the rubric of socialisation of investment, along with 'labour market' and industrial policies as exemplified above.

Socialisation of investment was, of course, very much one of Keynes' (1936) policy prescriptions when he suggested that '....a somewhat comprehensive socialisation of investment will prove the only means of securing an approximation to full employment; though this need not exclude all manner of compromises and of devices by which public authority will co-operate with private initiative' (p.378). In another passage at a later date, Keynes made more explicit his notion of socialisation:

> If two-thirds or three-quarters of total investment is carried out or can be influenced by public or semi-public bodies, a long-term programme of a stable character should be capable of reducing the potential range of fluctuations to much narrower limits than formerly, when a smaller volume of investment was under public control and when even this part tended to follow, rather than correct, fluctuations of investment in the strictly private sector (Keynes, 1980, p.322).

In this way socialisation of investment is seen as filling the gap left by private investors, and also as encouraging more private investment by reducing uncertainty through the creation of a more stable environment. In addition, it should act as an inducement to unions to engage in incomes planning. Furthermore, socialisation of investment would remove the obstacles referred to above, in terms of achieving and maintaining full employment, especially as the dislike of the socio-political changes normally associated with attempts to sustain full employment disappear altogether. Changes of this nature would now be welcomed by the unions since they strengthen the position of the working class by enhancing their industrial muscle. Finally, it can be argued that socialisation of investment goes a long way to meeting the Marxist critique of post-Keynesian economics that it '... cannot resolve the struggle over the distribution of factor shares between capital and labour, nor over control of the labour process that gives rise to profits' (Chernomas, 1982, p.139). It clearly can within the parameters set by the socialisation of investment process.

SUMMARY AND CONCLUSIONS

In the inevitably short space available in a book such as this, I have attempted to summarise the post-Keynesian economics school of thought. This has been done from the points of view of methodology, the theoretical constructs of this way of thinking as to how the economy works, and the policy implications as they emerge from the theoretical premises.

The major policy implication of post-Keynesian thinking, as exemplified in this chapter, would appear to be some form of socialisation of investment. In this sense Keynes (1936,1980) would seem more prophetic than is generally recognised. But socialisation ought to be accompanied by some form of planning of incomes under the umbrella of a 'social contract' among unions, industry and state, which are generally recognised as the three all-important groups in any economic system. In this environment, wage pressures that damage profitability and accumulation can be avoided, especially if there is a commitment to full employment by governments. These policies should also be accompanied by appropriate industrial policies to promote participation of the workforce in decision-making.

There are two well-documented examples where socialisation of investment has been successfully implemented within capitalist economies: Sweden, which is probably the most well-known example (Arestis, 1986, 1989b), and Austria, where Tichy (1984) claims that a successful form of 'social control' of investment has taken effect. As it happens these economies belong to that group of countries which have been doing particularly well in terms of economic performance in the turbulent recent, and not so recent, past. In this sense one might conclude by suggesting that the likelihood of the type of analysis explored in this chapter becoming more influential on economic policy looks very promising.

NOTES

1.   I am grateful to Malcolm Sawyer and Len Shackleton for comments and discussion. They are in no way held responsible for any remaining errors and omissions.
2.   If post-Keynesian methodology is, as described by Hamouda and Harcourt (1988), a 'horses for courses' approach, it is sensible to argue that the Lakatosian criterion for evaluating a research programme (with its associated hard cores and protective belts) may not be appropriate. For an interesting analysis where a post-Keynesian research programme is identified, see Brown (1981) and Lavoie (1989). The latter offers an interesting synthesis of post-Keynesianism and neo-Ricardianism to produce a post-classical mode of thought. There is also the argument that even neo-classical methodology cannot be Lakatosian either. See Lavoie (1989) who summarises this argument neatly and goes on to contend that the core of neo-classical economics is essentially Walrasian, whilst the less theoretically rigorous but quantitatively-biased aspects of it comprise its protective belt.
3.   This is another area for possible future developments within post-Keynesian literature.
4.   Lexicographic ordering means that rules, based on non-numerical criteria, exist for arranging goods into categories with an appropriated taxonomy. In other words, just as there are rules for arranging words in a lexicon, similarly there are rules for the order of listing categories of goods. For a comprehensive application of this notion in post-Keynesian economic analysis of consumer choice, see Eichner (1987).
5.   There are, of course, many ways of classifying post-Keynesian thought. Indeed there are economists who do not fall into one or another category (for example, Kaldor, Pasinetti, Goodwin and Godley all of whom are discussed in Hamouda and Harcourt, 1988, pp.19–24), yet whose thinking has been of paramount importance in the development of post-Keynesianism.
6.   Dow and Earl (1982) cite *five* financial failures in an attempt to elucidate how financial crises can be caused by the workings of a free financial system. They also discuss how intervention by monetary authorities can mitigate the depth of these crises.
7.   Dow has argued that the degree of openness of an economy and the distinction between fixed and flexible exchange rates are important considerations in relation to the demand and supply of finance and money.
8.   The theoretical propositions put forward in the section on 'Main Theoretical Constructs' provide the basis for the empirical model recently constructed and estimated, as reported in Arestis (1989a).

11. The New Industrial Economics

Brian Haines and J R Shackleton

In this chapter the authors draw attention to recent theoretical developments in industrial economics and link these to the dramatic changes in policy since the 1970s. They begin by outlining new ways of looking at market structure, particularly noting the revival of 'Austrian' ideas and the development of the 'contestable market' approach. They then look at the current emphasis on the internal structure of the firm, drawing on transactions costs, agency and property rights literature. Competition policy, deregulation and privatisation are then discussed in the light of these ideas.

INTRODUCTION

Industrial economics is the theoretical and empirical study of the structure of the firm and industry, the conduct of buyers and sellers, and consequent effects on economic performance and welfare. It has both positive and normative aspects: our understanding of how firms and industries operate has clear implications for public policy, as we shall indicate.

Despite – or, perversely, perhaps *because of* – its practical relevance, industrial economics had a low profile and lower status amongst academics for many years. George Stigler wrote in 1968 that 'much of the literature of industrial organisation has been so nontheoretical, or even antitheoretical, that few economic theorists were attracted to it' (Stigler, 1968, p. 1). Since then, as in other areas of economics, sophisticated mathematical and statistical analysis has revolutionised the surface appearance of the literature: many journal articles and textbooks are no longer accessible except to the specialist. In this essay, we attempt to communicate the flavour of recent developments in industrial economics, which are too important to be left to the experts.

We concentrate on three broad aspects of the New Industrial Economics. First, we look at developments in the analysis of market structure. These are conveniently discussed as challenges to the 'structure-conduct-performance' paradigm which dominated thinking until quite recently. Second, we review changes in our understanding of the internal structure of the firm, changes which

179

are particularly interesting for the light they throw on the nature of so-called anti-competitive practices, but which also tie in with new thinking in other sub-disciplines such as labour economics. Third, we discuss the relevance of these developments to economic policy, with particular reference to the controversial issues of competition policy, privatisation and deregulation.

MARKET STRUCTURE

Since the dawn of systematic economic thinking, market dominance has been seen as a problem. At its simplest, this is shown in the elementary textbook's comparison of 'pure' monopoly and 'perfect' competition, which in its modern guise dates back to the 1920s, and in cruder form to Adam Smith. Here stress is laid on the allocative inefficiency resulting from market power. In a tightly-specified (and highly unrealistic) model, a profit-maximising monopolist can be shown to produce a smaller output at a higher price than a competitive industry facing identical technological and demand parameters. Thus monopoly misallocates resources.

Structure-Conduct-Performance

This rather abstract analysis was given practical significance by the *Harvard School* 50 years ago. Recognising that in the real world there were no simple dichotomies between competition and monopoly, such writers as Mason (1939) and Bain (1949, 1956) drew attention instead to the degree of concentration in an industry as an indicator of market power and hence of undesirable effects on economic welfare. This 'structure-conduct-performance' analysis is usually outlined by means of a flow diagram like Figure 11.1. The arrows suggest a causal sequence. Basic market conditions determine structure, which in turn affects conduct; finally conduct determines performance. This appears to present a testable hypothesis. We can find measures of concentration summarising market structure, and examine their relationship to indicators of conduct (for example pricing policy) and, most importantly, performance (profitability). If the expected relationships are found, there are clear implications for competition policy: the approach has been used to justify vigorous anti-trust action in the United States. Similar reasoning lies behind the emphasis in the UK on the proportion of the market (25%) controlled by a supplier as a criterion for referral to the Monopolies and Mergers Commission.

Evidence on the supposed relationship between market concentration and industry-average profitability is, however, underwhelming. Cross-sectional studies until the early 1970s seemed to indicate the existence of a weak positive correlation. However in the last 15 years, more sophisticated industry-level studies in the US and the UK have led one commentator to the conclusion that

Figure 11.1 The structure-conduct-performance approach

BASIC MARKET CONDITIONS

SUPPLY
Elasticities, costs
technology etc

DEMAND
Elasticities, marketing,
tastes etc

MARKET STRUCTURE
Market concentration, product differentiation, barriers to entry and exit,
vertical integration and diversification

CONDUCT
Goals of the firm, pricing and output strategies, degree of cooperation
amongst firms, anti-competitive practices,
research and innovation, advertising

PERFORMANCE
Output, growth, profitability, technical progress, employment, efficiency

'it is hard to find such a correlation in many data sets' (Schmalensee, 1988, p. 667).

Experience has shown there to be many problems in applying the structure-conduct-performance approach in practice. First there are the limitations of the microeconomic theory normally applied. Many industries are essentially oligopolistic in nature, and no generally accepted theory of oligopoly exists: see Burke *et al* (1988) for an account of the various suggestions. Much was once hoped for from applications of game theory, but such optimism is no longer common.

Firms are normally assumed to seek maximum profits, but even within this framework there may be different optimal strategies in the short run from those favoured in the long run. Much microeconomic theory is static in nature: clearly there are many situations where a dynamic approach is really needed to analyse changes over time (see Auerbach, 1988, for a detailed assessment of static and dynamic approaches). A simple example is that of *limit pricing*, the concept discussed by Bain and many subsequent writers. Firms may set prices below those necessary to maximise profits in the short run, if by doing so they can keep new firms from entering. Lower profits today mean higher profits in the future. Furthermore, goals of firms may in any case range through profit maximisation, sales revenue maximisation and growth maximisation to satisficing behaviour. This means there is no necessary connection between market power and performance as shown by conventional indicators.

So the structure-conduct-performance model does not give unambiguous predictions. Even were we to agree on a precise form in which it could be tested, the practical difficulties are considerable.

First of all, there are data problems. For instance, market structure is usually described by an index of seller concentration. Commentators agree that such a measure should reflect the number and size distribution of firms in an industry. Hall and Tideman (1967) listed six ideal properties that a measure of concentration should possess, and then proceeded to appraise the two most popular measures: the Concentration Ratio (CR) and the Herfindahl-Hirschman Index (HHI). The CR is the fraction of industry size held by the largest X firms, where X is usually 4, 5 or 8. The HHI is the sum of squared fractions of industry size held by all N firms within the industry. Thus:

$$CR_4 = \Sigma_{i=1}^4 S_i \quad \text{and} \quad HHI = \Sigma_{i=1}^n S_i^2$$

Hall and Tideman demonstrate the superiority of HHI over CR: the former is the only available measure satisfying all the properties of an ideal index. This should make CR redundant in empirical work. However, in practice Concentration Ratios are used far more frequently. Why? Because of data availability. Census of Production data generally contain information on the proportion of industry size contributed by the largest X firms, but the absence of readily available data on small-sized firms makes accurate calculation of the Herfindahl-Hirschman Index extremely difficult as the relative size of every firm within the industry is required. The infrequency with which production censuses are undertaken compounds the difficulties of research in this area. Moreover, it is not easy to define the appropriate boundaries of markets: government statistics are notoriously arbitrary. This is particularly a problem when examining the evolution of market structures over time.

Data problems mean that empirical results must accordingly be interpreted with extreme caution in industrial economics. Much often depends on the predilections of the researcher. The Harvard School, together with its more recent derivative the 'Structuralist' School, has historically been associated with a strong belief in the connection between concentration and market power. This has been reflected in their research findings, as well as in their strong support for the *per se* doctrine, an important feature of the American anti-trust legal tradition. This doctrine holds market dominance to be harmful in itself; it should therefore be illegal. By contrast, in the more pragmatic 'cost-benefit' tradition of the UK, the Monopolies and Mergers Commission is obliged to weigh the disadvantages of market power against possible compensating advantages.

The Chicago View

The Harvard approach has not had the academic field to itself. Throughout the postwar period there has been a strong rival tradition in the form of the *Chicago School*. Chicago economists, most notably George Stigler, have taken the view that concentrated markets are not necessarily evil in themselves. Rather stress is placed on the benefits of economies of scale and superior efficiency accruing to large firms. In any case, the strong belief in market forces associated with Chicago economics leads these researchers to claim that the 'barriers to entry' emphasised by the Harvard and Structuralist schools are more apparent than real. In the long run, competition is sufficiently powerful to undermine attempts by firms to rig markets.

A couple of examples serve to illustrate the differences between the schools. First, take the case of exclusive dealing (a contractual arrangement where retailers or distributors promise a supplier not to handle competing products). Such contracts obviously protect suppliers; the benefit to retailers is usually in the form of a franchise to be the sole outlet in a particular area. However, Harvard/Structuralist writers would point out the potential harm to consumers in the form of higher prices, and condemn such arrangements as anti-competitive. Not so the Chicagoans. Marvel (1982) has argued that it is only fair and just that suppliers should seek exclusive dealerships in compensation for their investment in advertising and sales promotion. Without exclusive dealership, retailers could 'free ride' on promotional investment. With it, producers find it worthwhile to enter new markets and develop new products. Marvel concludes that such arrangements should not be regarded as anti-competitive.

A second example is the well-known practice of vertical integration (where firms attempt to control a number of different production stages between the extraction of raw materials and the sale to the public of finished products). Whereas the Harvard/Structuralist writers see this practice as anti-competitive, Chicago authors such as Bork (1954) have argued forcefully that it does not threaten consumer welfare. Bork believes that even if a particular industry is characterised by monopoly at all stages of production, there is no reason why entry should not occur. Profitable opportunities exist which should attract capital and new entry. Bork acknowledges that entry will probably have to be by vertically-integrated concerns, but believes that this will be forthcoming unless there are capital market imperfections. If no entry occurs, and supernormal profits persist, the capital market cannot be working correctly – but it will be this, rather than vertical integration, which is the problem. He goes on to point out that vertical integration can bring positive benefits to the consumer in the form of lower costs, and should not be seen as a threat to competition.

Neo-Austrian Economics

In recent years the attack on the structure-conduct-performance paradigm has been joined by a resurgence in 'Austrian' approaches to competition. Few 'neo-Austrians' have any connection with geographical Austria, but they take their inspiration from the ideas of Austrian economists of the past: Menger, von Mises, Schumpeter and Hayek.[1] Austrians have always been associated with a robustly free-market stance, and perhaps even more strongly with an abhorrence of government involvement in the economy. Thus they tend to play down the need for government intervention to prevent market concentration.

Neo-Austrians are sceptical of the existence of long-run market power, and certainly of the link between market concentration and market power postulated by the Harvard School. They believe, with Demsetz (1982), that a high level of concentration in a particular market merely reflects underlying cost conditions in the absence of any legal entry barriers. Indeed, virtually no genuine economic entry barriers are believed to exist.

According to neo-Austrians, persistent examples of the abuse of market power by producers only tend to arise where enterprises are protected from competition by the state – for example, nationalised industries. By contrast firms in a genuinely free market are unable to maintain supernormal profits for very long, as such profits attract new entrants. These may not – and this is a crucial point – be producers of identical products, but rather products in a related field. Thus conventional measures of market concentration may remain unchanged, but the boundaries of the 'real' market may shift. Word processors compete with typewriters; spicey corn chips with potato crisps; video games with board games.

So neo-Austrians worry little about market concentration if free entry is feasible. Supernormal profits are temporary and a spur to competition. Government intervention may actually make markets work less well. For instances, price or profit controls on regulated industries reduce the attractiveness of new entry and thus paradoxically protect the position of incumbents. Firms contemplating innovation and invention may be deterred if the profits they can make are threatened by state regulators. As leading British neo-Austrian Steven Littlechild has argued, it is all very well complaining about the high price of a product if the alternative is a lower price under competition, but if the alternative is that no product is available because nobody has an incentive to invent it, things look different (Littlechild, 1981).

Moreover, neo-Austrians distrust the way in which regulators operate. Because firms know more about their costs and technologies than regulators, it is too easy for them to use this knowledge asymmetry to their advantage in pleading the necessity for higher prices and other privileges.

Neo-Austrians are therefore highly sceptical of active government intervention to break up private sector concentrations of market power or to prevent mergers. Instead they lay great emphasis on reducing the state's role in the economy, promoting privatisation and deregulation as the key to competition. Where some regulation is nevertheless called for, there should be no attempt to control prices and behaviour in detail. Rather governments should set rules which allow regulated firms to innovate and seek maximum profits. For example, Steven Littlechild was largely responsible for the acceptance of the 'RPI-X' rule applied to British Telecom and subsequently to other privatised firms. Under this rule (Littlechild, 1983), a weighted average of the prices of BT's regulated services was set to fall by at least X% per annum in real terms over a five-year period: it could choose the profit-maximising way to do this for itself.

Such policy recommendations depend on a strong faith in the virtues of the free market and private enterprise, a faith which is not subject to empirical testing: Austrians have historically denied that there are quantifiable regularities in economic life and eschewed econometrics. This is a defensible view, but not one which the uncommitted always find easy to accept.

Market Contestability

Another way to look at market power involves the 'contestable market' approach developed by the American economist William J. Baumol (Baumol *et al*, 1982). In Baumol's view also, economists have been wrong to worry too much about market concentration: the number of firms in an industry at a particular moment is irrelevant if they are free to enter and (very importantly) leave the market without making substantial losses. Such freedom of entry and exit makes possible a 'hit and run' competitive strategy. Firms enter when producers are making supernormal profits, and leave as those profits disappear. This is only possible in the absence of *sunk costs*, i.e. those which cannot be recouped on leaving the industry. Sunk costs, which should be clearly distinguished from the fixed costs (which do not vary with output changes) of standard neo-classical theory, are those which arise from investing in specific assets which have little or no value in other uses.

A market where sunk costs are low, where investment in specific assets is minimal, is what Baumol means by a contestable market. In such a case, *even if there are only one or two active producers*, supernormal profits cannot persist. Were they to do so, new firms would enter and compete away the excess. As existing firms are assumed to be aware of this, they will refrain from exploiting their apparent market power even in the absence of new entrants. We should not assume that the existence of a high degree of concentration in an industry will be associated with abnormally high profits or other indicators of market power.

This result depends on the plausibility of the assumption that sunk costs are unimportant. An example given by Baumol is the case of an unregulated airline route. Even if an airline is the only operator on this route, it cannot charge excessive prices because new airlines could enter. They would need to invest in aircraft, but these are not sunk costs as they could be used elsewhere: there is a lively secondhand market in planes. If abuse of market power by airlines is nevertheless observed, this suggests that government regulatory intervention is to blame.

By contrast, other markets may not be contestable if they involve heavy investment in specific assets. For example, constructing a railway involves heavy spending (on constructing bridges, tunnels and embankments) which cannot be recouped on leaving the industry. Consequently existing railways are less likely to be faced with 'hit and run' entrants.

For Baumol, then, sunk costs are a 'barrier to exit' rather than a 'barrier to entry'. The greater its sunk costs, the greater the risks to a potential entrant – and the more likely it is that supernormal profits will be maintained. The question of the empirical relevance of Baumol's approach might seem easy to determine, by examining the cost structure of different industries. However a question arises about the appropriate definition of costs. One view – that of the Austrians[2] – is that costs are ultimately impossible to measure objectively. This is particularly so with investment in specific human assets – skills, knowledge and experience which are valuable to one firm but not transferable elsewhere. The existence of sunk human capital costs may deter entry even though the physical assets of the firm are non-specific, but demonstrating this quantitatively is impossible.

So the relevance of Baumol's argument remains debatable. As with the neo-Austrians, a certain act of faith is required to assert that the contestable market analysis obviates the need for any government intervention in the private sector to promote competition. Few industrial economists are prepared to go that far, though it is now widely accepted that Baumol's analysis is useful in suggesting new ways of looking at the perennial problem of promoting competition.

THE INTERNAL STRUCTURE OF THE FIRM

Hoary tradition in economics treats the firm as a 'black box' into which inputs of the services of labour, capital and natural resources are made, and from which emerges saleable output. This is treated formally in neo-classical economics as a situation where firms maximise profits, given a technological production function relating inputs uniquely to outputs, and a set of prices at which inputs can be purchased and outputs sold.

What goes on in the black box is ignored. The instrumentalist methodology of Chicago's Milton Friedman (see Blaug, 1980), with its insistence that the economy behaves 'as if' profits are maximised, has been highly influential. This is justified by the claim that the literal descriptiveness of theory is irrelevant: all that matters are the predictions which it generates and against which it can be tested.

However, as already suggested, empirical evidence has rarely been decisive in adjudicating between competing schools of thought in industrial economics. There has therefore always been some interest in examining the internal workings of firms and in exploring alternative behavioural assumption. Earlier insights have recently been formalised into a 'new institutional economics' applying rigorous microeconomic reasoning to explain the structures and practices of firms rather than treating them as given, as well as drawing attention to the incentives facing individuals working in them. Amongst the various different strands of this literature, some of the more important are as follows.

Transaction Costs

Why do firms exist? In neo-classical economics, where until recently full information and constant returns to scale were normally assumed, it is unclear what functions firms can serve. Markets are seen as the ideal means of coordinating private economic activity, and inputs are costlessly converted to produce outputs. A network of atomistic producers supposedly forms and reforms automatically in response to shifts in demand and supply. However many years ago, Ronald Coase (1937) attempted to shed light on the emergence of firms by contrasting markets and firms as organisational forms. Others have followed him lately.

Without firms, producing all but the simplest goods would involve a complex web of bilateral contracts between otherwise isolated producers. For instance, take the production of a good involving five distinct processes – say, a simple wooden toy which has to be cut out, nailed, glued, painted, etc. Adam Smith's analysis of the division of labour suggests that each process is best done by a separate individual. In the absence of a firm, each individual producer would need to form a contract with each other individual. As illustrated in Figure 11.2(a), this would require ten separate contracts. This is the 'market' solution. However, if one of the producers (in this case individual C) sets up a firm and employs all the other producers, only four contracts need be formed. This is shown in Figure 11.2(b). In general, with n individuals the 'market' solution requires $n(n-1)/2$ contracts, while the 'firm' solution only needs $(n-1)$ (see Ricketts, 1987, ch. 2 for a fuller analysis). If forming contracts were costless, there would of course be nothing to choose between the 'market' of autonomous individuals and the 'firm'. However, in the real world there are *transactions costs*

Figure 11.2   The firm versus the market

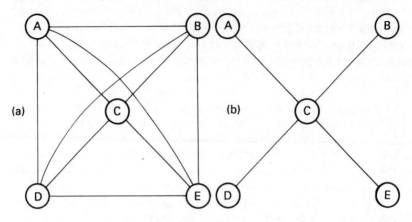

to forming contracts. These include search costs (having to find suitable partners), costs of negotiation etc. Clearly where there are positive transactions costs,
a form of organisation which minimises these is attractive, and thus the firm finds
a *raison d'être*.

The foremost recent advocate of the explanatory power of transactions costs
is O. E. Williamson. He has claimed that 'the modern corporation is mainly to be
understood as the product of a series of organisational innovations that have had
the purpose and effect of economising transactions costs' (1985, p. 273). On the
basis of analysis which assumes self-interested behaviour and bounded rationality,[3] he builds up a plausible explanation of many aspects of firm behaviour. This
provides a number of interesting theoretical insights; for instance, he gives a
powerful critique of the view that vertical integration is technologically determined (*ibid*, ch. 4).

Williamson's policy conclusions are sometimes controversial. He argues that
some phenomena which appear to be anti-competitive may have an 'efficiency
rationale' in minimising transactions costs and should be permitted. For example
he offers an alternative justification for exclusive contracts between firms, which
may sometimes be necessary in order for production to take place at all. Without
assurances of exclusivity, firms will be unwilling to invest in highly specific
capital – for instance, a machine to make automobile parts which can only be sold
to a very few car producers. If the firm cannot be assured of a regular outlet for
its product, it will not invest because the transactions costs involved in renegotiating a contract with some other car producer will be prohibitive.

Principal-Agent Theory

Developments in this area can be traced back to the classic discussion of the divorce between ownership (shareholders) and control (management) in the large firm by Berle and Means (1932). This spawned a substantial literature in the 1950s and early 1960s looking at managerial behaviour and considering alternative objectives to profit maximisation which might be pursued in 'managerial' firms.

More recently, this issue has been subsumed under the wider topic of principal-agent theory (Spence and Zeckhauser, 1971). In many areas of economic life, but especially in this context within firms, remote 'principals' employ as 'agents' people whose motives and pecuniary interests may differ from theirs. Given a world of imperfect information, principals have difficulty in monitoring how well agents are serving their interests. Resources have to be devoted to monitoring and to devising contracts which provide incentives for agents to act as principals intend.

Particular emphasis is placed on the observation that different individuals and groups within the firm have access to different types of information. They can use this access opportunistically in a way which serves their own interest, rather than that of the firm. Thus structures and incentives have to be devised to channel self-serving behaviour in the appropriate direction. For example, managerial remuneration may be linked to profit performance. Stock options are recommended to make managers share in the risks facing the firm. Lower down the organisation hierarchy, appropriate pay schemes will need to recognise the difficulties and costs associated with monitoring performance. In some contexts piece-rate based schemes may be an appropriate response, though elsewhere team-based production may call for different solutions. Theoretical developments in other areas of economics tie in here. For instance the analysis of 'implicit contracts' (see Chapter 7) can be linked to an understanding of the difficulties firms face in motivating workers.

Most pertinently for our purposes, the principal-agent literature has shed light on institutional innovations on which traditional theory has little to say, and much of that misleading. Take for example the case of franchising, one of the most rapidly growing forms of business expansion in recent years. Fast-food outlets, photographic processing, vehicle servicing, cosmetics, underwear and other types of retail sales have been examples of this. A common response has been to see the restrictive contracts which franchisors typically impose – tying franchisees to a particular source of supply, for example – as anti-competitive. However in an agency framework, franchises can be interpreted as a means of motivating managers of outlets by making them share the business risks: the alternative of employing salaried managers may be significantly less efficient. Apparently restrictive contracts prevent opportunistic franchisees from reneging on quality standards, whereas without restrictions, the value of the franchise generally would decline, and with it the benefits to be obtained by all parties.

In the public sector, principal-agent theory has been used to lend support to institutional changes which were a feature of the 1980s in a number of countries, most notably the UK. Management buy-outs (used in the private sector also, of course) proved an effective way of reviving some moribund public enterprises. The contracting-out to private companies of public services (hospital cleaning, refuse collection etc.) previously performed in-house by salaried employees has been strongly advocated. This has the potential to motivate better performance and greater efficiency. However it should be pointed out that many contracts have been badly designed from the viewpoint of agency theory, and the results in practice have therefore not always been very happy.

Property Rights

The need to develop incentives to promote efficiency is a subject also dealt with in another body of literature, that concerned with property rights. Economists have long understood that a stable framework of laws, including laws about ownership, is necessary in order for markets to flourish. Industrial economists have been prominent in drawing attention to aspects of this need. Certain systems of property rights encourage innovation and invention, while others do not, despite their other attractions. A familiar case is that of patent law. A system which vigorously protects the right of investors to the profits of their inventions provides strong incentives to the development of new processes and products. On the other hand, it can be pointed out that permissive patent laws may favour more rapid dissemination of innovation.

Alchian and Demsetz (1972) discuss another aspect of production within a firm which ties in with the transactions costs and agency literature. Granted that there are transactions-costs advantages to be gained from producing in teams organised by one individual rather than by a series of separately negotiated contracts, what structure of property rights promotes productivity? Alchian and Demsetz point out that there is a 'public good' problem within production teams which involve joint efforts and where output is not directly attributable to individuals. Everybody gains if all members of the team work hard, but opportunistic individuals may recognise that if they work less hard their own income may be little different from what it would be otherwise: they may be tempted to take a free ride on the rest of the team. Clearly, if many of the group behave like this total output suffers.

What is needed is someone to monitor the team to check that satisfactory effort is maintained. However, monitors themselves need incentives to maintain a high standard of vigilance: for *'quis custodiet ipsos custodes?'* as Roman economists might have said. Alchian and Demsetz argue that the strongest incentive is provided where monitors are 'residual claimants'. That is, they own the product which other members of the team are paid a wage to produce. The monitor can therefore claim the residual – what is left out of sales proceeds after paying the wage-earners. Such a monitor has a strong interest in ensuring that workers work as hard as they can within the terms of the employment contract.

A firm with a single owner-controller can have a comparative advantage in this respect over some other types of organisation, such as the labour-managed cooperative. This point has been explored by various writers, notably Furubotn and Pejovich (1974). It has also been part of a critique of the public sector in the 1980s. It has been claimed that nationalised firms, for instance, have a structure of property rights ('state ownership') providing inadequate incentives to efficiency.

Another aspect of property rights is their exchangeability. Ownership itself may provide incentives, but transferability of property rights accentuates this as assets can pass into the hands of those most likely to make effective use of them. This is a key element in recent discussions of the stock market or *market for corporate control*. Where company ownership (in the form of shares of equities) is freely traded in active stock markets, incumbent managements face a strong incentive to efficiency. If a firm is being badly run, share prices will fall and there is a strong possibility of a hostile takeover. The new owners would impose more dynamic management and raise profitability: because the existing management know and fear this, they are kept on their toes. By contrast in closed or private companies, where ownership is not freely traded (for instance there may be requirements that shareholders cannot sell their holdings without the agreement of other investors), this spur to efficiency is missing. For a discussion of the market for corporate control in the UK, see Chiplin and Wright (1987).

Another theme in the property rights literature is environmental pollution. The existence of 'negative externalities' in production have often been seen as a market failure, justifying state intervention – to regulate emissions of pollutants, impose fines and restrictions, forbid certain types of production and nationalise others. However, economists since Coase (1960) have proposed alternative policies which draw on the analysis of property rights.

One reason why the market fails to take adequate account of environmental factors is that nobody 'owns' important aspects of the environment. Rubbish is not normally tipped on my lawn because I have a property right to it which the courts will uphold, and I can sue a firm which decides to use my land as a garbage dump. However, a smoky factory or a noisy road can poison the air and damage my peace, and I am powerless to do anything about it. Neither I nor my neighbours have a 'right' to a pleasant environment which can be enforced at law.

Economists have argued that many environmental problems would be mitigated with an appropriate system of property rights. A clean environment is rather like the 'public good' of team effort mentioned earlier. In order to promote it we need an appropriate ownership structure – but one which recognises that there are conflicting rights involved, and thus an outright ban on economic activity is rarely sensible. For example, there have been experiments in the USA with the sale of pollution permits. These limit the total amount, say, of some chemical emission with harmful consequences. But each producer has a right to trade its permit with other producers. Thus a firm which employs a relatively harmless production process can sell its permit to another producer with higher emission levels. This provides incentives to firms to invest in pollution-reducing technologies, but without incurring the heavy economic costs in a total ban on production, which would also have the effect of punishing 'light' polluters as much as 'heavy' polluters. By varying the level of permitted pollutants, this procedure is potentially capable of fine-tuning environmental improvement. We are likely to hear much more of such indirect forms of industrial regulation in the environmentally-conscious 1990s.

POLICY ISSUES

The relationship between economic analysis and policy is not a simple one. Keynes believed that 'the power of vested interests is vastly exaggerated compared with the gradual encroachment of ideas' (1936/73, p. 383). In this light many of the policies adopted by governments in the 1980s might be traced directly to developments in the economic thinking of 'some academic scribbler of a few years back' (*ibid*). However, the direction of causation is surely less clear-cut than this. Disillusionment with much state involvement in the economy, and the associated policy changes from the mid-1970s onwards, arguably caused many economists radically to rethink ideas they had grown up with. And policy-makers, seeking an economic rationale for measures which they wished to pursue, were often able to find support amongst economists whose long-established ideas, until recently unpopular or simply obscure, seemed 'new' only by comparison with orthodoxy. The rise of the neo-Austrians is a good case in point.

In this section we briefly sketch some of the important policy trends of recent years, and indicate their relation to economic theory.

Competition Policy

What Americans call 'anti-trust' is usually referred to as competition policy in the UK. Whereas anti-trust dates back to the Sherman Act of 1890, action to combat concentrations of economic power in the UK is a post-World War II phenomenon.

By contract with the USA's emphasis on the *per se* doctrine, the British tradition has been to adopt a pragmatic, case-by-case approach. Rather than condemning outright a particular market structure or aspect of business conduct, the approach has been to weigh up the costs and benefits in terms of that flexible concept, the public interest. The original 1948 legislation, the Monopolies and Restrictive Practices Act, specified this approach. It has remained the determining factor despite criticisms which have increased in volume recently.

The Monopolies and Mergers Commission (MMC) is the UK's neutral investigatory body charged with examining monopolies and mergers according to certain criteria. The MMC came into being in its current form in 1965, when merger investigations were added to the powers of the former Monopolies Commission set up after the 1948 Act. Today the MMC's area of interest is considerably wider than that of the former Monopolies Commission. The latter was only intended to enquire into monopolies and restrictive practices in the production and supply of goods in the private sector of the economy. This was widened to include restrictive trade practices in 1956, mergers and monopolies in the service sector in 1965, restrictive labour practices in 1973 and (under the first Thatcher administration), anti-competitive practices and efficiency audits of nationalised industries in 1980.

Critics of the MMC have noted that its structure and procedures have remained substantially unchanged for many years despite enormous developments in the corporate environment. They charge that its effectiveness in dealing with the 'merger mania' of the 1980s has been extremely limited. A large increase in spending on domestic mergers and acquisitions has occurred, with the total figure rising from £5.5 billion in 1984 to £22.1 billion in 1988. These figures suggest that competition policy has had little or no effect in stemming the tide of merger activity. Industrial concentration has increased as larger merged units have been created. Commentators have pointed to the greatly increased workload and wondered if the MMC can cope.

Horizontal mergers have been the main type investigated by the MMC. Conglomerate mergers have been about half as numerous, while vertical mergers

Table 11.1 Outcome of MMC investigations, 1965–85

Structural Change	Referred	Aban-doned	Public Interest Conclusion		% Against
			Against	Not Against	
Horizontal	51	10	17	24	41
Vertical	6	1	1	4	20
Conglomerate	26	11	5	10	33
Total	83	22	23	38	94

Source: Chiplin and Wright (1987).

have been the occasion for relatively few investigations. The overall pattern is illustrated in Table 11.1, taken from Chiplin and Wright (1987), though this fails to demonstrate the increased relative importance of conglomerate mergers in the last decade. The MMC's activities have been examined by several writers. Shaw and Simpson (1986) analysed a sample of 28 markets investigated between 1959 and 1973 to see if concentration persisted where markets had been subject to investigation. They found evidence of a statistically significant decline in market share of firms investigated, but the decline was modest. Fairburn (1989) shows that, despite the wide powers of investigation the MMC nominally possesses, these have been used sparingly. From July 1965 to April 1969, for instance, only ten out of 350 mergers falling within the scope of the 1965 legislation were referred to the MMC. The qualifying assets criterion has been changed twice from £5 million to £15 million in April 1980 and to £30 million in July 1984, but this has failed to increase the proportion of qualifying mergers examined. Over the whole period 1965 to 1986, only 3% of all qualifying mergers were referred to the MMC.

Those economists who suspect that large numbers of mergers are potentially anti-competitive would like to see more investigations. They recognise that one reason why more cases are not examined is the sheer scale of the effort involved because the burden lies with the MMC to make out a case against a merger. George (1989) has advocated a reversal of the burden of proof, arguing that a bidding company is necessarily better informed than anyone else about the pros and cons of an acquisition. It seems reasonable, therefore, to expect it to be able to demonstrate benefits. This is a view with which Sir Gordon Borrie, Director-General of Fair Trading, has expressed sympathy.

However another suggestion is to alter the criteria for referral. Littlechild (1989), as a neo-Austrian, is sceptical of using measures of concentration or size of assets as indicators. He argues for a much narrower focus on those mergers particularly concerning barriers to entry, instances of which he expects to be few and far between.

This scepticism over concentration measures, which we have seen to be founded in various strands of new thinking about the nature of competition, is reflected in policy developments in other countries, notably the USA. Despite the long-standing *per se* principle, since the Sylvania decision in 1977 the Supreme Court has taken a much more lenient attitude towards vertical mergers. And under the Reagan presidency, the ideas of Chicago economists like Marvel and Bork became much more influential in determining the policy of the US Justice Department.

Argument over UK merger policy arises in part from the jurisdictional overlap with the European Community. Competition Policy is covered by article 86 of the Treaty of Rome. In principle the EC's Competition Directorate (DGIV) has considerably more power than the Office of Fair Trading and the MMC in the

UK. For example, DGIV has the authority to demand company information, to enter company premises and to impose heavy fines of up to 10% of annual turnover. DGIV is effectively investigator, prosecutor and judge. In comparison, any verdict by the MMC is simply a recommendation to the Secretary of State for Trade and Industry. Recommendations can be rejected; they frequently have been.

Until recently the powers of the DGIV have been used sparingly. This was partly because of the initial legal obscurity of its authority over mergers, and partly because its powers only related to goods and services traded between EC member countries. However, with the imminent advent of the Single Internal Market and a more active stance by DGIV, it is increasingly realised that UK competition policy cannot be conducted in isolation from the rest of Europe (Fleming and Swann, 1989).

If the detail of future mergers policy in the UK remains obscure, much more progress has been made in relation to other aspects of competition policy. As we have suggested in looking at theoretical developments, policy-makers are increasingly aware that size and concentration are only part of the problem, and arguably no longer the most important part. In the 1980s attention has been increasingly concentrated on what firms and other organisations actually *do*. Anti-competitive practices (see Burke *et al*, 1988, ch. 6), spelt out in the 1980 Act as practices operated by a single firm which have the effect of restricting, distorting or preventing competition in the supply of goods – have increasingly been stressed. Pricing practices and distribution arrangements, such as exclusive dealing and tie-in sales, are examples. Renewed attention has also been paid to the older idea of restrictive practices between firms, and a Review of Restrictive Trade Practices Policy was published by the Department of Trade and Industry in 1988. This Green Paper broadly recommended that the UK should adopt the European emphasis on the effects, rather than the form, of such practices, as spelt out in Article 85 of the Treaty of Rome. Section 3 of this Article spells out the grounds for exempting an agreement from illegality much more precisely than has previously been the case in the UK.

There is an important question that policy-makers in any country need to answer in order to decide on appropriate action. What exactly are the costs to society from monopoly power exercised by large organisations? Some writers, as we have seen, argue that monopoly brings benefits in scale economies or greater innovation. Against these benefits it is necessary to define the costs. Given the different points of view we have outlined, it is not surprising that estimates have varied widely.

Harberger's pioneering study (1954) has long been discussed. He claimed to have shown that the welfare loss from monopoly power was in fact extremely small, of the order of 0.1% of GNP for all manufacturing in the USA in the 1920s. More recently Cowling and Mueller (1978) claimed to have discovered evidence of much greater losses from monopoly power, producing an estimate of 13.1% of gross corporate product for the USA over the period 1963/66 (and a lower figure of 7.2% of gross corporate product for the UK using 1968/69 data).

From the Austrian perspective, Littlechild (1981) scathingly criticised such estimates, arguing that all studies from Harberger onwards have failed to recognise that much supernormal profit is a reward for risk and innovation rather than simply the result of monopoly power. He believes that all earlier studies are totally misleading about the location, extent, duration and costs of monopoly power and are quite inappropriate as a basis for public policy measures. In his view Cowling and Mueller's figures are 'gross overestimates' (see Clarke, 1983, for a fuller discussion).

Looking back on the 1980s, though, future historians of competition policy will surely pay less attention to policy on mergers and restrictive practices than to the much more radical break with the past represented by privatisation and deregulation. Whereas competition policy has traditionally stressed the need for governments to control the private sector to promote the public interest, the last decade has seen a switch towards trying to reduce the power of the state in many areas of economic life. We now turn to consider these aspects of policy.

Privatisation

Few readers can be unaware of the worldwide significance of privatisation in the 1980s. Its most familiar aspect in the UK, and the one on which we concentrate, has been the sale of shares in previously nationalised industries such as British Telecom, British Gas and British Airways. However, the term also covers sales of assets directly to other firms, management buy-outs of state enterprises, the 'contracting-out' of government services to the private sector, the sale of local authority public housing to occupiers and so forth. The economics of privatisation have been widely examined (a compendious introduction is provided by Swann, 1988); we shall not tarry over now-familiar ground. But a number of points should be made which are of particular relevance in the context of this essay.

For one thing, the political origins of privatisation tend to cast doubt on any simplistic view of the influence of economic thinking. Kay and Thompson (1986) referred to privatisation as 'a policy in search of a rationale'. The privatisation programme in the UK began as a modest attempt to tidy up the fringes of the public sector by denationalising a number of smallish enterprises which for historical reasons had ended up in state ownership: something similar had occurred in the early stages of the Heath administration in 1970/74. As it progressed other objectives accrued. It was seen variously as a welcome source of public sector finance (rising to well over £5 billion per annum in recent years), a means of breaking trade union power, a device for spreading share ownership, and finally an ideological objective in its own right.

However, government ministers also sought to rationalise privatisation as a technical solution to the economic problems of the public sector. An increasing number of economists, becoming persuaded of the merits of this viewpoint, were able to draw arguments from many of the newer ideas in industrial economics which we have already outlined. Policy and economic analysis fed off each other.

Fifteen years ago, the picture was very different. In Britain and Western Europe, though to a considerably lesser extent in the USA, the existence of state enterprise was taken for granted by economists as a necessary response to perceived market failures such as natural monopoly and externalities (though the basis for this assumption was always flimsy: see Shackleton, 1986). Most intellectual effort was devoted to devising appropriate theoretical pricing rules or investment appraisal techniques. Excellent examples of the kind of work this generated are to be found in Rees (1976). It was generally assumed that managers only needed to be aware of the appropriate decision rules. They would then make appropriate decisions and efficiency would be maximised. Economists' advice was heeded by UK governments: White Papers were published in 1961, 1967 and 1978 laying down appropriate guidelines for the operation of nationalised industries.

But these industries – and the public sector more generally – did not perform well in the 1970s, despite economists' advice (Pryke, 1981). In retrospect, much writing on the subject failed adequately to consider some of the topics discussed earlier in this essay: incentive structures (few managers or workers stood to gain directly from enterprise success); the difficulties of monitoring performance (nationalised industries were overseen by remote ministers, themselves nominally answerable to Parliament but in practice unwilling to allow detailed outside supervision; informational asymmetry (managers knew more about their businesses than the civil servants who ultimately controlled them).

Belated awareness of these problems has led many to jump on the bandwagon and promote privatisation as a virtual panacea for all the difficulties of the public sector. *Government* failure rather than *market* failure was the issue of the 1980s. For once Anglocentrism seemed justified, for the anti-statist mood of this decade reached its most developed form in the UK.

It was claimed that privatisation, particularly when coupled with market liberalisation (so that enterprises faced genuine new competition), would provide incentives to managers who had previously been dominated by a civil service mentality. By making their environment less cosy, by forcing enterprises to take risks and suffer the consequences of their own mistakes, it was argued that a new spur to efficiency could be created. Even where technical conditions ruled out product market contestability, it was claimed that the advent of a market for corporate control – the possibility of takeover – would goad managers into action. And by 1985 Mrs Thatcher's government was arguing that, even where threat of takeover was implausible, 'we believe that it is possible to privatise natural monopolies in such a way that their customers, the employees and the economy as a whole will all benefit...privatisation policies have now been developed to such an extent that regulated private ownership of natural monopolies is preferable to nationalisation' (Moore, 1985, pp. 94–5).

In a political sense, UK privatisation has clearly been a success. It has removed from day-to-day politics the problems of many nationalised industries which plagued British governments of both parties for most of the postwar period. It has brought in substantial sums to the Exchequer. And it has been part of a major cultural shift back towards the market and away from the defensive postures of public sector management and trades unions.

However, in narrowly economic terms, the position is less clear-cut. Privatised companies have certainly experienced increases in profits, output per head and total factor productivity.[4] But as one recent study noted (Bishop and Kay, 1988, p. 87), these improvements 'do not appear to bear any obvious relationship to privatization': similar improvements in performance have been noted in industries which (so far) remain in the public sector.

Critics have drawn attention to the substantial costs associated with the privatisation programme – costs of marketing and handling share issues, writing-off millions of pounds worth of debts and deliberate underpricing of shares in order to ensure a successful launch. They have observed, as did the late Lord Stockton, that selling off profitable assets in any case resembles selling off the family silver – an income boost today, but at the cost of having less to enjoy in the future.

More importantly, it has been observed that the urge for instant political success has often led to the form of privatisation being ill-adapted to the promotion of long-term efficiency. For example, most commentators now agree that the privatisation of British Gas and British Telecom could have been better handled if the promotion of competition and genuinely contestable markets had been prime objectives. These monopolistic giants, now happily ensconced in dominant positions in the private sector, could have been broken into smaller components, either regionally or by function. Competition between these groupings would have been encouraged, information about comparative performance would have been made readily available, and genuine new entry been much more feasible. However a short-term view was taken that a successful stock market flotation would be more likely if the former nationalised industries were sold virtually intact. The lesson seems to have been learnt with the planned privatisation of water and electricity, but ironically these sales seem at the time of writing to be more controversial than any which have gone before.

Finally, privatisation has not totally disposed of government interest in the great public utilities. While the Thatcher administration has stressed its concern with the failing of government rather than market failure, it has nevertheless recognised that natural monopolies pose continuing problems, and that externalities may be particularly important in industries which are crucial to the life of the nation. It has accordingly erected a new series of regulatory bodies – such as Oftel and Ofgas – which are intended to lay down guidelines about their conduct. We now turn to consider the economics of regulation.

Regulation and Deregulation

The regulation of economic activity by governments has a history going back hundreds – thousands – of years, and covers a much wider field than nationalised industries or direct state production have ever done. General regulation of industry includes such matters as health and safety at work, the environment, consumer protection and employment law. The economic rationale for this intervention includes potential market failures resulting from externalities or informational problems. These are also important issues in the case of regulation of specific industries such as telecommunications, transport, and public utilities like water and gas, although here problems of market power (particularly those arising from natural monopoly) are likely to be of paramount concern.

For a variety of reasons,[5] specific regulation has historically been more important in the US than in the UK and other European countries where industries have more frequently been nationalised. Thus although the USA is often thought of as the home of the free market, American industries have for decades been subject to a considerable degree of direct regulation over matters such as entry, pricing policy and output quality, as John Burton points out in Chapter 2. Federal bodies such as the Food and Drug Administration, Federal Communications Commission, the Interstate Commerce Commission, and the Securities and Exchange Commission have long had a high profile; significant regulatory powers also exist at state and local levels.

In the 1970s and 1980s both general and specific regulation came under increasing attack from economists as well as politicians. One line of attack was on the economic rationale for direct state intervention, the argument being that the private sector is not as prone to market failure as its critics claim. For example, it has been suggested (Allen, 1984) that regulations on quality control are unnecessary in markets where firms compete for customers who make repeat purchases of products so that quality is easily judged. A firm's reputation will be a valuable market asset which it will wish to protect by maintaining high standards: the UK's Marks and Spencer and Sainsburys would serve as good examples. It has also been claimed that the informational problems which consumers face can be overcome by private provision of consumer advice: the UK Consumers' Association is a case in point. And we have seen already that many environmental issues may be resolved by an appropriate definition of property rights. In each case it is claimed that the market can provide an appropriate pattern of incentives for firms to serve the public interest, and that continual state intervention is redundant.

Another line of attack concerned the record of regulation in practice. In the United States it was pointed out that (i) regulation intended to protect the consumer had often aided the producer, for example by excluding competition from new entrants unable to meet the restrictive standards imposed by regulations; (ii) cross-subsidisation in regulated industries had reduced allocative efficiency and perpetuated outmoded patterns of provision and perverse transfers of real income from one group of consumers to another; (iii) the advent of new technologies and new products had been retarded; (iv) regulated industries were frequently overstaffed, and labour unions had acquired excessive powers. This list of complaints closely resembles that made against nationalised industries in Europe.

American commentators have long complained of the phenomenon of 'regulatory capture', where regulatory agencies gradually come to equate the public interest with that of the industries they oversee. Shared backgrounds of producers and regulators, overlapping careers (where a gamekeeper can turn poacher or vice-versa with startling rapidity), and the need for rapport with people whom you frequently contact, all play a part. It is not surprising that, as Kay and Vickers observe, 'industries are generally opposed both to the introduction of new regulation and to the dismantling of old regulation' (Kay and Vickers, 1988, p. 312).

Some have claimed that there is a deeper reason for regulatory failure: regulation was never really intended to serve the public interest in the first place. Thus Stigler (1971) analysed regulation in the context of the familiar framework of rational, self-interested utility maximisers. There is a 'demand' for regulation by firms themselves wishing to control entry, fix prices and receive various subsidies, together with a 'supply' offered by politicians and bureaucrats who obtain favours in return. All sorts of ideological flimflam may be used to disguise this reality, but Stigler argues that it is difficult to see the persistent distortion or failure of regulation as an accident: 'If an economic policy has been...persistently pursued by a society over a long span of time, it is fruitful to assume that the real effects were known and desired' (Stigler, 1975, p. 140). This cynical view of the political process has been criticised in detail (Posner, 1974; Wilson, 1980), but it has been very influential.

For various reasons, then, market regulation became unpopular in the USA in the later 1970s and 1980s. A period of considerable deregulation ensued, including the dismantling of the Bell telephone system; liberalisation of interstate trucking, broadcasting and domestic airlines; relaxation of controls over oil and natural gas, and the promotion of greater competition in the financial sector. For an interim appraisal of these initiatives, see Bailey (1986).

In the UK the picture has been less clear-cut. In spite of considerable ideological sympathy between US and UK governments in recent years, some rather different political and economic pressures operate. The Thatcher administration's measures to promote competition in, for example, bus and airline transport and professional and financial services, display clear parallels with US policy. However, there has been a simultaneous increase in the number of regulatory bodies, for three reasons. First, the utility privatisations have created a need for specialist regulatory institutions such as Oftel and Ofgas. Second, the long-established British practice of self-regulation – particularly marked in finance and the professions – has been increasingly criticised, compelling the government to impose its own regulatory framework to assist the change to greater competition. This was particularly marked in the case of 'Big Bang" in the financial sector (see Goodhart, 1987), where the need to open up markets to world competition created opportunities for sharp practice. There are arguments, as we have suggested, for believing that fears of such market failure may be exaggerated. But in an area where investor confidence is so vital, it is understandable that the UK government felt obliged to 'reregulate'. Finally, the growing importance of European legislation as 1992 approaches has led to a significant increase in government regulation.

However, even where regulation has increased, some lessons have been learnt from American experience and from new economic thinking. For example, increasing stress has been placed on structural considerations, on the need to promote new entry and greater competition, rather than on detailed regulation of conduct. Where conduct regulation exists, it is confined to a limited set of rules – most notably the price cap (or RPI-X) rule. This avoids some of the difficulties of rate-of-return regulation of the kind used by US regulators in the past. Under rate-of-return regulation, firms were limited to a given rate of return on capital, but were allowed to raise prices to pay for the cost of new investment. This provided an incentive to over-investment in capital equipment. Under the price cap rule, firms are allowed to increase their prices on a key range of products and services by no more than X percentage points less than the retail price index. With a positive 'X', real prices must fall over time. Firms have an incentive to minimise costs rather than engage in unnecessary investment. The rule is not perfect, for firms can still manipulate their output mix and quality standards in order to increase profits in a way unintended by the regulators. Moreover, setting an appropriate 'X' factor depends on a knowledge of cost structures which regulators do not possess, and firms have an incentive to conceal. However, these problems are known and understood, and the UK's new breed of regulators seem more economically sophisticated than their predecessors.

Industrial Support

A final area for comment is that rather vague collection of policies which come under the heading of industrial support. They include regional policy, research and development, industrial reorganisation, tariff and other protection policies, and education and training. In the UK such policies have often been associated with the left, but this is by no means the case worldwide. Japan's industrial policy (Patrick, 1985), for example, has often been seen as an important element in the country's economic success, although it was certainly not the product of socialist thinking. Even in the United States, the early 1980s saw an interest in such policies developing across the political spectrum, although it turned out to be something of a damp squib (Norton, 1986).

Hay (1987) distinguishes three possible rationales for industrial support. The first stresses the risks involved in research and development and long-term investment. Private firms are accused of 'short-termism'; a more sophisticated variant looks at investment in R & D as a form of strategic competition engaged in by firms, where imperfect information can lead to inappropriate levels of investment. A second reason stresses the need to smooth the adjustment of declining industries given rigidities in labour and capital markets which may produce long periods of unemployment and excess capacity in the face of economic change. Finally there is the traditional 'infant industry' argument: a country may in time possess comparative advantage from particular industries in which meanwhile there is a substantial element of 'learning by doing'. Firms may need a period of protection behind tariff barriers, or some other form of industrial support, while they learn.

It is clear that such arguments fit uneasily with the emphasis in the last decade on competition and deregulation, and the belief that government failure is a greater threat than market failure. Accordingly, interest in industrial support has declined considerably in the UK. To take one example, despite persistent regional unemployment differentials, regional assistance declined by more than two-thirds in real terms between 1979–80 and 1987–88 (Shepherd, 1987, p. 61). This is defended by pointing out that much regional support in the past went on investment in capital equipment and did little to reduce unemployment; it is also argued that regions are in any case inappropriate categories. Often there can be as much variation in economic performance within regions as between them.

Attempts to protect UK firms from external competition are in any case more difficult to justify as world markets become more integrated and as the country becomes more enmeshed in the European Community. It is certainly possible for the EC as a whole to develop its regional support policies to a greater extent (a recurrent fear of American governments), but it is doubtful that a consensus exists on the form such intervention should take.

One area where UK industrial support *has* increased considerably in the last decade, however, is vocational education and training. It has been argued that too few resources have gone into preparing young people for work and for providing continuing training for those at work. However the arguments used to justify largely indiscriminate spending in this area have been exhortatory rather than analytical: they have not adequately spelt out the sources of market failure which lead the private sector to undersupply training. In particular, there have frequently been references to skill shortages in engineering which do not seem to correspond to anything measurable in terms of abnormally high pay for existing engineers. There is also a failure to realise the importance of Gary Becker's (1964) distinction between general training (where market failure is possible) and specific training (where is is extremely difficult to understand): both have been subsidised. It seems likely that in the not-too-distant future this policy will have to be reexamined in a more critical manner.

CONCLUDING COMMENTS

We have tried to show the extent to which both theoretical and policy aspects of industrial economics have changed dramatically in recent years, with politicians' disillusionment with government intervention going hand-in-hand with new theoretical developments stressing the resilience and inventiveness of the private sector and the inherent weaknesses of government intervention.

Human nature being what it is, it would be sensible to expect some reaction against these changes. It is certainly possible to visualise some sort of political backlash: apart from the inevitable swings and roundabouts of party politics, there are issues such as increasing environmental concern, fear about the power of the big utility monopolies and the pressure for supranational regulation coming from the EC (with a possible defensive reaction in the USA and Japan). Concern about these matters may lead to an increase in demands for government regulation and other forms of intervention.

Amongst economists, the reaction may be rather different, involving more detailed analysis of information problems which might still suggest serious potential market failures, and with attempts to design public sector interventions which avoid the worst errors of policies followed in the 1960s and 1970s. However, these developments will build on what has been learnt in recent years: industrial economics is unlikely to slip back into the slough of which Stigler complained 20 years ago.

NOTES

1.   See Littlechild (1978) for an excellent short introduction to these ideas.
2.   For a collection of papers on Austrian-style cost theory, see Buchanan and Thirlby (1973).
3.   Bounded rationality involves choosing the most attractive of a range of *known* alternatives: in a world where information has a cost, individuals will not normally find it worthwhile to explore every feasible alternative.
4.   Total factor productivity is a measure of output divided by an index of all the factor inputs used in the productive process. In principle it is a better efficiency indicator than the more common labour productivity: comparisons of labour productivity between two firms or industries are of little value if there are major differences in, say, capital employed per head.
5.   See Shackleton (1985).

References

Abraham, K.G. and Katz, L.F. (1986) 'Cyclical Unemployment: Sectoral Shifts or Aggregate Disturbances?' *Journal of Political Economy*, 94, June, pp. 507–22.

Adam Smith Institute (1989) *The First Hundred*, Adam Smith Institute, London.

Akerlof, G.A. and Yellen, J.L. (1985) 'A Near-rational Model of the Business Cycle with Wage and Price Inertia' *Quarterly Journal of Economics*, 100, pp. 823–38.

Alchian, A.A. and Demsetz, H. (1972) 'Production, Information Costs and Economic Organisation' *American Economic Review*, 62, pp. 777–95.

Alesina, A. (1989) 'Politics and Business Cycles in Industrial Democracies' *Economic Policy*, 8.

Allen, F. (1984) 'Reputation and Product Quality' *Rand Journal of Economics*.

Alt, J.E. and Chrystal, K.A. (1983) *Political Economics*, Wheatsheaf, Brighton.

Amel, D.F. *et al.* (1989) 'Trends in Banking Structure' *Federal Reserve Bulletin*, March, pp. 120–33.

Anderson, M. (1988) *Revolution*, Harcourt Brace Jovanovitch, New York.

Arestis, P. (1986) 'Post Keynesian Economic Policies: The Case of Sweden' *Journal of Economic Issues*, September.

Arestis, P. (1989a) 'On the Post Keynesian Challenge to Neoclassical Economics: A Complete Quantitative Macro-Model for the UK Economy' *Journal of Post Keynesian Economics*, Summer.

Arestis, P. (1989b) 'Economic Policies in a Post-Keynesian World' (mimeo).

Arestis, P. and Driver, C. (1987) 'The Effects of Income Distribution on Consumer Imports' *Journal of Macroeconomics*, Winter.

Arestis, P. and Eichner, A.S. (1988) 'The Post-Keynesian and Institutionalist Theory of Money and Credit' *Journal of Economic Issues*, December.

Argy, V. (1986) 'The Effects of Monetary and Fiscal Policy with Flexible Exchange Rates and Imperfect Asset Substitutability' *International Economic Research Papers*, No. 52

Argy, V. (1988) 'A Postwar History of the Rules Versus Discretion Debate' *Banca Nazionale del Larovo Quarterly Review*, June.

Argy, V. and Salop, J. (1979) 'Price and Output Effects of Monetary and Fiscal Policy under Flexible Exchange Rates' *IMF Staff Papers*, 26, pp. 224–56.

Auerbach, P. (1988) *Competition: The Economics of Industrial Change*, Basil Blackwell, Oxford.

Azariadis, C. (1975) 'Implicit Contracts and Unemployment Equilibria' *Journal of Political Economy*, 83, December, pp. 1183–1202.

Azariadis, C. (1982) 'Implicit Contracts and Related Topics; A Survey' in Hornstein, Z., Grice, J. and Webb, A. (eds.) *The Economics of the Labour Market*, HMSO.

Azariadis, C. and Cooper, R. (1985) 'Nominal Wage-Price Rigidity as a Rational Expectations Equilibrium' *American Economic Review*, Papers and Proceedings, 75, May, pp. 31–35.

Backhouse, R. (1985) *A History of Modern Economic Analysis*, Basil Blackwell, Oxford.

Bailey, E.E. (1986) 'Price and Productivity Change Following Deregulation: the UK Experience' *Economic Journal*, March.

Bailey, R.W. *et al.* (1982) 'The Information Content of Monetary Aggregates in the UK' *Economic Letters*, 9, pp. 61–67.

Bain, J.S. (1949) 'A Note on Pricing in Monopoly and Oligopoly' *American Economic Review*, March.

Bain, J.S. (1956) *Barriers to New Competition*, Harvard University Press, Cambridge, Mass.

Baltensperger, E. and Dermine, J. (1987) 'Bank Deregulation' *Economic Policy*, 4, April, pp. 63–109.

Bank of England (1984) 'Funding the Public Sector Borrowing' *Bank of England Quarterly Bulletin* (BEQB), 24/4, December, pp. 482–92.

Bank of England (1986) 'Financial Change and Broad Money' *Bank of England Quarterly Bulletin*, 25/4, December, pp. 499–507.

Bank of England (1987a) 'Measures of Broad Money' *Bank of England Quarterly Bulletin*, 27/2, May, pp. 212–19.

Bank of England (1987b) *Bank of England Quarterly Bulletin*, 27/3, August, pp. 365–70.

Bank of England (1987c) 'Supervision and Central Banking' *Bank of England Quarterly Bulletin*, 27/3, August, pp. 380–85.

Bank of England (1988) 'The Co-ordination of Regulation' *Bank of England Quarterly Bulletin*, 28/3, August.

Bank of England (1989a) 'Statistical Consequences of the Conversion of the Abbey National Building Society to a Public Limited Company' *Bank of England Quarterly Bulletin*, 29/3, August, pp. 352–53.

Bank of England (1989b) 'The Future of Monetary Arrangements in Europe' *Bank of England Quarterly Bulletin*, 29/3, August, pp. 368–74.

Barnett, W.A. (1980) 'Economic Monetary Aggregates' *Journal of Econometrics*, 14, September, pp. 11–48.

Barnett, W.A. (1987) 'The Microeconomic Theory of Monetary Aggregation' in

Barnett, W.A. and Singleton, K.J. (eds.) *New Approaches to Monetary Economics*, Cambridge University Press.

Barro, R.J. (1974) 'Are Government Bonds Net Wealth?' *Journal of Political Economy*, 82, pp. 1095–1117.

Barro, R.J. (1977) 'Unanticipated Money Growth and Unemployment in the United States' *American Economic Review*, 67, pp. 101 115.

Barro, R.J. (1979) 'Second Thoughts on Keynesian Economics' *American Economic Review*, 69, No. 2, Papers and Proceedings, May, pp. 54–59.

Barro, R.J. (1986) 'Recent Developments in the Theory of Rules Versus Discretion' *Economic Journal*, 96 (supplement), pp. 23–37.

Barro, R.J. (ed.) (1989) *Modern Business Cycle Theory*, Basil Blackwell, Oxford.

Barro, R.J. and Gordon, D.A. (1983) 'Rules, Discretion and Reputation in a Model of Monetary Policy' *Journal of Monetary Economics*, 17, pp. 101–122.

Barro, R.J. and Grossman, H.I. (1971) 'A General Equilibrium Model of Income and Employment' *American Economic Review*, 61, pp. 82–93.

Barro, R.J. and Grossman, H.I. (1976) *Money, Employment and Inflation*, Cambridge University Press.

Barro, R.J. and King, R.G. (1984) 'Time-Separable Preferences and Intertemporal-Substitution Models of Business Cycles' *Quarterly Journal of Economics*, 99, pp. 817–39.

Barry, N.P. (1987) *The New Right*, Croom Helm, London.

Batchelor, R.A. (1987) 'Monetary Developments' *City University Business School Economic Review*, 5/2, pp. 18–22.

Baumol, W.J. (1952) 'The Transactions Demand for Cash' *Quarterly Journal of Economics*, 67, pp. 545–56.

Baumol, W.J., Panzar, J.C. and Willig, R.D. (1982) *Contestable Markets and the Theory of Industry Structure*, Harcourt Brace and Jovanovich, San Diego.

Beaver, W.H. (1981) 'Market Efficiency' *The Accounting Review*, 56, pp. 23–27.

Becker, G. (1985) 'A Theory of Competition Among Pressure Groups for Political Influence' *Quarterly Journal of Economics*, 98, No. 3.

Becker, G.S. (1964) *Human Capital: A Theoretical and Empirical Analysis*, Columbia University Press.

Begg, D.K.H. (1982) *The Rational Expectations Revolution in Economics*, Philip Allan, Deddington, Oxford.

Benassy, J.P. (1986) *Macroeconomics: An Introduction to the Non-Walrasian Approach*, Academic Press, New York.

Benston, G.J. and Smith, C.W. (1976) 'A Transactions Cost Approach to the Theory of Financial Intermediation' *Journal of Finance*, 31, pp. 215–31.

Berle, A. and Means, G. (1932) *The Modern Corporation and Private Property*, Macmillan, London.

Bernanke, B.S. (1983) 'Nonmonetary Effects of the Financial Crisis in the Propagation of the Great Depression' *American Economic Review*, 73/3, June, pp. 257–76.

Bernanke, B.S. and Gertler, M. (1987) 'Banking and Macroeconomic Equilibrium' in Barnett, W.A. and Singleton, K.J. (eds.) *New Approaches to Monetary Economics*, Cambridge University Press.

Bharadwaj, K. (1983) 'On Effective Demand: Certain Recent Critiques' in Kregel, J.A. (ed.) *Distribution, Effective Demand and International Economic Relations*, Macmillan, London.

Bilson, J.F. (1980) 'Recent Developments in Monetary Models of Exchange Rate Determination' *IMF Staff Papers*, December.

BIS (Bank for International Settlements) (1986) *Recent Innovations in International Banking*, April.

Bishop, M. and Kay, J. (1988) *Does Privatization Work? Lessons from the UK*, London Business School.

Black, D. (1985) *A Theory of Committees and Elections* Cambridge University Press.

Blackburn, K. and Christenson, M. (1988) 'Macroeconomic Policy Games and Reputational Equilibria in a Contracting Model', University of Southampton, Discussion Paper No. 8621.

Blackburn, K. and Christenson, M. (1989) 'Monetary Policy and Policy Credibility' *Journal of Economic Literature*, XXVII:1, pp. 1–45.

Blanchard, O.J. (1985) 'Debt, Deficits and Finite Horizons' *Journal of Political Economy*, 93, pp. 223–47.

Blanchard, O.J. and Kahn, C.M. (1980) 'The Solution of Linear Difference Models under Rational Expectations' *Econometrica*, July.

Blanchard, O.J. and Kiyotaki, N. (1987) 'Monopolistic Competition and the Effects of Aggregate Demand' *American Economic Review*, 77, Sept. pp. 647–66.

Blanchard, O.J. and Summers, L.H. (1986) 'Hysteresis and the European Unemployment Problem' *NBER Macroeconomics Annual*, 1, pp. 15–77.

Blanchard, O.J. and Summers, L.H. (1987) 'Hysteresis in Unemployment', *European Economic Review*, 31, Feb/March, pp. 288–95.

Blanchard, O.J. and Summers, L.H. (1988) 'Why is Unemployment So High in Europe?' *American Economic Review*, Papers and Proceedings, 78, No. 2, May, pp. 182–93.

Blanchard, O.J. and Watson, M.W. (1982) 'Bubbles, Rational Expectations and Financial Markets' in Wachtel, P. (ed.) *Crises in the Economic and Financial Structure*, Lexington Books, Lexington.

Blaug, M. (1980) *The Methodology of Economics*, Cambridge University Press.

Blinder, A.S. (1988) 'The Challenge of High Unemployment' *American Economic Review*, Papers and Proceedings, 78, No. 2, May, pp. 1–15.

Blinder, A.S. and Fischer, S. (1981) 'Inventories, Rational Expectations and the Business Cycle' *Journal of Monetary Economics*, November, pp. 277–304.

Boaz, D. (ed) (1988) *Assessing the Reagan Years*, Cato Institute, Washington DC.

Bohara, A.K. *et al.* (1987) 'New Evidence on Targets for Monetary Policy' *Southern Economic Journal*, 53/3, pp. 591–604.

Bork, R. (1954) 'Vertical Integration and the Sherman Act: The Legal History of an Economic Misconception' *University of Chicago Law Review*, 22, pp. 157–201.

Boschen, J.F. (1988) 'Should We Reduce the Role of Banks in the Monetary Policy Process?' *Federal Reserve Bank of Kansas City Economic Review*, February, pp. 18–28.

Box, G.E.P. and Jenkins, G.M. (1976) *Time Series Analysis: Forecasting and Control*, Holden-Day, San Francisco.

Boyd, J.H. and Prescott, E.C. (1986) 'Financial Intermediary Coalitions' *Journal of Monetary Theory*, 38, pp. 211–32.

Brandsma, A. and Hallett, A. (1984) 'Optimal Policies for Interdependent Economies' in Basan, T. and Paw, L. (eds.) *Dynamic Modelling and Control of National Economies,* Pergamon Press.

Brennan, G. and Buchanan, J.M. (1985) *The Reason of Rules*, Cambridge University Press.

Breton, A. and Weintrobe, R. (1982) *The Logic of Bureaucratic Conduct*, Cambridge University Press.

Brittan, S. (1984) 'The Politics and Economics of Privatisation', *Political Quarterly*, Vol 55, No 2, April-June.

Britton, A. (1986) *The Trade Cycle in Britain 1958–82*, NIER Occasional Paper XXXIX, Cambridge University Press.

Broaddus, A. (1985) 'Financial Innovation in the US' *Federal Reserve Bank of Richmond Economic Review*, January/February, pp. 2–22.

Brooks, M. and Heijdra, B.J. (1988) 'In Search of Rent-Seeking' in Rowley, C.K., Tollinson, R.D. and Tullock, G. (eds.) *The Political Economy of Rent-Seeking*, Kluwer, Boston.

Brown, E.K. (1981) 'The Neoclassical and Post-Keynesian Research Programs: The Methodological Issues' *Review of Social Economy*, October.

Brunner, K. and Meltzer, A.H. (1971) 'The Uses of Money' *American Economic Review*, 61, pp. 784–805.

Bryant, R.C. (1983) 'Money and Monetary Policy' *The Brookings Review*, Spring, pp. 6–12.

Bryant, R.C. and Portes, R. (eds.) (1987) *Global Macroeconomics*, Macmillan, London.

Bryant, R.C. *et al.* (1988) *Empirical Macroeconomics for Interdependent Economies*, The Brookings Institution, Washington.

Buchanan, J.M. (1975) *The Limits of Liberty: Between Anarchy and Leviathan*, Chicago University Press.

Buchanan, J.M. (1984) 'Politics Without Romance: a Sketch of Positive Public Choice Theory and its Normative Implications' in Buchanan, J.M. and Tollinson, R. (eds.) *Public Choice Theory II*, University of Michigan Press, Ann Arbor.

Buchanan, J.M. (1986) *Liberty, Market and the State*, Harvester, Brighton.

Buchanan, J.M. (1987) 'The Constitution of Economic Policy' American Economic Review, 77, No. 3, pp. 243–50.

Buchanan, J.M. and Tullock, G. (1962) *The Calculus of Consent*, University of Michigan Press, Ann Arbor.

Buchanan, J.M. and Thirlby, G.F. (eds.) (1973) *LSE Essays on Costs*, London School of Economics and Weidenfeld and Nicolson.

Buchanan, J.M., Tollinson, R.D. and Tullock, G. (eds.) (1980) *Toward a Theory of the Rent-Seeking Society*, Texas A and M Press, College Station.

Buchanan, J.M. *et al.* (1989) *Reaganomics and After*, Institute of Economic Affairs, London.

Buiter, W. (1981) 'Time Preference and International Lending and Borrowing in an Overlapping-Generations Model' *Journal of Political Economy*, 89, pp. 769–97.

Bulow, J. and Summers, L.H. (1986) 'A Theory of Dual Labour Markets with Application to Industrial Policy Discrimination and Keynesian Unemployment' *Journal of Labor Economics*, 4, July, pp. 376–414.

Burke, T., Genn-Bash, A. and Haines, B. (1988) *Competition in Theory and Practice*, Croom Helm, Beckenham.

Burton, J. (ed) (1984) *Hayek's "Serfdom" Revisited*, Hobart Paperback 18, Institute of Economic Affairs, London.

Burton, J. (1985) *Why No Cuts?* Institute of Economic Affairs, London.

Caldwell, B.J. (1989) 'Post-Keynesian Methodology: An Assessment' *Review of Political Economy*, March.

Canzoneri, M.B. (1983) 'Two Essays on Monetary Policy in an Interdependent World', Federal Reserve Board, *International Finance Discussion Paper No. 219*.

Canzoneri, M.B. and Henderson, D.W. (1988) 'Is Sovereign Policymaking Bad?' *Carnegie-Rochester Conference Series on Public Policy*, 28, pp. 93–140.

Carlozzi, N. and Taylor, J. (1985) 'International Capital Mobility and the Coordination of Monetary Rules' in J. Bhandari (ed.) *Exchange Rate Management under Uncertainty*, MIT Press, Cambridge Massachusetts.

Cecchini, P. (1988) *The European Challenge*: 1992, Wildwood House, Aldershot, Hants.

Central Statistical Office (1975) 'Cyclical Indicators for the United Kingdom Economy' *Economic Trends*, March, pp. 95–99.

Chernomas, B. (1982) 'Keynesian, Marxist and Post-Keynesian Policy: A Marxist Analysis' *Studies in Political Economy*, 10.

Chick, V. (1986) 'The Evolution of the Banking System and the Theory of Saving, Investment and Interest,' *Economies of Societies*, Cahiers de l'IS-MEA, Série Monnaie et Production, No. 3.

Chiplin, B. and Wright, M. (1987) *The Logic of Mergers*, Hobart Paper 107, Institute of Economic Affairs.

Clarke, R. (1983) *Industrial Economics*, Basil Blackwell, Oxford.

Coase, R. (1937) 'The Nature of the Firm' *Economica*, 4, p. 86.

Coase, R. (1960) 'The Problem of Social Cost' *Journal of Law and Economics*, 3, No. 1.

Congdon, T. (1990) 'We're Doing Better Than Europe' *Spectator*, 3 February, pp. 8–10.

Connolly, R.A. (1989) 'An Examination of the Robustness of the Weekend Effect' *Journal of Financial and Quantative Analysis*, 24, pp. 133–70.

Cooper, R.N. (1969) 'Macroeconomic Policy Adjustment in Interdependent Economies' *Quarterly Journal of Economics,* 82.

Cooper, R.N. (1984) 'Economic Interdependence and Co-ordination of Economic Policies' in Jones, R.W. and Kenen, P.B. (eds.) *Handbook in International Economics Vol. II*, Elsevier Science Publishers, Amsterdam.

Copeland, T.E. and Weston, J.F. (1979) *Financial Theory and Corporate Planning*, Addison Wesley, Reading.

Corden, W. Max (1984) 'On Transmission and Co-ordination' in Buiter, W. and Marston, R.C. (eds.) *International Economic Policy Co-ordination.*

Coughlin, P. (1982) 'Pareto Optimality of Policy Proposals with Probabilistic Voting' *Public Choice*, 39, No. 3, pp. 247–63.

Cowling, K. and Mueller, D.C. (1978) 'The Social Costs of Monopoly Power' *Economic Journal*, 91, pp. 727–48.

Cross, R.B. (ed) (1988) *Unemployment, Hysteresis and the Natural Rate of Unemployment*, Basil Blackwell, Oxford.

Cullis, J.G. and Jones, P.R. (1987) *Microeconomics and the Public Economy: In Defence of Leviathan*, Basil Blackwell, Oxford.

Cuthbertson, K. (1988) *The Supply and Demand for Money*, Blackwell, Oxford.

Currie, D.A. and Levine, P. (1985) 'Macroeconomic Policy Design in an Interdependent World' in Buiter, W.H. and Marston, R.C. (eds.) *International Economic Policy Coordination*, Cambridge University Press, Cambridge and New York.

Dale, R. (1984) *The Regulation of International Banking*, Woodhead Faulkner, Cambridge.

Davidson, J.E.H., Hendry, D.F., Srba, F. and Yeo, S. (1978) 'Econometric Modelling of the Aggregate Time-Series Relationship Between Consumers' Expenditure and Income in the United Kingdom' *Economic Journal*, 88, pp. 661–92.

Davidson, P. (1978) *Money and the Real World*, Second Edition, Macmillan, London.

Davidson, P. (1982) *International Money and the Real World*, Macmillan, London and Basingstoke.

Davidson, P. (1988) 'A Technical Definition of Uncertainty and the Long-Run Non-Neutrality of Money' *Cambridge Journal of Economics*, 12.

Davis, T.E. (1952) 'The Consumption Function as a Tool for Prediction' *Review of Economics and Statistics*, 34, pp. 270–77.

Deaton, A.S. (1977) 'Involuntary Saving through Unanticipated Inflation' *American Economic Review*, Dec., pp. 899–910.

De Cecco, M. (ed) (1987) *Changing Money: Financial Innovation in Developed Countries*, Blackwell, Oxford.

Delors, J. (1989) *Report on economic and monetary union in the European Community*, Committee for the Study of Economic and Monetary Union, Commission of the European Communities, Brussels.

Demsetz, H. (1982) 'Barriers to Entry' *American Economic Review*, 72, pp. 47–57.

Diamond, D.W. (1984) 'Financial Intermediation and Delegated Monitoring' *Review of Economic Studies*, 51, pp. 394–414.

Diamond, P. (1965) 'National Debt in a Neo-Classical Growth Model' *American Economic Review*, 55, pp. 1126–50.

Dixit, A.K. (1978) 'The Balance of Trade in a Model of Temporary Equilibrium with Rationing' *Review of Economic Studies*, October, pp. 393–404.

Dooley, M. and Isard, P. (1980) 'Capital Controls, Political Risk, and Deviations from Interest Parity' *Journal of Political Economy*, 88, pp. 370–84.

Dorn, J.A. and Schwartz, A.J. (eds.) (1957) *The Search for Stable Money*, University of Chicago Press.

Dornbusch, R. (1974) 'Real and Monetary Aspects of the Effects of Exchange Rate Changes' in Aliber, R.Z. (ed.) *National Monetary Policies and the International Financial System*, Chicago University Press.

Dornbusch, R. (1976) 'Expectations and Exchange Rate Dynamics' *Journal of Political Economy*, December, pp. 1161–1176.

Dornbusch, R. (1980) 'Exchange Rate Economics: Where Do We Stand?' *Brookings Papers on Economic Activity*, 1, pp. 143–185.

Dornbusch, R. and Fischer, S. (1980) 'Exchange Rates and the Current Account' *The American Economic Review*, December, pp. 960–971.

Dotsey, M. and King, R.G. (1988) 'Rational Expectations Business Cycle

Models: A Survey' *Federal Reserve Bank of Richmond Economic Review*, 74:2, pp. 3–15.

Dow, J.C.R. and Saville, I.D. (1988) *A Critique of Monetary Policy*, Clarendon Press, Oxford.

Dow, S.C. (1985) *Macroeconomic Thought: A Methodological Approach*, Basil Blackwell, Oxford.

Dow, S.C. (1988) 'Post-Keynesian Economics: Conceptual Underpinnings' *British Review of Economic Issues*, Autumn.

Dow, S.C. and Earl, P.E. (1982) *Money Matters: A Keynesian Approach to Monetary Economics*, Martin Robertson, Oxford.

Downs, A. (1957) *An Economic Theory of Democracy*, Harper and Row, New York.

Duesenberry, J.S. (1949) *Income, Saving, and the Theory of Consumer Behaviour*, Harvard University Press, Cambridge, Massachusetts.

Eastwood, R.K. and Venables, A.J. (1982) 'The Macroeconomic Implications of a Resource Discovery in an Open Economy' *Economic Journal*, June.

Eatwell, J. (1983) 'Theories of Value, Output and Employment' in Eatwell, J. and Milgate, M. (eds.) *Keynes's Economics and the Theory of Value and Distribution*, Duckworth, London.

Economist (1989) 'Margaret Thatcher's Ten Years', 29 April, 19–26.

Eichner, A.S. (1976) *The Megacorp and Oligopoly: Micro Foundations of Macro Dynamics*, Cambridge University Press.

Eichner, A.S. (1987) *The Macrodynamics of Advanced Market Economies*, M.E. Sharpe, Armonk.

Eichner, A.S. and Kregel, J.A. (1975) 'An Essay on Post-Keynesian Theory: A New Paradigm in Economics' *Journal of Economic Literature*, December.

Evans, G.W. (1989) 'Output and Employment Dynamics in the United States: 1950–1985' *Journal of Applied Econometrics*, 4, pp. 213–37.

Evans, M.K. (1969) *Macroeconomic Activity*, Harper and Row, New York.

Fairburn, J. (1989) 'The Evolution of Merger Policy in Britain' in Fairburn, J. and Kay, J. *Mergers and Merger Policy*, Oxford University Press.

Fama, F.F. (1970) 'Efficient Capital Markets: A Review of Theory and Empirical Work' *Journal of Finance*, 25, pp. 383–417.

Figlewski, S. (1980) 'Market Efficiency in a Market with Heterogeneous Information' *Journal of Political Economy*, 86, pp. 581–97.

Fischer, S. (1977) 'Long-Term Contracts, Rational Expectations and the Optimal Money Supply Rule' *Journal of Political Economy*, 85, pp. 191–205.

Fischer, S. and Cooper, J.P. (1973) 'Stabilisation Policy and Lags' *Journal of Political Economy*, July/August, 81, pp. 847–77.

Fleming, J. (1962) 'Domestic Financial Policies Fixed and Under Floating Exchange Rates' *IMF Staff Papers*, November, pp. 369–379.

Fleming, M. and Swann, D. (1989) 'Competition Policy – The Pace Quickens and 1992 Approaches' *The Royal Bank of Scotland Review*, June.

Foot, M.D.F. *et al.* (1979) 'Monetary Base Control' *Bank of England Quarterly Bulletin*, 19/2, pp. 149–59.

Frenkel, J.A. (1976) 'A Monetary Approach to the Exchange Rate: Doctrinal Aspects and Empirical Evidence', ch. 1 in Frenkel, J. and Johnson, H.G. *The Economics of Exchange Rates*, Chicago University Press.

Frenkel, J.A. (1981) 'Flexible Exchange Rates, Prices and the Role of News: Lessons from the 1970s' *Journal of Political Economy*, August.

Frenkel, J.A. and Engel, C.M. (1984) 'Do Asset-Demand Functions Optimise over the Mean and Variance of Real Returns: A Six Currency Test' *Journal of International Economics*.

Frenkel, J.A. and Razin, A. (1985) 'Government Spending, Debt and International Economic Interdependence' *Economic Journal*, 95, pp. 619–36.

Frenkel, J.A. and Razin, A. (1986a) 'Fiscal Policies in the World Economy' *Journal of Political Economy*, 94, pp. 564–94.

Frenkel, J.A. and Razin, A. (1986b) 'Real Exchange Rates, Interest Rates and Fiscal Policies' *Economic Studies Quarterly*, 37, pp. 99–113.

Frenkel, J.A. and Rockett, K.E. (1988) 'International Macroeconomic Policy Coordination When Policy Makers Do Not Agree on the True Model' *American Economic Review*, 78, pp. 318–40.

Friedman, B. (1988) 'Monetary Policy without Quantity Variables' *American Economic Review*, 78, pp. 440–45.

Friedman, J.W. (1971) 'A Non-Cooperative Equilibrium for Supergames' *Review of Economic Studies*, 38, pp. 1–12.

Friedman, M. (1953) *Essays in Positive Economics*, Chicago University.

Friedman, M. (1957) *The Theory of the Consumption Function*, University Press for National Bureau of Economic Research, Princeton, NJ.

Friedman, M. (1968) 'The Role of Monetary Policy' *American Economic Review*, pp. 1–17.

Friedman, M. (1978) "The Role of Monetary Policy' in Tieden, R.L. (ed) *Readings in Money, Income and Stabilisation Policy*, Fourth Edition, Irwin, Homewood, pp. 365–74.

Friedman, M. (1987) 'Monetary Policy: Tactics Versus Strategy' in Dorn, J.A. and Schwartz, A.J. (eds.) *The Search for Stable Money*, University of Chicago Press, pp. 361–82.

Friedman, M. and Friedman, R. (1980) *Free to Choose: A Personal Statement*, Secker and Warburg, London.

Friedman, M. and Friedman, R. (1984) *The Tyranny of the Status Quo*, Secker and Warburg, London.

Friedman, M. and Friedman, R. (1988) 'The Turning Tide' in Anderson, A. and

Bark, D.L. (ed) *Thinking About America; the US in the 1990s* Hoover Institute, Stanford California.

Friedman, M. and Friedman, R. (1989) 'The "Tide in the Affairs of Men"' *Economic Impact*, No. 66, pp. 74–79.

Friedman, M. and Savage, L.J. (1948) 'The Utility Analysis of Choices Involving Risk' *Journal of Political Economy*, 56, pp. 59–96.

Friedman, M. and Schwartz, A.J. (1963) *A Monetary History of the United States*, Princeton University Press, Princeton NJ.

Friedman, M. and Schwartz, A.J. (1982) *Monetary Trends in the United States and the United Kingdom: Their Relation to Income, Prices and Interest Rates 1867–1975*, Chicago University Press.

Friedman, M. and Schwartz, A.J. (1986) 'Has Government any Role in Money?' *Journal of Monetary Economics*, 17, pp. 37–62.

Funabashi, Y. (1988) *Managing the Dollar From the Plaza to the Louvre*, Institute for International Economics, Washington.

Furobotn, E. and Pejovich, S. (eds) (1974) *The Economics of Property Rights*, Ballinger, Cambridge, Massachusetts.

Gamble, A. (1988) *The Free Economy and the Strong State: The Politics of Thatcherism*, Macmillan, Basingstoke.

Gamble, A. *et al.* (1989) *Ideas, Interests and Consequences*, Institute of Economic Affairs, London.

George, K.D. (1989) 'Do We Need a Merger Policy?' in Fairburn, J. and Kay, J. *Mergers and Merger Policy*, Oxford University Press.

Gertler, M. (1988) 'Financial Structure and Aggregate Economic Activity' *Journal of Money, Credit and Banking*, 20/3, August, Part 2, pp. 559–88.

Gertler, M. and Hubbard, R.G. (1988) 'Financial Factors in Business Fluctuations' in *Financial Markets Volatility*, Federal Reserve Bank of Kansas City, pp. 33–71.

Gilligan, T. *et al.* (1984) 'Scale and Scope Economies in the Multi-Product Banking Firm' *Journal of Monetary Economics*, 13/3, May, pp. 393–405.

Girton, L. and Roper, D. (1976) 'Theory and Implications of Currency Substitution' *Federal Reserve Board International Finance Discussion Papers*, No. 56.

Goodhart, C.A.E. (1975) *Money, Information and Uncertainty*, Macmillan, London.

Goodhart, C.A.E. (1984) *Monetary Theory and Practice*, Macmillan, London.

Goodhart, C.A.E. (1987) 'The Economics of the "Big Bang"' *Midland Bank Review*.

Goodhart, C.A.E. (1989) 'The Conduct of Monetary Policy' *Economic Journal*, 99, June, 293–346.

Goodwin, R.M. (1967) 'A Growth Cycle' in Feinstain, C.H. (ed) *Socialism, Capitalism and Economic Growth*, Cambridge University Press.

Gordon, D.F. (1974) 'A Neo-classical Theory of Keynesian Unemployment' *Economic Enquiry*, 12, pp. 431–49.

Gordon, R.A. (1976) 'Rigor and Relevance in a Changing Institutional Setting' *American Economic Review*, 66, March, pp. 1–14.

Granger, C.W.J. (1969) 'Prediction with a Generalized Cost of Error Function' *Operations Research Quarterly*, 20, pp. 199–207.

Green, D. (1987) *The New Right*, Wheatsheaf, London.

Greenfield, R.L. and Yeager, L.B. (1983) 'A Laissez-Faire Approach to Monetary Stability' *Journal of Money, Credit and Banking*, 15, August, pp. 302–15.

Greenwald, B.C. and Stiglitz, J.E. (1988) 'Examining Alternative Macroeconomic Theories' *Brookings Papers on Economic Activity*, 1:88, pp. 207–70.

Grossman, S.J. and Stiglitz, J.E. (1980) 'On the Impossibility of Informationally Efficient Markets' *American Economic Review*, 70, pp. 393–407.

Guimaraes, R.M., Kingsman, B.G. and Taylor, S.J. (eds.) (1989) *A Reappraisal of the Efficiency of Financial Markets*, NATO ASI Series, Proceedings of the NATO Research Workshop on A Reappraisal of the Efficiency of Financial Markets, Sesimbra, Portugal, April 11–15, 1988.

Hahn, F.H. (1987) 'On Involuntary Unemployment' *Economic Journal*, 97, Supplement, pp. 1–17.

Hall, Max (1987) *The City Revolution*, Macmillan, Basingstoke.

Hall, M. and Tideman, N. (1967) 'Measures of Concentration' *Journal of American Statistical Association*, 62, pp. 162–68.

Hamada, K. (1974) 'Alternative Exchange Rate Systems and the Interdependence of Monetary Policies' in Aliber, R. (ed.) *National Monetary Policies and the International Financial Systems*, University of Chicago Press.

Hamada, K. (1976) 'A Strategic Analysis of Monetary Independence' *Journal of Political Economy*, 84, pp. 677–700.

Hamada, K. (1985) *The Political Economy of International Monetary Interdependence*, MIT Press, Cambridge, Massachusetts.

Hamilton, J.D. (1988) 'A Neoclassical Model of Unemployment and the Business Cycle' *Journal of Political Economy*, 96:3, pp. 593–617.

Hamouda, O.F. and Harcourt, G.C. (1988) 'Post-Keynesianism: From Criticism to Coherence?' *Bulletin of Economic Research*, January; reprinted in Pheby, J. (ed.) *New Directions in Post-Keynesian Economics*, Edward Elgar Publishing Limited, Aldershot.

Harberger, A.C. (1954) 'Monopoly and Resource Allocation' *American Economic Review*, Proceedings, pp. 727–48.

Harrington, R. (1987) *Asset and Liability Management by Banks*, OECD, Paris.

Hart, O. (1987) 'Incomplete Contracts' in Eatwell, John, Milgate, Murray and Newman, Peter (eds) *The New Palgrave: A Dictionary of Economics*, Macmillan Press, London, pp. 752–58.

Hart, O. and Holmstrom, B. (1987) 'The Theory of Contracts' in Bewley, T. (ed)

Advances in Economic Theory, Cambridge University Press.

Hay, D. (1987) 'Competition and Industrial Policies' *Oxford Review of Economic Policy*, 3, No. 3, Autumn.

Hayek, F.A. (1933) *Monetary Theory and the Trade Cycle*, Cape, London.

Hayek, F.A. (1935) *Prices and Production*, (2nd edn), Routledge and Kegan Paul, London.

Hayek, F.A. (1944) *The Road to Serfdom*, Routledge and Kegan Paul, London.

Healey, N. (1989) 'Is Monetarism at last Dead?' in Campbell, M. *et al.* (eds) *Controversies in Applied Economics*, Harvester Wheatsheaf, Hemel Hempstead.

Helliwell, J. and Padmore, T. (1985) 'Empirical Studies of Macroeconomic Interdependence' in Jones, R.W. and Kenen, P.B. (eds.) *Handbook of International Economies*, Vol II, Elsevier Science Publishers.

Hendry, D.F. (1980) 'Econometrics: Alchemy or Science?' *Economica*, 47, pp. 387–406.

Hendry, D.F. (1983) 'Econometric Modelling: The Consumption Function in Retrospect' *Scottish Journal of Political Economy*, Nov, pp. 193–220.

Hendry, D.F. (1985) 'Monetary Economic Myth and Econometric Reality' *Oxford Review of Economic Policy*, 1/1, pp. 72–84.

Hendry, D.F. and Ericsson, N.R. (1983) 'Assertion without Empirical Basis' in Bank of England Panel of Academic Consultants,*Monetary Trends in the UK*, Panel Papers 22, pp. 45–101.

Hendry, D.F. and Mizon, G.E. (1985) 'Procustrean Econometrics: Or Stretching and Squeezing Data' *CEPR Discussion Paper 68*, Centre for Economic Policy Research, London.

Hendry, D.F. and Richard, J.F. (1983) 'The Econometric Analysis of Economic Time Series' *International Statistical Review*, 51, pp. 111–63.

Hester, D.D. (1982) 'Innovations and Monetary Control' *Brookings Papers on Economic Activity*, 1, pp. 141–89.

Hibbs, D. (1977) 'Political Parties and Macroeconomic Policy' *American Political Science Review*, 71, pp. 1467–87.

Hicks, J.R. (1950) *A Contribution to the Theory of the Trade Cycle*, Clarendon Press, Oxford.

Hicks, J.R. (1974) *The Crisis in Keynesian Economics*, Basil Blackwell, Oxford.

Hillman, A.L. and Katz, E. (1984) 'Risk-Averse Rent-Seekers and the Social Cost of Monopoly Power' *Economic Journal*, 94, March, pp. 104–10.

Hinich, M.J. (1977) 'Equilibrium in Spatial Voting: The Median Voter Result is an Artifact' *Journal of Economic Theory*, 16, pp. 104–110.

H.M. Treasury (1980a) *Financial Statement and Budgetary Report 1980/81*, HMSO, London.

H.M. Treasury (1980b) *Monetary Control*, HMSO, London, Cmnd 7858.

H.M. Treasury (1989) *Financial Statement and Budgetary Report 1989/90*, HMSO, London.

Holden, K., Peel, D.A. and Thompson, J.L. (1985) *Rational Expectations: Theory and Evidence* Macmillan, London.

Hollis, M. and Nell, E.J. (1975) *Rational Economic Man*, Cambridge University Press.

Holtham, G. and Hughes Hallett, A.J. (1987) 'International Policy Cooperation and Model Uncertainty' in Bryant, R. and Portes, R. (eds.) *Global Macroeconomics Policy Conflict and Cooperation*, Macmillan, London.

Humphrey, T.M. (1987) 'The Theory of Multiple Expansion of Deposits' *Federal Reserve Bank of Richmond Economic Review*, March/April, pp. 3–11.

Humphrey, T.M. (1988) 'Rival Notions of Money' *Federal Reserve Bank of Richmond Economic Review*, September/October, pp. 3–9.

Ikenberry, D. and Lakonishok, J. (1989) 'Seasonal Anomalies in Financial Markets: A Survey' in Guimaraes, R.M., *et al* (ed.), *op. cit.*

Isard, P. (1977) 'How Far Can We Push the Law of One Price?' *American Economic Review*, December.

Ishii, N., McKibbin, W. and Sachs, J.D. (1985) 'The Economic Policy Mix, Policy Cooperation, and Protectionism: Some Aspects of Macroeconomic Interdependence Among the United States, Japan, and other OECD Countries' *Journal of Policy Modelling*, Vol. II, No. 4, pp. 533–72.

Jackson, P. (1982) *The Political Economy of Bureaucracy*, Philip Allan, Oxford.

Johnson, H.G. (1976) 'The Monetary Approach to Balance of Payments Theory' in Frenkel, J. and Johnson, H.G. *The Economics of Exchange Rates*, Chicago University Press.

Johnston, R.B. (1984) 'The Demand for Non-Interest Bearing Money in the UK', Government Economic Service *Working Paper*, No. 66, HMSO.

Judd, J.P. and Scadding, J.L. (1982) 'The Search for a Stable Money Demand Function' *Journal of Economic Literature*, 20/3, pp. 993–1023.

Kaldor, N. (1940) 'A Model of the Trade Cycle' *Economic Journal*, March.

Kalecki, M. (1943) 'Political Aspects of Full Employment' *Political Quarterly*, 14, No. 4.

Kalecki, M. (1971) *Selected Essays on the Dynamics of the Capitalist Economy, 1933–70*, Cambridge University Press.

Kane, E.J. (1983) 'Policy Implications of Financial Changes' *American Economic Review*, 73, pp. 96–100.

Kane, E.J. (1988) 'Interaction of Financial and Regulatory Innovation' *American Economic Review*, 78, pp. 328–34.

Katz, L.F. (1986) 'Efficiency Wage Theories: A Partial Evaluation' *NBER Macroeconomic Annual*, 1, pp. 235–75.

Katz, L.F. (1988) 'Some Recent Developments in Labor Economics and Their

Implications for Macroeconomics' *Journal of Money, Credit and Banking*, 20, No. 3, August, Part 2, pp. 507–22.

Kay, J.A. and Thompson, D.J. (1986) 'Privatisation: A Policy in Search of a Rationale' *Economic Journal*, March, pp. 18–33.

Kay, J.A. and Vickers, J. (1988) 'Regulatory Reform in Britain' *Economic Policy*, No. 7, October.

Keynes, J.M. (1936) *The General Theory of Employment, Interest and Money*, 1973 Edition, Royal Economic Society/Macmillan, London.

Keynes, J.M. (1973) *The General Theory and After*, Collected Writings, XIV, Macmillan, London.

Keynes, J.M. (1980) *Activities, 1940–46: Shaping the Post-War World: Employment*, Collected Writings, XXVII, Macmillan, London.

Kim, K. (1988) *Equilibrium Business Cycle Theory in Historical Perspective*, Cambridge University Press.

King, D. (1987) *The New Right*, Macmillan, London.

King, R.G. and Plosser, C.I. (1984) 'Money, Credit and Prices in a Real Business Cycle' *American Economic Review*, 74, pp. 363–80.

Kingston, G.H. and Turnovsky, S.J. (1977) 'Monetary and Fiscal Policies under Flexible Exchange Rates and Perfect Myopic Foresight' *Scandinavian Journal of Economics*, September.

Klamer, A. (1984) *The New Classical Macroeconomics*, Wheatsheaf, Brighton.

Kravis, I. and Lipsey, R.G. (1978) 'Price Behaviour in the Light of Balance of Payments Theories' *Journal of International Economics*, March.

Krueger, A.O. (1974) 'The Political Economy of the Rent-Seeking Society' *American Economic Review*, 74, pp. 291–303, reprinted in Buchanan, Tollinson and Tullock, (1980), *op. cit.*

Kydland, F.E. and Prescott, E.C. (1977) 'Rules Rather than Discretion: the Inconsistency of Optimal Plans' *Journal of Political Economy*, 85, pp. 473–92.

Kydland, F.E. and Prescott, E.C. (1982) 'Time to Build and Aggregate Fluctuations' *Econometrica*, 50, pp. 1345–70.

Lavoie, M. (1984) 'The Endogenous Flow of Credit and the Post Keynesian Theory of Money' *Journal of Economic Issues*, September.

Lavoie, M. (1989) 'Towards a New Research Programme for Post-Keynesianism and Neo-Ricardianism' paper delivered at the *Post-Keynesian Conference*, Great Malvern, UK, August 15th-17th.

Lawson, T. (1983) 'Different Approaches to Economic Modelling' *Cambridge Journal of Economics*, March.

Lawson, T. (1989) 'Realism and Instrumentalism in the Development of Econometrics' *Oxford Economic Papers*, January.

Ledyard, J.O. (1984) 'The Pure Theory of Large Two-Candidate Elections' *Public Choice*, 44, No. 1, pp. 7–41.

Levačić, R. (1987) *Economic Policy Making*, Wheatsheaf, Brighton.

Levitas, R. (ed) (1987) *The Ideology of the New Right Polity*, Cambridge Massachusetts.

Leijonhufvud, A. (1987) 'Natural Rate and Market Rate' in Eatwell, J., Milgate, M. and Newman, P. (eds.) *The New Palgrave: A Dictionary of Economics*, Macmillan, London.

Leland, H.E. and Pyle, D.H. (1977) 'Informational Asymmetries, Financial Structure and Financial Intermediation' *Journal of Finance*, 32/2, May, pp. 371–87.

Levine, P. (1987) 'Does Time Inconsistency Matter?' *CEF Discussion Paper*, No. 19, London Business School.

Lewis, M.K. and Davies, K.T. (1987) *Domestic and International Banking*, Philip Allan, Oxford.

Lichtenstein, P.M. (1983) *An Introduction to Post-Keynesian and Marxian Theories of Value and Price*, Macmillan, London.

Lilien, D.M. (1982) 'Sectoral Shift and Cyclical Unemployment' *Journal of Political Economy*, 90, August, pp. 777–93.

Lindbeck, A. and Snower, D.J. (1986) 'Wage Setting, Unemployment and Insider-Outsider Relations' *American Economic Review*, 76, No. 2, Papers and Proceedings, May, pp. 235–39.

Lindbeck, A. and Snower, D.J. (1988) 'Cooperation, Harassment and Involuntary Unemployment: An Insider-Outsider Approach' *American Economic Review*, 78, March, pp. 167–88.

Littlechild, S. (1981) 'Misleading Calculations of the Social Costs of Monopoly Power' *Economic Journal*, 91, pp. 348–63.

Long, J.B. and Plosser, C.I. (1983) 'Real Business Cycles' *Journal of Political Economy*, 91, pp. 39–69.

Lucas, R.E. (1975) 'An Equilibrium Model of the Business Cycle' *Journal of Political Economy*, 83, pp. 1113–44.

Lucas, R.E. (1981) *Studies in Business Cycle Theory*, The MIT Press, Cambridge, Massachusetts.

Lucas, R.E. (1982) 'Interest Rates and Currency Prices in a Two-Country World' *Journal of Monetary Economics*, 10, pp. 355–60.

Lucas, R.E. (1987) *Models of Business Cycles*, Basil Blackwell, Oxford.

MacInnes, P. (1987) *Thatcherism at Work*, Open University Press, Milton Keynes.

McKibbin, W.J. and Sachs, J.D. (1986) 'Comparing the Global Performance of Alternative Exchange Rate Arrangements' *Brookings Papers in International Economics*, No. 49, August.

McKinnon, R.I. (1984) 'An International Standard for Monetary Stabilisation' *Policy Analyses in International Economics*, Institute for International Economics, No. 8, March, Washington.

McLean, I. (1987) *Public Choice: An Introduction*, Basil Blackwell, Oxford.

McPherson, D. (1984) 'Limits on Self-Seeking: The Role of Morality in Economic Life' in Colander, D. (ed.) *Neoclassical Political Economy*, Balinger, Cambridge Massachusetts.

Maddala, G.S. (1988) *Introduction to Econometrics*, Macmillan, London.

Mankiw, N.G. (1989) 'Real Business Cycles: A New Keynesian Perspective' *NBER Working Papers*, No. 2882.

Margolis, H. (1982) *Selfishness, Altruism and Rationality*, University of Chicago Press.

Marshall, A. (1890) *Principles of Economics*, Macmillan, London.

Marston, R. (1985) 'Stabilization Policies in Open Economies' in Jones, R. and Kenen, P. (eds.) *Handbook of International Economics*, 2, Amsterdam and North Holland.

Marvel, H.P. (1982) 'Exclusive Dealing' *Journal of Law and Economics*, April.

Mason, E.S. (1939) 'Price and Production Policies of Large-Scale Enterprise' *American Economic Review*, Supplement 29, pp. 61–74.

Melitz, J. (1988) 'Monetary Discipline and Cooperation in the European Monetary System: A Synthesis' in Giavazzi, P., Micossi, S. and Miller, M. (eds.) *The European Monetary System*, Cambridge University Press.

Mester, L. (1987) 'Efficient Production of Financial Services' *Federal Reserve Bank of Philadelphia Business Review*, January/February, pp. 15–25.

Meulendyke, A. (1980) 'A Review of Federal Reserve Policy Targets and Operating Guides in Recent Decades' *Federal Reserve Bank of New York Quarterly Review*, Autumn, pp. 6–17.

Miles, D.K. (1989) 'Recent Developments in the Pattern of UK Interest Rates; Bank of England *Discussion Papers*, No. 36, February.

Minford, A.P.L. (1983) *Unemployment: Cause and Cure*, Martin Robertson, Oxford.

Minford, A.P.L. and Peel, D.A. (1983) *Rational Expectations and the New Macroeconomics*, Martin Robertson, Oxford.

Minsky, H.P. (1982) *Can 'It' Happen Again? Essays on Instability and Finance*, M.E. Sharpe, Armonk, New York.

Minsky, H.P. (1986) 'The Evolution of Financial Institutions and the Performance of the Economy' *Journal of Economic Issues*, June.

Mitchell, W.C. (1988) 'Virginia, Rochester and Bloomington: 25 Years of Public Choice and Political Science' *Public Choice*, 56, No. 2.

Moore, B.J. (1986) 'How Credit Drives the Money Supply: The Significance of Institutional Developments' *Journal of Economic Issues*, 20/2, June.

Moore, B.J. (1988) *Horizontalists and Verticalists: The Macroeconomics of Credit Money*, Cambridge University Press.

Moore, J. (1985) 'The Success of Privatisation' in Kay, J., Mayer, C. and

Thompson, D. (eds.) *Privatisation and Regulation – the UK Experience,* Oxford University Press.

Morris, D. (1988) *Government Debt in International Financial Markets,* Pinter, New York.

Muellbauer, J. and Portes, R. (1978) 'Macroeconomic Models with Quantity Rationing' *Economic Journal,* December, pp. 788–821.

Mueller, D.C. (1989) *Public Choice II,* Cambridge University Press, New York.

Mundell, R.A. (1961) 'A Theory of Optimum Currency Areas', *American Economic Review.*

Mundell, R.A. (1963) 'Capital Mobility and Stabilisation Policy under Fixed and Flexible Exchange Rates' *Canadian Journal of Economics and Political Science,* November.

Mundell, R.A. (1968) *International Economics,* Macmillan, New York.

Mussa, M. (1979a) 'Empirical Regularities in the Behaviour of Exchange Rates and Theories of the Foreign Exchange Market' in Brunner and Meltzer (eds.) 'Policies for Employment, Prices and Exchange Rates' *Carnegie-Rochester Conference Series on Public Policy.*

Mussa, M. (1979b) 'Macroeconomic Interdependence and the Exchange Rate Regime' in Dornbusch, R. and Frenkel, J. (eds.) *International Economic Policy: Theory and Practice,* John Hopkins University Press, Baltimore MD.

Mussa, M. (1986) 'Nominal Exchange Rate Regimes and the Behaviour of Real Exchange Rates: Evidence and Implications' *Carnegie-Rochester Conference Series on Public Policy,* 25, pp. 117–213.

Muth, J.F. (1961) 'Rational Expectations and the Theory of Price Movements' *Econometrica,* 29, pp. 13–49.

Neary, J.P. and Purvis, D.D. (1981) 'Sectoral Shocks in a Dependent Economy; Long Run Adjustment and Short Run Accommodation' Institute for International Economic Studies, *Seminar Paper,* No. 188, Stockholm.

Neary, J.P. and Van Winjbergen, S. (1984) 'Can an Oil Discovery lead to a Recession?' *Economic Journal,* June, pp. 390–395.

Nell, E.J. (1980) 'The Revival of Political Economy' in Nell, E.J. *Growth, Profits and Property,* Cambridge University Press.

Nelson, C.R. and Plosser, C.I. (1982) 'Trends and Random Walks in Macroeconomic Time Series: Some Evidence and Implications' *Journal of Monetary Economics,* 10, pp. 139–62.

Niehans, J. (1975) 'Some Doubts about the Efficacy of Monetary Policy under Flexible Exchange Rates' *Journal of International Economics,* 5, August.

Niehans, J. (1978) *The Theory of Money,* Johns Hopkins University Press, Baltimore MD.

Niehans, J. (1982) 'Innovations in Monetary Policy' *Journal of Banking and Finance,* 6, pp. 9–28.

Niskanen, W.A. (1971) *Bureaucracy and Representative Government*, Aldine-Atherton, Chicago.

Niskanen, W.A. (1988) 'Reflections on Reaganomics' in Boaz, D. (ed)*Assessing the Reagan Years*, Cato Institute, Washington DC.

Nordhaus, W, (1975) 'The Political Business Cycle' *Review of Economic Studies*, 42, pp. 169–90.

North, D. (1986) 'The New Institutional Economics' *Journal of Institutional and Theoretical Economics*, No. 1, 142, March.

Norton, R.D. (1986) 'Industrial Policy and American Renewal' *Journal of Economic Literature*, March.

Nutter, G.W. (1978) *Growth of Government in the West*, American Enterprise Institute, Washington DC.

Okun, A. (1981) *Prices and Quantities*, Brookings Institution, Washington, DC.

Olson, M. (1965) *The Logic of Collective Action*, Harvard University Press, Massachusetts.

Olson, M. (1982) *The Rise and Decline of Nations: Growth, Stagnation and Social Rigidities*, Yale University Press, New Haven.

Oudiz, G. (1985) 'European Policy Coordination: An Evaluation' Centre for Economic Policy Research, *Discussion Paper*, No. 81, October.

Oudiz, G. and Sachs, J.D. (1984) 'Macroeconomic Policy Coordination Among the Industrial Economies' *Brookings Papers on Economic Activity*, 1, pp. 1–64.

Oudiz, G. and Sachs, J.D. (1985) 'International Policy Coordination in Dynamic Macroeconomic Models' in Buiter, W.H. and Marston, R.C. (eds.) *International Economic Policy Coordination*, Cambridge University Press, Cambridge and New York.

Padoa-Schioppa, T. (1988) 'The European Monetary System: a Long-Term View' in Giavazzi, F. et al. (eds.) *The European Monetary System*, Cambridge University Press.

Pagan, A. (1987) 'Three Economic Methodologies: A Critical Appraisal' *Journal of Economic Surveys*, 1, pp. 3–24.

Paish, F.W. (1968) 'The Limits of Incomes Policies' in Paish, F.W. and Hennessy, J. *Policy for Incomes* (4th edn.), Institute of Economic Affairs, Hobart Paper 29, 1968, pp. 13–49.

Pasinetti, L.L. (1974) *Growth and Income Distribution: Essays in Economic Theory*, Cambridge University Press.

Pasinetti, L.L. (1981) *Structural Change and Economic Growth*, Cambridge University Press.

Patrick, D. (1985) 'Japanese Industrial Policy' in Bornstein, M. (ed.) *Comparative Economic Systems*, (5th edn) Richard D. Irwin, Homewood Illinois.

Peacock, A.T. (1983) 'Public x-inefficiency: informational and institutional constraints' in Hanusch, H. (ed.) *Anatomy of Government Deficiencies*,

Springer-Verlag, Berlin.

Pecchioli, R.M. (1987) *Prudential Supervision in Banking*, OECD, Paris.

Peltzman, S. (1976) 'Towards a More General Theory of Regulation' *Journal of Law and Economics*, 19, August, pp. 211–40.

Persson, T. (1985) 'Deficits and Intergenerational Welfare in Open Economics' *Journal of International Economics*, 19, pp. 67–84.

Phelps, E.S. (1968) 'Money Wage Dynamics and Labor Market Equilibrium' *Journal of Political Economy*, 76, pp. 687–711.

Phillips, A.W. (1954) 'Stabilisation in a Closed Economy' *Economic Journal*, 64, pp. 290–305.

Phillips, A.W. (1958) 'The Relationship Between Unemployment and the Rate of Change of Money Wage Rates in the United Kingdom, 1861–1957' *Economica*, 25, pp. 283–99.

Pirie, M. (1988) *Micropolitics: The Creation of Successful Policy* Wildwood House, Aldershot Hants.

Pissarides, C.A. (1989) 'The Search Equilibrium Approach to Fluctuations in Employment' *American Economic Review*, 78, Papers and Proceedings, May, pp. 363–68.

Pissarides, C.A. (1989) 'Unemployment and Macroeconomics' *Economica*, 56, No. 221, February, pp. 1–13.

Podolski, T.M. (1986) *Financial Innovation and the Money Supply*, Basil Blackwell, Oxford.

Pokorny, M.J. (1987) *An Introduction to Econometrics*, Basil Blackwell, Oxford.

Poole, K.T. and Romer, T. (1985) 'Patterns of Political Action Committee Contributions to the 1980 Campaigns for the US House of Representatives' *Public Choice*, 47, No. 1, pp. 63–111.

Portes, R. and Swoboda, A.K. (eds) (1987) *Threats to International Financial Stability*, Cambridge University Press.

Posner, R.A. (1971) 'Taxation by Regulation' *Bell Journal of Economics*, 2, pp. 22–50.

Posner, R.A. (1974) 'Theories of Economic Regulation' *Bell Journal of Economics*, 5, pp. 335–58.

Prescott, E.C. (1986) 'Theory Ahead of Business Cycle Measurement' *Carnegie-Rochester Conference on Public Policy*, Autumn, pp. 11–44.

Pryke, R. (1981) *The Nationalised Industries: Policies and Performance since 1968*, Martin Robertson, Oxford.

Ramakrishan, R.T.S. and Thakor, A.V. (1984) 'Information Availability and a Theory of Financial Intermediation' *Review of Economic Studies*, 51, pp. 415–32.

Rasche, R.H. (1987) 'M1-Velocity and Money-Demand Functions: Do Stable Relationships Exist?' *Carnegie-Rochester Conference Series on Public Pol-*

icy, 27, pp. 9–88.

Rasche, R.H and Johannes, J.M. (1987) *Controlling the Growth of Monetary Aggregates*, Kluwer Academic Publishers, Boston, Massachusetts.

Rawls, J. (1971) *A Theory of Justice*, Belknap Press, Cambridge Massachusetts.

Rees, R. (1976) *Public Enterprise Economics*, Weidenfeld, and Nicolson, London.

Reisman, D. (1990) *The Political Economy of James Buchanan*, Macmillan, London.

Reynolds, P.J. (1990) 'Kaleckian and Post-Keynesian Theories of Pricing: Some Extensions and Implications' in Arestis, P. and Kitromilides, Y. (eds.)*Theory and Policy in Political Economy: Essays in Pricing, Distribution and Growth*, Edward Elgar Publishing, Aldershot.

Ricketts, M. (1987) *The Economics of Business Enterprise*, Wheatsheaf Books, Brighton Sussex.

Riddell, P. (1983) *The Thatcher Government*, Martin Robertson, Oxford.

Riker, W.H. (1962) *The Theory of Political Coalitions*, Yale University Press, New Haven.

Riley, C.J. (1982) 'Non-Traded Goods and the Long Run Effects of Macroeconomic Policy' *Manchester School*, September.

Robinson, J. (1956) *The Accumulation of Capital*, Macmillan, London.

Robinson, J. (1973) *Collected Economic Papers*, 4, Basil Blackwell, Oxford.

Rogers, S.C. (1989) *Money, Interest and Capital: A Study in the Foundations of Monetary Theory*, Cambridge University Press.

Rogoff, K. (1985) 'Can International Monetary Policy Coordination be Counter Productive?' *Journal of International Economics*, 18, pp. 199–217.

Rogoff, K. (1987) 'Reputational Constraints on Monetary Policy' in *Carnegie-Rochester Conference Series on Public Policy*, 2b, pp. 141–81.

Romer, P.M. (1989) 'Capital Accumulation in the Theory of Long-Run Growth' in Barro, R.J. (ed.) *Modern Business Cycle Theory*, Basil Blackwell, Oxford.

Romer, T. (1988) 'Nobel Laureate: On James Buchanan's Contributions to Public Economics' *Journal of Economic Perspectives*, 2, No. 4, pp. 165–79.

Roncaglia, A. (1978) *Sraffa and the Theory of Prices*, John Wiley and Sons, New York.

Rosen, S. (1985) 'Implicit Contracts: A Survey' *Journal of Economic Literature*, 23, pp. 1144–75.

Rowley, C.K. (1987) 'The Calculus of Consent' in Rowley, C.K. (ed.) *Democracy and Public Choice: Essays in Honor of Gordon Tullock*, Basil Blackwell, Oxford.

Rowley, C.K. and Elgin, R. (1988) 'Government and its Bureaucracy; a Bilateral Bargaining Versus a Principal-Agent Approach' in Rowley, C.K., Tollinson, R.D. and Tullock, G. (eds.) *The Political Economy of Rent-Seeking*, Kluwer, Boston.

Rowthorn, B. (1981) 'Demand, Real Wages and Economic Growth' *Thames Papers in Political Economy*, Autumn.

Rubenstein, M. (1975) 'Securities Market Efficiency in an Arrow Debren Economy' *American Economic Review*, 65, pp. 812–24.

Rush, M. (1986) 'Unexpected Money and Unemployment' *Journal of Money, Credit and Banking*, 18:3, pp. 259–74.

Rush, M. (1987) 'Real Business Cycles' *Federal Reserve Bank of Kansas City Economic Review*, 72, pp. 20–32.

Sachs, J.D. (1990) 'East Europe's Economies: What Is To Be Done?' *Economist*, 13 January, pp. 23–26.

Sachs, J.D. and McKibbin, W.J. (1986) 'Macroeconomic Policies in the OECD and LDC External Adjustment' in Colaco, F. and Van Wijnbergen, S. (eds.) *International Capital Flows in Developing Countries*, MIT Press, Cambridge Massachusetts.

Sachs, J.D. and Wyplosz, C. (1984) 'Real Exchange Rate Effects of Fiscal Policy' *NBER Working Paper*, No. 1255, January.

Salin, P. (ed) (1984) *Currency Competition and Monetary Union*, Nijhoff, The Hague.

Salter, W.E.G. (1959) 'Internal and External Balance: The Role of Price and Expenditure Effects' *Economic Record*, August.

Samuels, J. and Mercuro, N. (1984) 'A Critique of Rent-Seeking Theory' in Colander, D. (ed.) *Neoclassical Political Economy*, Ballinger, Cambridge Massachusetts.

Samuelson, P. (1954) 'The Pure Theory of Public Expenditure' *Review of Economics and Statistics*, 36, November, pp. 386–89.

Sargent, T. and Wallace, N. (1976) 'Rational Expectations and the Theory of Economic Policy' *Journal of Monetary Economics*, April, pp. 169–83.

Sawyer, M.C. (1985a) *The Economics of Industries and Firms*, 2nd edition, Croom Helm, London.

Sawyer, M.C. (1985b) *The Economics of Michal Kalecki*, Macmillan, London.

Schefold, B. (1985) 'Cambridge Price Theory: Special Model or General Theory of Value?' *American Economic Review*, May.

Schmalensee, R. (1988) 'Industrial Economics: An Overview' *Economic Journal*, September.

Seldon, A. (ed) (1985) *The New Right Enlightenment*, Economic and Literary Books, Sevenoaks, Kent.

Selgin, G.A. and White, L.H. 'The Evolution of a Free Banking System' *Economic Enquiry*, 35, July, pp. 439–57.

Shackle, G.L.S. (1958) *Time in Economics*, North Holland, Amsterdam.

Shackleton, J.R. (1985) 'UK Privatisation: US Deregulation' *Politics*, October.

Shackleton, J.R. (1986) 'Back to the Market' *Public Policy and Administration*, 1, No. 3, Winter, pp. 20–40.

Shaw, R.W. and Simpson, P. (1986) 'The Persistence of Monopoly: An Investigation of the Effectiveness of the U.K. Monopolies Commission' *Journal of Industrial Economics*, XXXIV, No. 4, pp. 355–72.

Sheffrin, S.M. (1984) *Rational Expectations*, Cambridge University Press.

Shepherd, J. (1987) 'Industrial Support Policies' *National Institute Economic Review*, November.

Shiller, R.J. (1978) 'Rational Expectations and the Dynamic Structure of Macroeconomic Models – A Critical Review' *Journal of Monetary Economics*, 4, pp. 1–44.

Shoup, C.S. (1965) 'Production from Consumption' *Public Finance*, 20, No. 1–2, pp. 178–202.

Siegel, B.N. (ed) (1984) *Money in Crisis*, Ballinger, Cambridge Massachusetts.

Sims, C.A. (1977) 'Exogeneity and Causal Ordering in Macroeconometric Models' in Sims, C.A. *New Methods in Business Cycle Research*, Federal Reserve Bank of Minneapolis.

Sims, C.A. (1983) 'Is There a Monetary Business Cycle?' *American Economic Review*, Papers and Proceedings, 73, pp. 469–81.

Smith, D. (1987) *The Rise and Fall of Monetarism*, Penguin, Harmondsworth.

Smith, D. (1988) *Mrs Thatcher's Economics*, Heinemann, Oxford.

Solow, R.M. (1980) 'On Theories of Unemployment' *American Economic Review*, 70, March, pp. 1–11.

Solow, R.M. (1985) 'Insiders and Outsiders in Wage Determination' *Scandinavian Journal of Economics*, 87, No. 2, pp. 411–28.

Solow, R.M. (1986) 'Unemployment: Getting the Questions Right' *Economica*, 53, Supplement, pp. 23–34.

Spence, A.M. and Zeckhauser, R. (1971) 'Insurance, Information and Individual Action' *American Economic Review*, 61, pp. 380–87.

Spencer, P.D. (1984) 'The Effect of Oil Discoveries on the British Economy' *Economic Journal*, September, pp. 554–69.

Spencer, P.D. (1986) *Financial Innovation, Efficiency and Disequilibrium*, Clarendon Press, Oxford.

Spencer, P.D. (1989) *Financial Innovation and Monetary Statistics: a New Measure of the UK Money Supply*, Credit Suisse First Boston.

Stigler, G.J. (1954) 'Early History of Empirical Studies of Consumer Behaviour' *Journal of Political Economy*.

Stigler, G.J. (1968) *The Organisation of Industry*, Richard D. Irwin, New York.

Stigler, G.J. (1971) 'The Theory of Economic Regulation' *Bell Journal of Economics*, 2, No. 1.

Stiglitz, J. (1986) *Economics of the Public Sector*, Norton, New York.

Stockman, A. (1980) 'A Theory of Exchange Rate Determination' *Journal of Political Economy*, 88, pp. 673–97.

Stockman, D.A. (1986) *The Triumph of Politics: The Crisis in American Government and How It Affects the World*, Harper and Row, New York.

Swann, D. (1988) *The Retreat of the State: Deregulation and Privatisation in the UK and US*, Harvester Wheatsheaf, Hemel Hempstead.

Taylor, J.B. (1979) 'Estimation and Control of a Macroeconomic Model with Rational Expectations' *Econometrica*, September.

Taylor, J.B. (1985) 'International Coordination in the Design of Macroeconomic Policy Rules' *European Economic Review*, 28.

Taylor, M.P. (1987) 'Financial Innovation, Inflation and the Stability of the Demand for Broad Money in the UK' *Bulletin of Economic Research*, 39/3, pp. 225–33.

Tichy, G. (1984) 'Strategy and Implementation of Employment Policy in Austria: Successful Experiments with Unconventional Assignment of Instruments to Goals' *Kyklos*, 3:37.

Tobin, J. (1970) 'Money and Income: Post Hoc Ergo Propter Hoc?' *Quarterly Journal of Economics*, 84:2, pp. 301–17.

Tollinson, R.D. (1987) 'Is the Theory of Rent-Seeking Here to Stay?' in Rowley, C.K. (ed.) *Democracy and Public Choice*, Basil Blackwell, Oxford.

Trehan, B. (1988) 'The Practice of Monetary Targeting: A Case Study of West German Experience' *Federal Reserve Bank of San Francisco Economic Review*, Spring.

Tullock, G. (1967) 'The Welfare Costs of Tariffs, Monopolies and Theft' *Western Economic Journal*, 5, June, pp. 224–32, reprinted in Buchanan, Tollinson and Tullock (1980), *op. cit.*

Tullock, G. (1981) 'Why So Much Stability?' *Public Choice*, 37, No. 2, pp. 189–202.

Veljanowski, C. (1989) 'Privatisation; Monopoly Money or Competition?' in Veljanowski, C. (ed) *Privatisation and Competition: a market prospectus*, Institute of Economic Affairs, London.

Volcker, P.A. (1986) 'Statements to Congress' *Federal Reserve Bulletin*, April, pp. 233–41.

Wagner, R.E. (1988) 'The Calculus of Consent: A Wicksellian Perspective' *Public Choice*, 56, No. 2, February.

Wagner, R.E. and Gwartney, J.D. (1988) 'Public Choice and Constitutional Order' in Wagner, R.E. and Gwartney, J.D. (eds.) *Public Choice and Constitutional Economics*, JAI Press, London.

Wall, K.D. *et al.* (1975) 'Estimates of a Simple Control Model of the UK Economy' in Renton, G.A. (ed.) *Modelling the Economy*, Heinemann Educational Books, London.

Walter, J.R. (1989) 'Monetary Aggregates: A User's Guide' *Federal Reserve Bank of Richmond Economic Review*, January/February, pp. 20–28.

Wellisz, S. (1982) 'The Political Economy of Protectionism: Comment' in Bhagwati, J.N. (ed.) *Import Competition and Response*, Chicago University Press, Chicago.

Wenniger, J. (1988) 'Money Demand – Some Long-Run Properties' *Federal Reserve Bank of New York Quarterly Review*, Spring, pp. 23–40.

White, L.H. (1987) 'Accounting for Non Interest Bearing Currency' *Journal of Money, Credit and Banking*, 19/4, November, pp. 449–68.

van Wijnbergen, S. (1986) 'On Fiscal Deficits, the Real Exchange Rate and the World Rate of Interest' *European Economic Review*, 30, pp. 1013–23.

Wilkinson, P. and Lomax, D.F. (1989) 'Lessons for Banking from the 1980s and the Recent Past' *National Westminster Bank Quarterly Review*, May, pp. 2–16.

Williamson, O.E. (1985) *The Economic Institutions of Capitalism*, Free Press, New York and London.

Williamson, S.D. (1987a) 'Financial Intermediation, Business Failures and Real Business Cycles' *Journal of Political Economy*, 95:6, pp. 1196–1216.

Williamson, S.D. (1987b) 'Transactions Costs, Inflation, and the Variety of Intermediary Services' *Journal of Money, Credit and Banking*, 19/4, November, pp. 484–98.

Wilson, J.Q. (ed.) (1980) *The Politics of Regulation*, Basic Books, New York.

van Winden, F. (1988) 'The Economic Theory of Political Decision-Making: A Survey and Perspective' in Van den Broeck, J. (ed.) *Public Choice*, Kluwer, London.

Yao, Y.C. (1985) 'A Libertarian Approach to Monetary Theory and Policy' *Hong Kong Economic Papers*, 15, pp. 1–24.

Yeager, L.B. (1985) 'Deregulation and Monetary Reform' *American Economic Review*, 75, pp. 103–107.

Yellen, J. (1984) 'Efficiency Wage Models of Unemployment' *American Economic Review*, 74, No. 2, pp. 202–205.

Young, P. (1986) 'Privatisation Around the Globe' *NCPA Policy Report*, National Center for Policy Analysis, Dallas.

Zarnowitz, V. (1985) 'Recent Work on Business Cycles in Historical Perspective: A Review of Theories and Evidence' *Journal of Economic Literature*, XXII: June, pp. 523–80.

Index

Abraham, K G 120
accelerator hypothesis 89–90, 108n
Adam Smith Institute 7, 13
adaptive expectations 73–4, 94–5
agency theory *see* principal-agent theory
aggregate supply function 28
Akerlof, G A 101, 116
Alchian, A A 190–91
Allen, F 199
Alt, J E 106
Amel, D F 35
Anderson, M 16, 17, 18, 22, 26n
anticompetitive practices 180, 181, 188,
    189, 193, 195
Arestis, P 111, 168, 169, 176, 178, 178n
Argy, V 52, 60, 104
asset markets 60, 81–2
Auerbach, P 181
Austrian economics 3, 5, 6, 93–4, 96,
    179, 184–5, 192, 194, 204
    see also Hayek, F.A.
autocorrelation 128, 129
Azariadis, C 100

Backhouse, R 16n, 108n
Bailey, E E 200
Bailey, R W 40
Bain, J S 180, 182
Baltensperger, E 46
banking system 30–33
Barnett, W A 40
barriers to entry 181, 183, 184, 186, 194
Barro, R J 56, 57–8, 97, 98, 105, 112
Barry, N P 24, 26n
Batchelor, R A 40
Baumol, W J 185–6
Beaver, W H 85n
Becker, G 151, 203
Begg, D K H 54
Benston, G J 36

Bernanke, B S 36
Bharadwaj, K 164
Bilson, J F 50
Bishop, M 198
Black, D 147, 159n
Blackburn, K 81, 105
Blanchard, O J 56, 62, 99, 118, 119
Blaug, M 9, 187
Blinder, A S 98, 121
Bohara, A K 39
Böhm-Bawerk, E von 108n
Bork, R 183–4, 194
Borrie, G 194
Boschen, J F 47n
Box, G E P 131
Box-Jenkins, methodology 6, 124,
    131–2, 135
Boyd, J H 36
Brandsma, A 53
Brennan, G 142, 145, 153, 155, 158,
    159n
Breton, A 156
British Telecom 20, 185, 196, 198
Brittan, S 20
Britton, A 108n
Brooks, M 150
Brown, E K 165, 178n
Brunner, K 33
Bryant, R C 39, 46, 61
Buchanan, J M 5, 6, 15, 17, 19, 22, 106,
    141–5, 149, 150, 153, 154, 158,
    159, 159n, 204n
Buiter, W 56
Burke, T 181, 195
Burns, A F 17
Burton, J 13, 25n
business cycles 88–108, 113, 114, 116,
    125, 173, 175

Caldwell, B J 162

Canzoneri, M B 53, 58, 59
Carlozzi, N 64
Cecchini, P 64
central limit theorem 73
Chernomas, B 177
Chicago School 183–4, 194
    see also Friedman, M., Stigler, G J.,
        Becker, G.S.
Chick, V 168
Chiplin, B 191, 193, 194
Christenson, M 81, 105
Chrystal, K A 106
Classical Liberalism 10–26
Coase, R 187, 191
cointegration 92, 108
competition 152, 180, 184, 186, 194,
    198, 200
competition policy 180, 192–6
concentration ratio 182, 194
Congdon, T 19, 23
Connolly, R A 84
Constant Monetary Growth Rule 95, 103,
    105, 108n
constitutionalism 5, 11, 15, 17, 19, 45,
    47n, 105, 140, 142, 145, 152–5,
    157
consumption function 124, 126–30,
    132–8
contestable market 34, 179, 185–6
Cooper, R N 53
Copeland, T E 82
Corden, W 53
corporate control, market for 21, 191,
    197
Coughlin, P 148
Cowling, K 195–6
credibility 5, 75, 81, 104–5, 107
    see also reputation
Cullis, J G 156
Currie, D A 57, 59
Cuthbertson, K 47n

Dale, R 46
Davidson, J E H 132–9 passim
Davidson, P 164, 166, 168
Davies, K T 35
Davis, T E 127
Deaton, A S 139n
Delors, J 67n
demand shocks 109, 118, 119, 120, 122
Demsetz, H 184, 190–91

deregulation see regulation
Dermine, J 46
Diamond, D W 36
Diamond, P 56
distribution of income 170–72
divisia aggregates 40
Dooley, M 60
Dorn, J A 47n
Dornbusch, R 50, 51, 54, 55, 59
Dow, J C R 39, 42
Dow, S C 162, 178n
Downs, A 141, 142, 143, 147, 148
Driver, C 169

Earl, P E 178
Eastern Europe, collapse of communism
    in 3, 7, 12, 13, 24, 25, 157, 158
Eastwood, R K 55
Eatwell, J 164
econometrics 6, 28–9, 73, 94, 96, 107,
    124–39, 144, 162, 185
education 154, 202, 203
efficiency wage hypothesis 101, 115–17,
    118
efficient market hypothesis 60, 72, 81–2,
    84
Eichner, A S 161, 162, 168, 169, 170,
    173, 178n
Engel, C M 60
environmentalism 8, 191–2, 199–200,
    203
equilibrium business cycles 92–100, 102,
    130
Ericsson, N R 28
Eurocurrency markets 37
European community 8, 12, 64, 153–4,
    158, 194–5, 202
European Monetary System 53, 54, 153,
    158
European Monetary Union 46, 158
Evans, G W 92
Evans, M K 129
exchange rates 48–71 passim, 168
    monetary theory of 50
    overshooting 54–5, 59, 65
ERM (exchange rate mechanism) 8, 46,
    49, 105
exclusive dealing 183, 188
externalities 142, 147, 191–2

Fairburn, J 194

false trading 121, 123n
Fama, F F 81–2
Figlewski, S 83
financial markets 27–47 passim, 81–2
fiscal policy 42, 51, 53–4, 56–7, 60, 61, 65
Fischer, S 55, 98, 102, 103, 104
Fisher, I 108n
fix price markets 100
Fleming, J 48, 51–5
Fleming, M 195
flexprice markets 100
Foot, M D F 39
forecasting 75, 83, 130–33, 134, 135, 137, 138
franchising 189
Frenkel, J 50, 56, 57, 59
Friedman, B 41
Friedman, M 3, 4, 13, 14–15, 17, 25n, 26n, 28, 29–30, 38–9, 41, 45, 77–8, 83, 94–6, 100, 143, 162, 187
Friedman, R 14–15
Funabashi, Y 64
Furobotn, E 191

Gamble, A 19
game theory 53–4, 57–8, 65–6, 67–71, 154, 181
George, K D 194
Gertler, M 36
Gilligan, T 34
Godley, W 178n
Goodhart, C A E 29, 33, 39, 41, 46, 47n, 201
Goodwin, R M 173, 178n
Gordon, D F 57–8
Gordon, R A 122
Granger, C W J 85n
Green, D 25
Greenfield, R L 47n
Greenspan, A 17
Greenwald, B C 98
Grossman, S J 85n
Guimaraes, R M 84

Hall, Max 35
Hall, M 182
Hallett, A 53, 59
Hamada, K 53, 66
Hamilton, J D 99

Hamouda, O F 160–62, 178n
Harberger, A C 195–6
Harcourt, G C 160–62, 178n
Harrington, R 35, 38
Harris, C Lowell 17
Hay, D 202
Hayek, F A 3, 3, 11, 13–14, 15, 25n, 26n, 89, 93–4, 96, 98, 108n, 184
Harvard School 180–83
Heijdra, B J 150–51
Helliwell, J 61
Henderson, D W 58, 59
Hendrification 139n
Hendry, D F 6, 29, 124, 132–9 passim
Herfindahl-Hirschman Index 182
Heritage Foundation 7
Hester, D D 33
Hibbs, D 106
Hicks, J R 67n, 89–90, 121
Hillman, A L 151
Hinich, M J 147
Holden, K 84
Hollis, M 166
Holtham, G 59
Hubbard, R G 36
Hume, D 3, 10
Humphrey, T M 46, 47n
hysteresis 118–20

Ikenberry, D 84
implicit contracts 100–101, 112–14, 189
import controls 149–50
Industrial support policies 178, 202–3
inflation 27–47 passim, 57, 76–80, 95, 104–5, 106–7, 137–8, 153
insider-outsider analysis 117–18, 119, 121
Institute of Economic Affairs 7, 13
institutional economics 5, 36, 152, 159, 166, 186–92 passim
Isard, P 50, 60
Ishii, N 62
IS-LM analysis, 52, 67n, 89, 111

Jackson, P 156
Jefferson, T 140
Jevons, W S 88
Johannes, J M 38
Johnson, H G 49
Johnston, R B 44, 47n
Jones, P R 156

Judd, J P 28
Juglar, C 88

Kahn, C M 55
Kaldor, N 111, 173, 178n
Kalecki, M 160, 165, 173, 175
Kane, E J 34, 35
Katz, E 151
Katz, L F 120
Kay, J A 26n, 196, 198, 200
Keynes, J M 2, 6, 14, 73, 90, 109, 110,
    112, 160, 164, 165, 166, 173,
    176–7
Keynesianism 3, 4, 5, 6, 9n, 51–5, 67n,
    76, 88, 89–90, 93, 94, 96, 97,
    100–102, 107, 108n, 109–23, 125,
    130, 160–78
Kim, K 94, 108n
King, D 24
King, R G 97, 99
Kingston, G H 51
Klamer, A 108n
Klaus, V 25
Kravis, I 50
Kregel, J 162
Kydland, F E 57, 80, 98, 104

labour turnover 115, 116
labour unions *see* trade unions
Laffer, A 17
Lakatos, I 178n
Lakonishok, J 84
Lavoie, M 160, 161, 168, 178n
law of one price 49, 50
Lawson, T 162
Ledyard, J O 148
Leijonhufvud, A 93
Leland, H E 36
Levačić, R 25n, 156
Levine, P 57, 58, 59
Lewis, M K 35
lexicographic ordering 163, 178n
liberalism, market *see* Classical Liberal-
    ism
Lichtenstein, P M 166
life-cycle hypothesis 128
Lilien, D M 120
limit pricing 182
Lindahl equilibrium 146
Lindbeck, A 117
Lipsey, R G 50

Littlechild, S 185, 194, 196, 204n
Liverpool University Forecasting Model
    74, 83
Locke, J 3
Lomax, D F 36
London Business School Forecasting
    Model 74
Long, J B 98
Lucas critique 6, 7n, 124, 130
Lucas, R E 3, 6, 7n, 56, 57, 89, 95, 96–8,
    108, 124, 130
Lucas supply function 97

Maddala, G S 108
Madison, J 140
majority voting 146, 147–8
malinvestment 93
Mankiw, N G 99
marginal propensity to consume 126,
    128–9, 169
Margolis, H 155
Marshall, A 6, 9n 165
Marston, R 52
Marvel, H P 183, 194
Marx, K 88, 165
Marxism 11, 14, 165, 177
Mason, E S 180
mathematical economics 5–7, 9n, 145
McKibbin, W J 53, 61, 63, 64
McKinnon, R I 64–5
McLean, I 157
MCM model 61–3
McPherson, D 157
median voter models 106, 144, 147–8,
    149
Medium Term Financial Strategy 23, 41,
    45, 95
megacorp 160, 169–70
Melitz, J 54
Meltzer, A H 33
Menger, C 184
Mercuro, N 151–2
mergers 185, 192–6
Mester, L 34
Meulendyke, A 41
Miles, D K 43
Mill, J S 10
Minford, P 79, 85n
Minsky, H P 167, 168
Mises, L von 184
Mitchell, W C 145

Mizon, G E 139n
monetarism, monetarists 3, 4, 26n,
    28–30, 94–6, 103, 104, 107,
    176
monetary base control 32, 38–40, 41–4,
    45–6
monetary control 23, 29, 38, 41–4, 45–6,
    95–6, 103–5
monetary policy 27–47, 61, 64, 85n,
    178n
monetary targets 23, 27, 29–30, 39–40,
    95, 103–4
monetary theory of the balance of
    payments 49, 168–9
money, creation of 30–33
money supply 23, 29–33, 34–41 passim,
    94–6 passim, 166–9
Monopolies and Mergers Commission
    180, 183, 193–5
monopoly 152, 163, 180, 183, 193–6,
    198
Mont Pelerin Society 11, 17, 25n
Moore, B J 36, 38, 39, 41, 167, 168
Moore, J 198
Morris, D 51, 67n
Muellbauer, J. 51, 67n
Mueller, D C 144, 147, 148, 155, 159n,
    195
multiplier 67n, 108n, 126
Mundell, R A 48, 49, 51–5
Mundell-Fleming model 48, 51–5, 56,
    61, 65
Mussa, M 49, 50, 52
Muth, J F 74

Nash equilibrium 53–4, 57, 58, 60,
    67–71
National Institute for Economic and
    Social Research Forecasting
    Model 74, 83
natural monopoly 152, 197, 198, 199
Neary, J P 55
Nell, E J 166
Nelson, C R 92, 108n
neo-Keynesians *see* Keynesianism
neo-Austrians *see* Austrian Economics
New Classical Economics 3, 4, 56–9, 88,
    93, 96–8, 104, 107, 108n, 114, 122
Niehans, J 33, 44, 50
Niskanen, W A 17, 18
Nordhaus, W 106

North, D 152
Norton, R D 202
Nutter, G W 13

Office of Fair Trading 194
oil price shocks 53, 90–92, 99, 118, 120
Okun, A 101, 117
Olson, M 143, 144
open economy 5, 48–71, 168–9
optimal control theory 80
ordinary least squares 128, 129, 130
Oudiz, G 53, 58, 59, 62, 63

Padoa-Schioppa, T 49
Padmore, T 61
Pagan, A 139
Paish, F W 76
Pareto-efficiency 53, 67n, 69, 145, 146
Pasinetti, L L 163, 172, 178n
patents, policy towards 80, 190
Patrick, D 202
Peacock,. A T 156
Pecchioli, R M 46
Peel, D 5, 84, 85n, 95, 112
Pejovich, S 191
Peltzman, S 151
permanent income hypothesis 128
Persson, T 56
Phelps, E S 100
Phillips, A W 76, 103
Phillips curve 72, 76–80, 95, 100, 106
Pirie, M 18, 22
Pissarides, C A 122
Plosser, C I 92, 98, 99,.108n
Podolski, T M 36, 37, 41, 44, 47n
Pokorny, M J 127, 129, 139n
Poland 12
policy coordination, gains from 48, 52–4,
    58–9, 61–4, 66, 67–71
political business cycles 105–7
Poole, K T 148
Portes, R 46, 51, 67n
portfolio balance 60
Posner, R A 25, 200
Post-Keynesianism 111, 160–78
Prescott, E C 36, 57, 80, 98, 99, 104
principal-agent theory 144, 179, 188–90
Prisoner's Dilemma 53, 105, 157
property rights 151–2, 156, 179, 190–92
privatisation 12, 18, 20–21, 23, 152, 180,
    185

Pryke, R 197
public choice 140–59
public goods 146–8, 149, 155, 191
public sector borrowing requirement
    41–4
Purvis, D D 55
Pyle, D H 36

quantity theory of money *see* monetarism

Ramakrishnan, R T S 36
Rasche, R H 29, 38
rational expectations 48, 50, 54–5, 57,
    65, 72–87, 96–7, 98, 100, 106,
    107, 112
Rawls, J 154
Razin, A 56
Reagan, R 12, 17, 194
Reaganomics 12, 16–19, 22–4
real business cycles 88, 92, 98–100, 107
Rees, R 197
regulation 7, 12, 18, 21, 25n, 26n, 35–6,
    149, 179, 185, 199–201
Reisman, D 153
rent-seeking 143, 148–52
reputation 57–9, 65, 81
    see also credibility
Reynolds, P J 169
Ricardian equivalence theorem 56–7
Ricardo, D 10
Riddell, P 19
Riker, W H 159n
Riley, C J 51
Roberts, P C 17
Robinson, J 111, 163, 165
Rockett, K E 59–60
Rogers, S C 162
Rogoff, K 58, 59, 64
Romer, P M 100
Romer, T 148, 159
Roncaglia, A 164
Rosen, S 122n
Rowley, C K 144, 159n
Rowthorn, B 161
Rubenstein, M 85n
rules (policy) 95, 103–4
Rush, M 98

Sachs, J D 12, 53, 58, 59, 60, 62, 63, 64
Salin, P 100n
Salop, J 52

Salter, W E G 48, 50, 56
Samuels, J 151–2
Samuelson, P 146–7
Sargent, T 104
Savage, L J 83
Saville, I D 39, 44
Sawyer, M C 170, 176, 178n
Say's Law 109, 110
Scadding, J L 28
Schefold, B 161
Schmalensee, R 181
Schultz, G 17
Schumpeter, J 149, 184
Schwartz, A 45, 47n, 94
sectoral shifts 120
Seldon, A 24
Selgin, G A 47n
Shackle, G L S 73
Shackleton, J R 178n, 197, 204n
Shaw, R W 194
Sheffrin, S M 80
Shepherd, J 202
Sherman Act 353
Shiller, R J 83
shirking 115, 116
Shoup, C S 123n
Siegel, B N 47n
Simon, W 17
Simpson, P 194
Sims, C A 96
Single European Market 49, 64, 195
Smith, A 10, 180, 187
Smith, C W 36
Smith, D 19, 26n
Snower, D 117
Solow, R 121
Solow residual 99
Spence, A M 189
Spencer, P D 40, 47n, 55
Sraffa, P 111, 165
Srba, F 132–9 passim
Stackelberg leader 70
statistical modelling 124, 131–2
Stigler, G J 139n, 179, 183, 200
Stiglitz, J 85n, 98, 147
Stockman, A 56
Stockman, D 16–19 passim
Stockton, Lord 198
structure-conduct-performance 179,
    180–83
Summers, L H 118–19

sunk costs 185–6
supply side shocks 64–5, 92, 98–9, 108n
Swann, D 13, 18, 195, 196
Swoboda, A K 46

Taylor, J B 55, 61, 63, 64
Taylor, M P 47n
Thakor, A V 36
Thatcher, M 12, 19–24, 105, 198, 201
Thatcherism 19–24
Thirlby, G F 204n
Thompson, D J 196
Thompson, J L 84
Tichy, G 178
Tideman, N 182
time-inconsistency 57–8, 65, 72, 80–81,
    104–5
Tobin, J 60, 94, 96
Tobin-Markowitz mean-variance asset
    market theory 60
Tollinson, R D 149, 152
trade unions 19, 77, 83, 104–5, 119, 169,
    174
training 117, 203
transaction costs 33–4, 152, 179, 187–8,
    190
Trehan, B 40
Tullock, G 106, 141, 143, 148, 149, 159n
Ture, N 17
Turnovsky, S J 51
type 1 and type 2 errors 60, 67

unanimity rule 142, 153–4
uncertainty 59–60, 164, 170
unemployment 51, 67n, 76–9, 101,
    109–23, 174
unit root 92, 108n

Veblen, T 166
Veljanovsky, C 20

Venables, A J 55
Vickers, J 26n
Volcker, P A 36
voting paradox 155

wage rigidity 100–102, 109–23 passim
Wagner, R E 159n
Wall, K D 139n
Wallace, N 47n, 104
Walras, L 92
Walras' Law 49
Walter, J R 38
Walters, A A 26n
Watson, M W 99
Weidenbaum, M 17
Weintrobe, R 156
Wellisz, S 299n
Wenniger, J 44
Weston, J F 82
White, L H 47
Wicksell, K 90, 93, 141, 146
van Wijnbergen, S 55, 56
Wilkinson, P 36
Williamson, O E 188
Williamson, S D 36
Wilson, J Q 200
van Winden, F 156
Wright, M 193, 194
Wyplosz, C 60

X-inefficiency 156

Yao, Y C 47n
Yeager, L B 47n
Yellen, J 101, 102, 116
Yeo, S 132–9 passim
Young, P 25n

Zarnowitz, V 99–100
Zeckhauser, R 189